KT-483-755

The SCOTTISH FISHING BOOK

SANDY FORGAN *with photographs by* GLYN SATTERLEY

This book is dedicated to anglers everywhere.
May their spirits soar in our wonderful aquatic environment.
This book is also dedicated to my wife Maureen and my daughters,
Elaine and Claire, whose patience and constant love make my spirit soar.

First published in Great Britain in 2001 by
Lomond Books
36 West Shore Road
Granton
Edinburgh EH5 1QD

Produced by Colin Baxter Photography Ltd

A CIP catalogue record for this book is available from the British Library.

ISBN 1-84204-020-0

Printed in Hong Kong

Page 1 photograph: Floors, River Tweed. Page 4 photograph: Loch Stack near Laxford Bridge, West Sutherland.

The SCOTTISH FISHING BOOK

SANDY FORGAN

with photographs by GLYN SATTERLEY

Foreword by Paul Young

LOMOND BOOKS
EDINBURGH • SCOTLAND

CONTENTS

FOREWORD

Gardenstown Pier, Banffshire: Where the love of the sport begins.

Fishing in Scotland. These three words suggest, to an angler, a cornucopia of piscatorial delights. We have, here in this most beautiful country, something to interest every fisher. That wildest of fish, the salmon, can be fished for in world famous rivers: Spey, Tweed and Tay, the Thurso, Helmsdale and Dee. Native brown trout can be caught in rivers and lochs in the Highlands and Lowlands. Coarse fish such as pike, perch and grayling are to be found in many rivers and lochs, and there is sea fishing all round our rugged and beautiful coastline.

As a youngster, I fished for trout on the Lyne Water, a tributary of the Tweed, and still remember a fish which took the brandling worm on a two hook Thomson tackle under a bush on the far bank. It came to the surface, jumped and threw the hook. I can still see the glorious colour of the fish and feel the deep sense of disappointment as it slid back into the depths.

I also remember landing several small perch from Duddingston Loch, near my home in Edinburgh. And pike swirling at my lure on a wee loch near Loch Awe. And catching mackerel from the promenade at Portobello. And the first time I saw a salmon being caught on the Tweed at Cardrona. Memories of fishing in Scotland.

I have been lucky enough to expand my fishing horizons over the years – fishing for exotic species in many other countries for our television programmes – but there has always been a loyalty to the country of my birth. Fishing in Scotland is what I love best, whether it be a hill loch for trout, a Highland river for salmon, a dainty stretch of water for grayling, the Sound of Mull for barn-door sized skate, Loch Awe for pike, or some small, unnamed loch for pugnacious perch.

Sandy Forgan's writing of the love of his sport and Glyn Satterly's photographs will, I'm sure, evoke what fishing in Scotland is all about. Because anyone can, and should, enjoy it; young, old, experienced or newcomer. I am sure you will enjoy this book. It is written and photographed showing a love of Scotland which I heartily endorse .

Paul Young

INTRODUCTION

It is perhaps inevitable that many Scots have an affinity with water and that, as a result, a disproportionately high number of Scots enjoy angling. After all, Scotland possesses an astonishing 31,469 freshwater lochs, 950 river systems and over 7,000 kilometres of sea coastline – more than enough for any lifetime of fishing! There is another factor, however, which is embedded much deeper in the Scottish psyche – perhaps a lingering echo of a time when Scots were prehistoric hunter-gatherers – something which turns someone from simply being aware of the rich aquatic environment surrounding them, into someone whose main recreational pleasure is derived within it, and their life is firmly influenced and steered by it.

Such is the case for Scottish anglers. They come in great diversity from the large urban sprawls and from the remotest and most inaccessible of islands and glens. They are male and female, young and old, kings and commoners, but what binds them together is their sheer delight in the quality of Scotland's fishing. And who can blame them, for our fishing is as varied as any on this planet; it is carried out within stunningly beautiful landscapes, and it generates unsurpassable pleasure for its participants.

The enchanting variety of our fishing derives, in significant part, from the complexities of our temperate oceanic climate and the geological form of our islands. The patterns of weather that rush headlong in from the vast expanses of the Atlantic Ocean are as ever-changing as the surging seas over which they develop. There is a saying that, in Scotland, we experience each of the year's seasons during every day.

Scotland's topography shows how countless aeons of geological turmoil have carved a land of character and diversity. It is easy to find great beauty in the wild vistas. Perhaps this is compounded by the constantly-changing hues and intensities of light, for the same scene transforms as we watch.

Loch Lomond:
One of the best known lochs in Scotland. Excellent fishing for trout, salmon, sea trout, pike and other coarse species.

Perhaps our five basic senses play a larger part on our fishing than we may first imagine. Clearly, sound adds greatly to our involvement within our angling environment. Our ears enjoy the sibilance of wind and its effect on water, ranging from the roar of breaking waves on the seashore to the soft, slide of the stream pouring over water-worn rocks. The raucous cry of seabirds, the mew of a buzzard or osprey, the constant arguing of ducks and coots, the splash of a rising trout, then the sudden scream of the reel's ratchet. Sound offers us one rich vein amongst our other pleasurable senses.

Our sense of smell also adds subliminally to our pleasure when fishing. There may be stark contrasts of scents in the air depending on the location, the time of day and the time of year. The strong salty-tang of the seashore contrasts with our soft West Highland air, scented by bog-myrtle, heather and peat smoke. Our rivers carry distinctive aromas too, especially when the early morning sun dries a film of spicy mud onto the stones; or in the still enchantment of dusk, when the bank-side vegetation releases the heady scent of wild blossom into the air. It may be the simple presence of the water itself in each of our angling landscapes, which adds a richness of texture of almost-mystical significance. Whatever the root cause, each of our senses are stimulated, inspired and charmed.

From Scotland's imposing sea lochs to the sweeping silver sands of countless deserted bays; from the majestic glides and dark pools of our major rivers, to the sparkle of our smallest burns; from the huge lowland lochs to the tiniest lochans set deep amongst the rocks of the mountain corries, our aquatic heritage is vast and utterly varied. For the angler it is quite simply heaven on earth!

The fish themselves exhibit boundless variety too. Our sea fishing is often spectacular and productive. Our so-called freshwater coarse fishing is much better than most appreciate, whilst our game fishing is justifiably famous. The artificial distinction given to those species known as 'game' fish – trout, sea trout and salmon – can be misleading. Why a trout should be regarded as a game fish, but a hard-fighting pike or tope is not escapes reason. The many marine species, which inhabit the waters around our shores, are worthy of inclusion in any sporting list.

The king of Scottish game fish, the silver Atlantic salmon, has a life-cycle that is genuinely astonishing. Hatching in the depth of icy winter amongst the gravel on the riverbed, they grow up as a freshwater species running the gauntlet of predation at every twist and turn. At the appointed time, they swim downstream to metamorphose into a saltwater species. They then migrate thousands of miles across the vast expanses of the northern oceans to their main feeding areas until they mature into adult fish. Ultimately, they return to the river of their birth to re-adopt their freshwater life and to head upstream against the incessant flow and countless obstacles to reproduce.

The salmon's close cousin, the richly-speckled, native brown trout and its migratory form the sea trout, are found wherever clean and suitable conditions are available. The more distant relations of salmon and trout – the grayling and charr – also provide fine angling opportunities. Many Scottish lochs and rivers have excellent stocks of coarse fish. Large pike and shoals of brightly-coloured perch and silvery roach are widely distributed. For those with a penchant for the unusual, there are other notable rarities like the powan and the ferox trout. This is an angling heritage of great diversity, worthy of cautious preservation and care.

It is not just the species that vary, the methods of fishing themselves are just as diverse. Other than the use of a rod and reel, there are few comparisons between seeking a great halibut or skate with heavy sea fishing tackle from a rolling boat off the north west coast, and attempting to entice a small, red-speckled brownie from a tumbling Borders burn. Similarly, small boys fishing for perch in their local pond are likely to experience just as much satisfaction and fun as their more-practised and refined fly-fishing elders, who skilfully cast great distances across the salmon pools of our rivers. These contrasting threads contribute to the intricate tapestry that is Scottish fishing in all its various colours, history, locations, equipment, procedures, expectations, laws, developments, failures and successes.

If this book carries a message, it is one of sharing. Mysteriously, this process of sharing is highly developed in anglers. The joy of passing someone your most-precious fly to tempt a wily salmon or trout; or the pleasure of pointing out the secret place where a big fish lies; or the joy of teaching a receptive novice give the provider great delight and satisfaction. In after-dinner company, the recounting of epic struggles with great fish, or the quiet solitary recollection of superb days by the river with close friends, signal the truth that angling is about sharing. Anglers are, almost without exception, unusually gracious and decent people disposed to help each other through sharing their knowledge and experiences.

We all love to fish the unsullied, deserted pool in utter peace and total solitude; or fish the bay where no footsteps have disturbed the sand. But the success which these idyllic dalliances provide give even greater pleasure when it is later shared. If this book does nothing else, I hope that when you put it down you will have shared some of my love of Scotland and its fishing.

Sandy Forgan

CHAPTER ONE

SPECIES AND HABITAT

Fishing is about choice. We must decide where and when to go, what tactics, methods and tackle to use, and what species we aim to catch. Scottish anglers are fortunate in having a wide range of species and places to enjoy. Curiously, this range is not exploited particularly widely, for few salmon anglers explore coarse fishing and many sea anglers fly-fish only rarely for trout. We should broaden our activities to gain wider technical experience and increase our enjoyment. For, while fishing *is* about choice, it is primarily about enjoyment.

River Thraill, Torridon, Wester Ross: Countless small west-coast spate rivers and burns run through countless glens in Scotland.

Scottish species may be divided into three categories. There are the 'game species' (salmon, trout and sea trout); 'coarse species' (pike, perch and roach); and numerous salt water species. These broad categorisations overlap, for salmon and some trout venture into the sea and marine species, like flounders and eels, regularly enter freshwater. The distinction between game and coarse species is equally unclear. Grayling are coarse species to some and game fish to others. In practical terms it rarely matters, with one major exception – the Law. Scots Law defines what may be fished for – when, where and how. If in doubt, ask!

Fish are found where conditions suit them. Freshwater may be sedate weedy streams or rapid, foam-flecked torrents. In the sea, the depth and type of bottom favours different species – flat-fish live on sandy bottoms, whilst cod and ling favour rocky areas. The availability of food is crucial to sustainability, as is avoiding predation. As with all things natural, each of these aspects changes over time and season. To be successful fishers, we must learn to 'read the water' and match our practices to the location and activities of the fish. It sounds so simple in a few words, but it isn't.

The Game Fish

There are five main species which make up the group commonly known as 'game fish' in Scotland. These are the Atlantic salmon *(Salmo salar)*; the brown trout *(Salmo trutta)* and its migratory sub-type the sea trout (also *Salmo*

trutta); the arctic charr *(Salvelinus alpinus)*, and the non-native, but widely distributed, rainbow trout *(Oncorhynchus mykiss)*. Placing wild animals into categories is always fraught with difficulty; attributing certain fish to the category of 'game species' is no exception. Many anglers hold the opinion that the grayling *(Thymallus thymallus)* should be included with the other game fish, while the increasing hybridisation of rainbow trout, North American brook trout and charr species has brought a plethora of interesting and exotic species to Scotland's stocked trout waters.

BROWN TROUT

Native brown trout, or as they are affectionately known in Scotland – 'broonies' – are found widely throughout running and still water. They need relatively few life requirements: cool, clean, oxygenated water; suitable food; a place to hide when predators threaten; and favourable conditions

to reproduce. If these elements are present, then a population of trout is likely to be present. Scotland's climate provides ample rainfall to keep most streams supplied with running water and its temperate climate does not suffer from extreme temperatures. Most of the lochs and rivers are free from major pollution, so food is relatively abundant, which enables the brown trout population to thrive.

Brown trout spawn primarily in running water in the closing months of the year. Spawning may be close to the area where they normally live, or may involve significant migration out of stillwater into headstreams, or further upstream in some river instances. The fry hatch in late winter to early spring when winter releases its grip and the availability of foodstuff increases. The tiny fry grow over two to three years into 'parr', often in close proximity to their salmon parr cousins. The mature brown trout may live for many years and growth reflects the abundance of feeding and the amount of energy output, which it needs to make in its adopted territory.

In rivers, brown trout take up 'lies' where they wait for food to be brought to them by the current. Often, you will see the same fish in the same 'lie' on many visits to a pool – they become 'auld freends'. The logical cause of this behaviour is that they adopt the optimum position to gain the best food supply, combined with a suitable deep or sheltered place to avoid predators and a comfortable flow of oxygenated water. There may be a distinct 'pecking order' in these trout lies, with the biggest trout taking the best place and progressively smaller fish trailing on behind – a case of 'the survival of the fittest'. Catch one brown trout from a certain lie and there is every likelihood that others will soon drop into the vacant place.

In lochs, predictably, trout tend to be found where the greatest quantity of food items are concentrated. In general, this occurs where sunlight fuels the life cycles of plants and the insects that feed upon them. Most of the trout's diet is composed of aquatic species which, in turn, live where their food items proliferate. Sunlight, generally, does not penetrate the water of Scottish lochs much deeper than ten to fifteen feet in

Sea Trout Flies

Sea trout are often selective about which artificial flies they will accept. This list of six traditional Scottish patterns should increase your chances of a decent catch. Try using them in different sizes, with larger ones (6, 8 and 10s) when the water conditions are heavy and stained, and smaller ones (10, 12 and 14s) when the river is low and clear. Each of these patterns may be tied on traditional single or double hooks. They are also highly effective when attached to small tubes.

STOAT'S TAIL

STOAT'S TAIL. The Stoat's Tail is probably the most effective sea trout pattern of them all. It may have a standard black body, or even better, a silver tinsel body, and it seems to benefit from the addition of jungle cock cheeks. The original, simple version is deadly, and its variations are even more so. Fish them with real confidence.

TEAL, BLUE AND SILVER

TEAL, BLUE AND SILVER. A traditional favourite, the Teal, Blue and Silver takes sea trout wherever it is used. It comes in many guises, from the conventional wet-fly dressing to the Medicine type of lure. The tinsel body and barred wing create the desired effect – sea trout chase it with gusto!

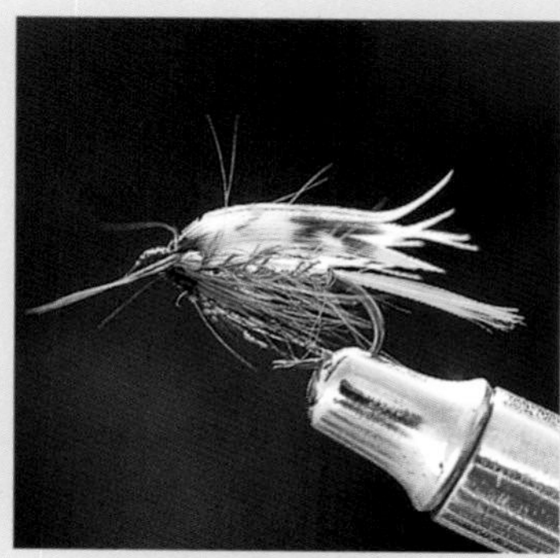

SILVER INVICTA

SILVER INVICTA. A real cracker, the tinsel bodied fly the Silver Invicta takes sea trout in both rivers and lochs. As soon as it gets dark, try it in larger sizes. If you are looking for a consistently successful fly, this is it.

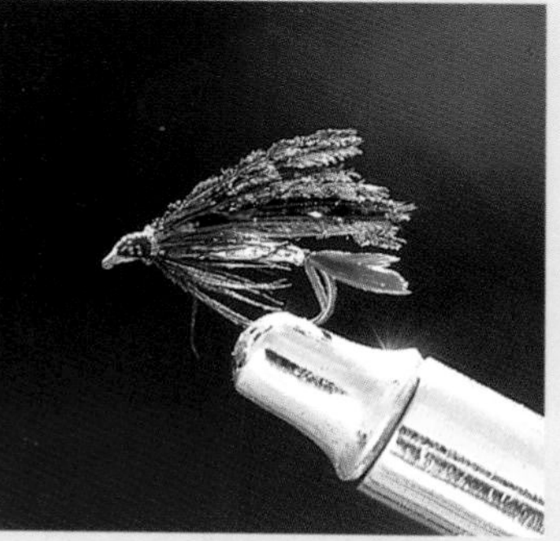

ALEXANDRA

ALEXANDRA. Yet another classic sea trout pattern with a tinsel body. The added advantage of red in the dressing also seems to help. It is no accident that many sea trout anglers have a good selection of the 'Alexandra' in their fly box.

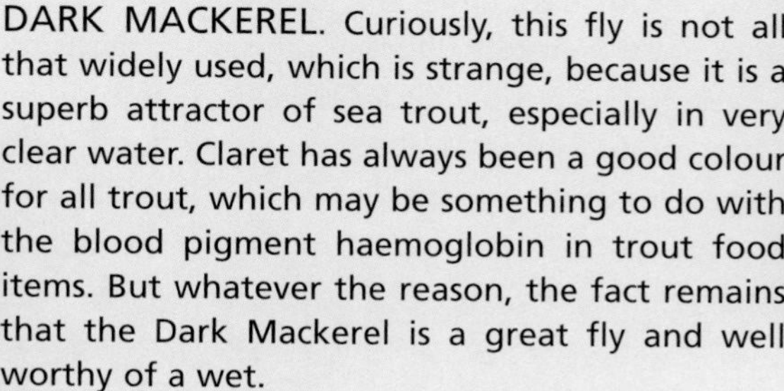

DARK MACKEREL. Curiously, this fly is not all that widely used, which is strange, because it is a superb attractor of sea trout, especially in very clear water. Claret has always been a good colour for all trout, which may be something to do with the blood pigment haemoglobin in trout food items. But whatever the reason, the fact remains that the Dark Mackerel is a great fly and well worthy of a wet.

DARK MACKEREL

DUNKELD. Similarly to the 'Teal, Blue and Silver', sea trout also favour the Dunkeld. It is fascinating to note that such traditional flies have retained their popularity in the face of all the new patterns that have emerged in Scotland.

Loch Watten, Caithness: Wild Brown Trout.

sufficient quality to sustain plant growth. At this depth, aquatic life tends to become less plentiful. Consequently, most trout are found in the marginal, shallower areas of lochs. However, this is a huge generalisation and trout often travel over deep water – so this exception exists to prove the rule.

The temperature of the water in lochs creates distinct warm and cold water layers – especially when winds are light. Over the winter months, layers tend to form at depth due to the greater density of cold water, with uppermost (less dense) layers comparatively warm. Winds can push this uppermost layer of warm water up against the lee (downwind) shore but this in turn tilts the whole layering system of the loch exposing the under-layer of cold water at the upwind shore. Feeding is more likely to be concentrated at the warmer end of the loch. However, even this 'rule' is broken by other effects. During very warm spells, the water heats up at the surface. Oxygen dissolves in water directly from the air but the warmer the water, the lower the oxygen content – so fish may have to swim deeper to find more comfortable conditions.

It is not uncommon for the wind to blow terrestrial insects like daddy-long-legs or heather flies, onto the water at the upwind shore where trout readily accept this concentration of food. At the other extreme, hatching aquatic insects may be blown into the shallows of the lee shore. Promontories and islands also tend to affect the concentration of food items, so it is not always straightforward to assess where most feeding is occurring. The species of insect which the trout eat, influences where and how they feed. It can be a very complex affair. Suffice it to say that there are logical systems at play, but feeding activities may be concentrated in different ways at different times. The trick is to be lucky, especially if you find difficulties in interpreting the complexities!

The range of habitat occupied by trout populations is diverse. They are found in the lochs and burns of the Highlands, often at considerable altitude, and are also present in lowland lochs and partly-saline estuaries. In northern and Highland waters, adult trout tend to be small due to prolonged winter cold and the short season when food is abundant. An adult brown trout in this type of water may reach around 20 centimetres after several years; whereas a trout of similar age in a richer lowland loch may be several times this size. In some lochs there are large trout, known as 'ferox', which have adopted a part-cannibalistic form of feeding and are the quarry of a special type of game fishing.

One of the attractions of wild Scottish trout is their range of colour and markings. In dark parts of rivers, usually gorges with deep overhung pools, they tend to adopt correspondingly dark brown/bronze-coloured camouflage; whereas in lochs, with bright sandy bottoms, the trout are butter-yellow with bright vermillion-red spots. In some waters they have shiny silver-lemon colouring and in others they have a wonderful golden sheen, which is highly attractive. The patterns of their markings also varies with some being very heavily-spotted, while others have lighter speckling or almost none at all.

Until recently, it was firmly believed that sea trout and river brown trout were separate species, but this has been disproved. Some brown trout offspring adopt migratory lifestyles – in other words, they become sea trout – while some of the offspring of sea trout may live all their days in the river as brown trout. Late twentieth-century technologies, such as DNA polymerase chain reaction and genetic probing, have enabled these fascinating findings to surface. Exactly what turns one fish into a migratory form, but does not influence its brothers, has yet to be determined. It may be the result of nature's heterogeneity creating the widest range of survival characteristics. For the wider the diversity of life traits that a species adopts, the higher its chances of overall survival – and trout have swum in Scottish waters for a very long time.

Most trout eat a varied diet. In lochs, the largest part of their diet is composed of aquatic insects, paticularly 'midges' (belonging to the order Chironomidae). The chironomids are also known coloquially as 'buzzers' due to their high pitched whine when they buzz close to, or into, your ear. Fortunately for anglers, the midges differ from their landward cousins because they do not bite humans. Anyone who has suffered the onslaught of the Scottish biting midge (*Culcoides impunctatus*) will know only too well their voracious appetite for human blood – although curiously, it is only the female that bites.

Trout eat most food items; it is unusual for a post-mortem examination to find only single species present in their alimentary canal. This opportunistic feeding is a result of the wide range of locally-available food, which includes: daphnia, shrimps and other small crustaceans; molluscs like freshwater snails and bivalve shells; the truly aquatic insects of the Chironomid species; the 'upwing', day-flies (Ephemeroptera); the 'sedge' and caddis' flies (Trichoptera); the 'stone flies' (Plecoptera); water-boatmen (Corixa) and the damselflies and dragonflies (Odonata). Added to this is the colossal variety of terrestrial insects like house flies and bluebottles (mostly of the order Diptera); bees, ants and wasps (Hymenoptera); butterflies and moths (Lepidoptera); beetles (Coleoptera); a few spiders (Arachnida); a grasshopper or two (Orthoptera); several small fish, an unfortunate tadpole, worms of various types and sizes and even the odd cigarette end!

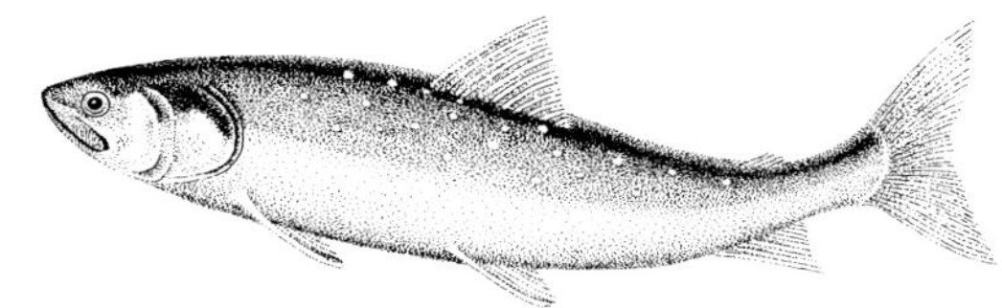

CHARR

Arctic charr are natural relics from the retreat of the last Ice Age. They are found in Scotland's deeper lochs, often in large shoals, although they tend not to be fished in the context of sport. In some countries around the Atlantic fringe, charr migrate into the sea and run the rivers to spawn. In Scotland they are 'land-locked' in the lochs. From time to time, they may be caught in rivers flowing out of the lochs where they normally live. They have beautiful colours and markings, particularly around spawning time, when they are deep blue-grey along the back with speckled bright orange-red flanks. The lower part of the pectoral, pelvic and anal fins and tail are sharply-edged with white. It is not unusual to catch charr when fly-fishing for trout in these lochs – this adds an extra dimension to a day afloat. They also make fine eating, especially if smoked. Ferox trout feed heavily on charr populations and some lochs, which have fish farm cages in them, hold larger charr that thrive on uneaten food falling from the cages.

THE SALMON

It is probably the Atlantic salmon that is most-closely identified with Scotland's fishing heritage. Here is a rich vein of Scottish outdoor culture, for there is a wealth of fact and fiction attached to this mystical and beautiful fish. We know a lot more about the salmon than we did previously – a great deal of research has been undertaken recently to understand its life cycle and biology – but it still remains enigmatic in many ways.

Salmon have been proven to consume nothing during the journey upstream, begging the question of why they take an artificial fly or fishing lure into their mouths. Many believe that they are curious about the unusual object that comes into view beside them and are trying to find out what it is. They sometimes seem to become irritated by it and chase after it, grabbing it aggressively. This is particularly true of male fish, which become very territorial and protective of their locality as they approach spawning maturity. Whatever the reason, salmon anglers the world over accept with gratitude that the mighty fish may sometimes be persuaded to accept their lure.

Standing at a pool-side watching salmon head upstream is utterly fascinating. Their great paddle tails are so powerful against the weight of the current. One decent thrust sends the fish off at high speed or careering out of the water in a spectacular, glittering leap. They may lie, finning quietly in the current, as though in a torpor, seemingly disregarding everything around them; then something breaks their reverie and they seem to startle into alertness; their whole demeanour changes from being inert into a state of quivering excitement. They are truly magnificent fish and a wonderful sporting quarry. Like the trout and charr, the salmon has swum in Scotland's rivers far longer than the riverbanks have been trodden by anglers. The Scottish salmon is so precious, a fascinating natural asset, and worth careful preservation and conservation.

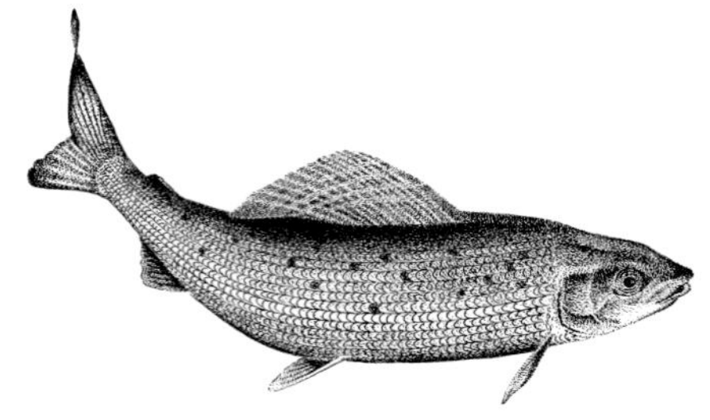

THE GRAYLING

This graceful fish is found in many of the Lowland rivers of Scotland. It is not a fish of rocky west coast spate rivers, where cascades and wild thrashing torrents abound, it is found in more sedate surroundings. The larger rivers of eastern Scotland have good grayling populations especially the Tay, Earn, Tummel, Isla and Tweed. Nevertheless, they are distributed widely wherever quieter streams are found. Affectionately known as the 'Lady of the Stream', the grayling offers fine angling opportunities for those who wish to fly-fish or use fine bait fishing techniques – especially when the trout season has closed.

The grayling occupies a similar ecological niche to river trout, therefore, although the trout's range is wider, grayling are often caught when fishing for trout. Trout and grayling co-exist without major difficulty, diversifying Scotland's game angling potential. The influence of eastern European fly-fishing techniques has impacted on grayling fishing in recent years, with the weighted and woven nymph patterns emanating from the former Czech Republic proving to be highly successful. This is due to the grayling's main feeding trait of taking the nymphs of aquatic flies and other species near the bottom. A pleasant alternative to fly-fishing is to trot a small worm, either using a small float or allowing the bait to run free, through likely pools and glides. Red and yellow-striped 'brandling' worms seem to work best. Grayling are shoal fish. Catch one, and you should be able to catch others. However, they are easily spooked and require to be fished for with care and skill – a demanding, attractive and worthy quarry.

THE RAINBOW TROUT

Originally introduced from North America, the now ubiquitous 'rainbow' is wholly established in Scottish fishing. In a way, it simply had to be, for the increased pressure of angling on brown trout would have jeopardised native stocks of brownies. Many waters could not have continued as fisheries had it not been for the availability and lower cost of stocking with fast-growing 'bows'. Initially, rainbow trout in Scotland were second-class citizens due to their poor quality. Now however,

fisheries stock with high-quality fish, fully worthy as an angling quarry. Consequently, a shift in the methods of Scottish trout fishing has occurred, fuelled by the powerful rainbow. Methods of catching rainbows differ from traditional methods of brown trout fly-fishing; a new generation of anglers has grown up who fish almost exclusively for 'bows'.

Rainbow trout have not naturalised after initial stocking in the way that they have done in other parts of the world. The reason for this is not clear, although small rainbow trout have appeared from time to time in Scottish rivers as though they had come from natural spawning. Similarly, rainbows that have migrated to sea – much in the same way as sea trout – have appeared in some of our rivers and these migratory fish are very like their North American counterparts, the legendary Steelhead Trout.

Rainbows are voracious feeding machines. They 'hoover-up' anything that is edible, and grow at prodigious rates under optimal conditions. This constant state of hunger makes them highly susceptible to the angler's fly – much more so than their cautious native cousin, the brownie. A well-conditioned rainbow is a sleek, powerful fish that fights strongly when hooked. Much depends on how well rainbows are reared. If they are kept in over-close proximity to each other, they damage their fins and tail. If they are overfed and under-exercised, they grow fat and deep. The best rainbow is torpedo shaped, fully-finned and brightly coloured. They are beautiful trout with iridescent purple-pink hues (hence their 'rainbow' description) along their flanks, are lightly speckled over the body, but heavily-speckled on tails and fins, and have bright-silver scales, which are sometimes matched by the rays of their fins that take on a silver colouration.

When you hook a decent 'bow' you soon know about it. They pull strongly and tend to leap out of the water more than brownies, adding to the excitement. They are shorter-lived than brown trout, often reaching only five or six years. Brownies may reach several times this age, but rainbows live life to the full and provide excellent sport. In the history of Scottish fishing, nothing has influenced and changed the course of this pastime more than the introduction of the rainbow trout. Love them – as many anglers do – or hate them, they are here to stay and form a huge part of our sport.

Atlantic Salmon, River Ettrick: The vigour and fighting qualities of a fresh Atlantic salmon are comparable to any fish anywhere in the world. Many anglers return most of their salmon to the water alive so that the species will continue to provide superb sport far into the future.

Coarse Fish

A Decent Pike: Found in many waters throughout the country, Scottish pike are large and strong and make excellent sporting quarry.

Angling for coarse fish – the wide range of fish families that are not recognised as game species – is a developing trend in Scotland. The reasons are clear. There are excellent coarse fisheries to enjoy. The influence of rapid access by road has meant that anglers from other parts of the UK have realised the potential that Scotland offers. This in turn has heightened the levels of interest.

Many young fishers cut their angling teeth and have great fun catching perch in their local pond, or worming for eels in the local burn. But their coarse fishing interest fades when what seem to be greater opportunities come along.

Quite a number of anglers, from around the UK and elsewhere, settle in Scotland and bring with them their angling interest and experience. These skills may not have much to do with traditional Scottish game angling or sea fishing but have a core of similarity. In turn, this cross-fertilisation of angling culture has encouraged many more Scots to adopt coarse fishing, especially during the game angling close season.

Scotland's coarse fishing scene consists of fishing in the lochs, canals and the slower reaches of rivers which are predominantly located in the central part of the country. There are several closely-guarded secrets in coarse angling – places where only the select few have found venues that offer excellent prospects. In a way, this is almost inevitable. But there is tremendous potential for exploration of the more remote areas, which are less well-known as coarse fisheries. Take care to obtain full permission however, for some waters are limited to game angling.

Not all coarse anglers who 'discover' lochs with good heads of pike or perch keep the information to themselves, and many are willing to help their fellow enthusiasts. There are clubs specialising in coarse angling and some of these clubs own or lease their own waters. They stock them with pike, perch, carp, roach and tench and create coarse fishing of significant quality.

The most well-known coarse fisheries tend to be those containing pike. Pike seem to attract a singular fascination. Perhaps this is because they can grow to a prodigious size, or maybe it is because they are seen to be fierce predators and worthy of an angling 'scrap'. The large lochs of the central area are fished for pike with consistent success, Loch Lomond and Loch Awe in particular, but others like those of the Trossachs deserve close attention. There are many lochs in Scotland that hold pike, but the fishing is underused and poorly understood.

The best part of pike fishing is its relaxing quality. Clambering up and down steep, rocky river banks is not for pike anglers; they tend to enjoy a more sedentary day out, restfully watching the float for the tell-tale pull; or quietly wading along a reedy loch margin to throw a 'wee spinner' in front of 'big Lucius'. The extra advantage of fishing well into the winter has great attraction too. After the salmon and trout seasons have closed, the pike comes to the fore as the quarry of late autumn and winter. Many a fine day has been had fishing for the 'freshwater shark' in crystal-clear, frosty weather, with a bright fire and freshly-brewed tea, and the superb aroma of bacon butties wafting along the loch-side.

Several of Scotland's rivers have a population of roach. The lower reaches of the River Tay are probably the most notable for roach angling and significant numbers of English roach fishers visit the river close to Perth to fish for the silver-scaled beauties. Some specimen roach have been caught and recorded here, and the traditional trout fly-fisher stands aside to watch, in awe of the intricacies of the use of swim feeders, quiver tips and other coarse angling technology.

Perch are found throughout much of the country. There can be few simpler or easier pleasures than catching fish after fish from a large shoal of decent sized perch. They are as bright as tropical fish, with a green and black-striped back, hot-orange fins, shiny flanks and prominent spiky dorsal fin. Are they easy to catch? Unquestionably yes. In fact, they can be a nuisance when they take a fly intended for a fine trout. Nevertheless, they are attractive fish especially for young and novice anglers. In the southern part of the country, most ponds, almost all lochs and a fair spread of the slower sections of river have perch. They are less well-distributed in the north.

Scotland sits on the northerly limit for many species, which are normally classified as coarse fish. There are no natural populations of tench, chub, carp, dace, rudd, or bream, but there are several waters, especially in the southern parts of Scotland, where some or all of these species have been introduced for fishing. This trend seems likely to increase. If global warming continues, it may well be that these species will adopt Scottish waters as their permanent, naturalised home. Too few anglers in Scotland realise the full potential of fishing for coarse species. It is a technical form of angling, often difficult and invariably challenging. More importantly, it is also highly enjoyable.

Eliburn Reservoir: A coarse fishery near Livingston in central Scotland. The potential for coarse fishing grows apace as more anglers become familiar with its many attractions.

Sea Fish

With almost four fifths of the Earth's surface covered by ocean it seems entirely reasonable to expect that sea fishing should be popular. Clearly, it is around our shallow shores that most of this is undertaken, and Scotland is extremely fortunate to have excellent sea fishing on the European continental shelf. The west coast is deeply etched with fjord-like lochs and many islands dotted in the sea. The North Sea, off the east coast, is one of the richest areas for white fish anywhere in the world.

It is food that sustains marine fish populations. The rivers pour minerals and organic matter into the sea, while the North Atlantic drift brings warm currents. These shallow waters are as rich as any in temperate regions.

The twice-daily swell and pull of the tides cleanses inshore areas, and organic matter drifts out to where it enriches the marine environment. The foraging fish of the shark, mackerel and tunny families range widely in these currents, while the littoral areas are populated by species of a more residential habit.

The shark family is well-represented. Porbeagle Sharks *(Lamna nasus)* are common and weigh between 100–200lbs, although specimens weighing 400lbs have been caught from time to time. Mako Sharks *(Isurus oxyrhinchus)* are often much larger, but are rarely caught on rod and line. Blue *(Prionace glauca)*, Thresher *(Alopius vulpinus)* and Hammerhead Sharks *(Sphyrna zygaena)* are uncommon visitors, but occasionally are rod-caught. The Tope *(Galeorhinus galeus)* and the Smooth Hounds *(Mustelus mustelus* and *Mustelus asterias)* are favourite rod fishing quarry, as are the Greater-Spotted *(Scyliorhinus canicula)* and Lesser-Spotted Dogfish *(Scyliorhinus stellaris)*.

Rays are relatively common, with the Thornback Ray *(Raja clavata)* the most likely to be encountered. Skate are caught around most of Scotland's shores – especially the Common Skate *(Raja batis)*. These great flatfish provide superb sport and are most unwilling to be dragged to the surface when hooked – you will have a major battle raising a Titanic version of a large Thornback or Skate!

Sea Fishing, Scotland: Out in a boat, the company are bright and humorous, with high prospects for a great fishing day. There are countless boats for charter around Scottish shores. Almost every small harbour has someone who knows the local area and will take you out to enjoy some first-class fishing.

A Decent Skate:
Catch and release. The fish is carefully measured, tagged and released back into the clear depths. Fish like these are a real asset in Scottish waters.

Perhaps the most common quarry is the ubiquitous cod *(Gadus morhua)* which is found and fished for over rocky reefs and along rocky shores. Pollack *(Pollachius pollachius)*, whiting *(Merlangius merlangus)*, ballan wrasse *(Labrus bergylta)*, ling *(Molva molva)*, coalfish *(Pollachius virens)*, and haddock *(Melanogramus aeglefinus)* are also found in rocky and weedy locations. Conger eels *(Conger conger)* enjoy the shelter of the many wrecks around Scotland's rocky shores, and are a difficult and challenging target species.

Mackerel *(Scomber scombrus)* shoal in huge numbers in high summer and are caught for use as bait. The sandy-bottomed bays have excellent populations of flounder *(Platichthyes flesus)*, dab *(Limanda limanda)* and plaice *(Pleuronectes platessa)*, with turbot *(Psetta maximus)* and our largest 'flattie', the halibut *(Hippoglossus hippoglossus)*, in deeper waters. Big halibut are fairly common, especially off our north-west coast, with specimens of 200lbs caught regularly; occasionally, one of three or even four times this weight turns up from time to time.

The streamlined-silver, and superb-to-eat, bass *(Dicentrachus labrax)* seem to be extending their range, which is excellent news for the surf and beach fisher. This may be due to global climate change because bass were previously found in southern waters. The thick-lipped grey mullet *(Chelon labrosus)* is similar as it is now found where warm water outflows come from industrial cooling and electricity power plants. Previously, it too was a southern water denizen.

One thing is for sure, you will never experience all that Scotland has to offer as far as sea fishing is concerned, it would simply be impossible to have the time for that. Select what you feel would suit you most – you have plenty to choose from.

Below: Boat fishing off the Isle of Mull, Inner Hebrides, West Scotland.
A rod bends into that wonderful curve which signals a big fish.

Fish Habitats

Fish are fairly simple creatures. They need only simple things to thrive. They need water containing sufficient dissolved oxygen to breathe, which should be within their optimum temperature range for survival – 0°C/25°C. The flow of the water should also suit their capabilities to swim and exist within it – too fast and the poorer swimmers will be swept away. There are recognisable zones within Scottish rivers where different conditions exist, each zone suiting different populations of fish. The zones are not sharply-defined, but overlap, their environmental conditions merging into each other.

The uppermost zone is the 'head-stream', which is often steep, fast-flowing and shallow, with extremely high oxygen-content due to the constant mixing of air and cool water. The average summer temperature rarely exceeds 10°C. This is the home of trout and salmon parr, minnows and stone loaches. These uppermost reaches of rivers do not support heavy vegetation, and their gravely pools are where salmon and trout deposit their eggs.

The middle zone is less turbulent and retains fairly high oxygen-content where the current mixes water and air. However, the water is likely to be heated during the height of summer – with mean temperatures of up to 15°C – thus reducing the oxygen dissolving capacity of the water. As guidance, water at 5°C will absorb oxygen up to 13 parts per million, but at 25°C the oxygen content will be below eight parts per million. The river may be deeper in places and consequently, the current is not as rapid. This is where shoals of grayling join the larger trout and salmon, and where perch and pike live in the slower sections. Various weeds grow in these slower runs, which are used for spawning by coarse species.

The lower zone has medium oxygen content but this shows layering – higher at the surface, but decreasing with depth. This is due to decay of organic matter at the bottom reducing the oxygen content, plus the effects of higher surface temperatures that often exceed 15°C. The water supports trout, pike and perch. Some rivers have populations of roach in the lower zones, and there is likely to be a good population of eels.

The estuarial zone becomes increasingly saline as it nears the sea and is influenced by backing–up by the tide. Here, the brackish water may be poorly oxygenated and verging on the toxic due to decay of organic matter, which causes high levels of dissolved carbon dioxide. The bottom is muddy and, although it may be rich in invertebrate food, it does not support the insect population that higher zones do. Consequently, the species here are mainly bottom feeders including flounders, mullet, bass and a few 'slob trout'.

Fish need a place to hide, or they may use other mechanisms, to avoid predators. Shoaling makes them look larger and a less-attractive meal to a potential predator. Although it means that a few of the shoal may be sacrificed, it enhances the chances of survival for the remainder of the shoal. Alternatively, they may adopt realistic

The River Dionard Estuary, Kyle of Durness, North West Sutherland: The estuarial zone of most rivers becomes increasingly saline as it nears the sea and is influenced by backing-up by the tide.

Loch Bad an Sgalaig, Gairloch, Wester Ross: There is a rich diversity of lochs in Scotland from the lovely natural west-coast lochs like this one, to the great expanses of reservoirs in the south and east.

Fish species have adapted to fill much of the available habitat that their aquatic environment provides. Some live and feed near the surface and range widely, while others lie on the bottom and live most of their lives in the same spot. Fish are great survivors. They have inhabited our planet for a very long time – 450 million years to be precise. Each species, or group of species, has developed ways of life that suit them. Anglers are more successful if they have some understanding of fish behaviour, and choose methods that have a basis in this knowledge.

The sea was the place where fish first developed and retains the greatest number and variety of species. Scotland is greatly favoured, as it sits between the cool north and the tropical south. This means that we have a large range of resident

camouflage and simply hide. Flat fish, like sole and flounders, demonstrate this beautifully; they are speckled and coloured exactly like the sand they live upon. When they wish to become invisible to escape a predator, or to lie in wait for unsuspecting food, they bury themselves just under the surface of the sand with their prominent eyes keeping a careful watch. Adaptation of form and behaviour suits their purpose – simple but effective.

River Laxford, West Sutherland: No trees here amongst the ancient rocks of the Laxford valley. This is a typical spate river – low when no rain falls, and in turbulent flood in times of high precipitation. Wild hard-stone rivers of this type do not have huge populations of large resident fish as feeding is relatively poor. They do however, enjoy excellent runs of migratory fish.

Loch Beinn a' Mheadhoin: Brown trout.

have developed to fill an ecological niche. This process has been assisted by Man from time to time, sometimes with beneficial outcomes and sometimes less so. Scotland is too far north – and too cold – for many coarse species, which occupy warmer southern waters. Nevertheless, the coarse fishing potential of Scotland is undervalued – probably due to the traditionalist attachment to game fishing. Many Scottish lochs have roach, perch and large pike. Carnivorous pike deserve their description as 'freshwater sharks' and to fish for them is to become part of 'nature, red in tooth and claw'. Many specimen sized pike are to be found in Scottish lochs.

Scottish rivers and lochs suit the different species that live within them. The lowland lochs, fringed with water lilies and reeds, are the home of large pike and shoals of green-striped, orange-finned perch. The more sedate rivers hold shoals of grayling. The rocky burns, which cascade over waterfalls into deep pools as they clatter downhill, suit the spirited red-speckled 'brownie'. The reasons for the selection of habitat are complex, although mostly based on the availability of food

marine species, swelled regularly by 'exotic visitors' from warmer climes. Sea angling around our shores is mainly for plentiful species such as: cod, haddock, ling, saithe, pollack, bass, conger and the various flat fish, plus the significant members of the shark family. As these species live in widely different habitats, Scottish sea angling is interesting and mixed.

Scotland's sandy-bottomed bays hold populations of flat fish including flounders, plaice, sole, rays and dabs, plus spotted dogfish, tope and bass. Rocky beaches are home to coalfish, cod, whiting, haddock, and pollack and are visited by glittering shoals of mackerel during the middle months of the year. Scotland's cliffs are great places to fish for cod and ling. Boat fishing often brings a colourful ballan wrasse amongst the cod, ling, coalfish, saithe and haddock. To fish for large 'flatties,' such as turbot, halibut, and skate, or encounter a large porbeagle shark at close quarters, requires the services of a specialised boat and skipper – the northern shores of Scotland have many places where this service excels.

In freshwater, both coarse and game species

River Thurso, Caithness: A fine salmon fresh in from the Pentland Firth tide.

supply and the water conditions. The mossy rocks around the tumbling mountain burn are home to stoneflies, dayflies and other items that trout favour. This kind of feeding and the speed and turbulence of the water would not suit species like perch, which need sedate flows or even still conditions.

Where one species thrives it wholly or partially excludes others from its habitat, unless they adopt some kind of symbiotic or predatory relationship. Each type of aquatic habitat typically fills with a small number of fish types, which become balanced in number and size. It is a question of population dynamics. Man intervenes however, and releases new species into the waters, or changes the environment so radically that the balances have to be redressed. Nature does this too, of course, but the effects of interference by Man seem sudden and often ill-advised. A typical example of this was the release of ruffe into Loch Lomond. These small coarse fish were used as live bait, but became naturalised in the loch where they had not existed previously. This new species proliferated, but consequently affected other well-established species in the loch. It is not difficult to introduce new species to an environment, but it is difficult to control them once they have become established.

Loch Watten, Caithness: A morning afloat on Loch Watten in Caithness provides sport to small floating fly-patterns.

Fish live where there is sufficient food to sustain them. The only significant exception to this rule is when reproductive requirements takes the place of nutritional appetite. Then, fish may range from their home station to reach localities where conditions favour juvenile fish. There the females release ova and the males fertilise spawn by releasing their milt. Some fish spawn in the same territory as they normally live. Others migrate to the shallows, or upstream to smaller parts of river systems. After reproduction, most fish are exhausted and are out-of-condition, so as soon as possible they return to the areas where rich feeding is available to restore themselves. The tiny progeny start on a journey through life, which is full of risk and dangers. Not many survive to maturity, but this is why adults produce so many offspring. It is the 'survival of the fittest' in a hazardous environment and the greatest danger of them all is undoubtedly Man!

Ghillie, North Uist.

Fish Behaviour

River Glass, near Cannich: The river has wide horizons and shimmering waters.

We catch fish by enticing them to take hold of a hook. Pretty simple stuff; nothing too complicated really. But the lengths that we have to go to, to entice the little silver darlings to grab a hook, are far beyond 'simple stuff'. This is probably because fish do not stick to one form of food; they are opportunistic feeders and will take just about any edible morsels whenever the chance comes along. What this means for anglers is that we try to imitate what we perceive to be natural food items and assume that this will entice the fish to grab our bait. Exactly how this relates to fancy fishing flies, which look nothing at all like natural food items, may become clearer in a moment.

Although many anglers use baits and lures which imitate food, there is an exception – the 'attractor' device. This may be a fluttering metal lure or a hook covered with brightly coloured feathers and furs. It may not be strictly imitative in any real sense, but has some general similarity to a food item. This kind of bait could be mistaken for a small fish glittering and swimming about as though it was wounded. It is more likely that fish see this peculiar object coming into their immediate locality and grab it in an attempt to establish if it is edible – a bit like us squeezing a pear to see if it is ripe. So the colour, size and motion of lures may attract without strict imitation. This is where fancy fishing flies come in. They are around the correct size of some food items, but they may be entirely the wrong colour and motion in the water. Nevertheless, fish will come towards them and may take them into their mouths to see if they really are edible.

Fish possess senses which are similar to our own, if not identical. They do have a sense of smell and can locate food at some distance through olfactory receptors. They clearly have eyes to see with, although their vision is not very like our own. They have different systems of detecting colour and motion, and images are processed by a much simpler brain than one belonging to a human being. However, if fish possess such simple brains, why do they outwit our attempts to catch them so easily? Fish also possess a sensitive capacity to register sound, although this is accomplished in a different way to dry land animals. Fish have pressure receptors sited in their skin, particularly concentrated along their lateral line, and these react to sound and pressure waves transmitted through the water.

When we try to outwit fish, making them believe that a bait is wholesome and not a thing of danger to them, we take a leap of faith and presume it is attractive to our intended catch. Our confidence is boosted by success – a fish biting seems to indicate that our faith was justified. But until the first interest, all we are left with is either previous experience that this particular bait worked at some time in the past, or an intuitive feeling that it should work now. It is gratifying to have your faith rewarded of course. You have presented the bait in the right way, in the right place, at the right time, to entice a wild creature to accept it – a satisfying achievement.

We go to extraordinary lengths to design, procure and manufacture the baits of choice. Salmon anglers will reject a fly for a multitude of reasons including: that it is too big, the wrong colour, the incorrect quantity of various materials or the wrong shape, only to tie on another creation, which is very similar when viewed through the eyes of a salmon. Sea anglers create recipes of bait, which they believe to be utterly infallible – strips of squid with peeler crab, topped off with a nice juicy ragworm; but when in nature was there such a dish of delights set before an unsuspecting cod? Coarse anglers have gone to even greater lengths with flavoured baits dyed in attractive hues and offered in the most unnatural of presentations. But each of these work, and that is what bait selection is all about – we must instinctively feel that the bait is worth trying, and often it will be. It starts with partial understanding – it can only ever be partially understood until we are able to enter the minds of fish – and culminates in what we think that fish would like to eat. Add to this the 'attractor' element which really has less to do directly with food, and we have the whole thing sewn up.

The life cycle of Scottish fish species is fairly standard. Regardless if the fish live in the sea, rivers or lochs, it goes more or less like this. The male and female pair up, find a suitable place for the female to discharge eggs, the male fertilises the eggs by releasing milt over them, they hatch out into tiny fry, then grow larger dependent on food supply and temperature until they reach maturity and they respond to the need to reproduce – then the cycle is complete. However, it is not quite so simple because fish, more than any other creature, are subject to being eaten by other living entities.

Birds catch many fish. In Scotland there are gulls, cormorants, shags, ducks, herons, kingfishers and ospreys, feeding on fish. Animals also catch fish. These include seals, otters, mink and the greatest predator of them all – Man. Even fish eat fish and cannibalistic predation by their own kind accounts for the disappearance of trout when ferox are present. Pike are notoriously voracious fish-eaters. In fact, most species will accept a smaller fish for supper if the opportunity comes along. What this all means is that to sustain a population of fish requires a huge overproduction of juveniles; their numbers are whittled down through predation and other natural losses.

Such are the losses in some species, that it takes several thousand hatched fry to end up with a single pair of reproductively-active adults. On the other hand, given ideal conditions, fish populations can flourish rapidly. It is a matter of natural balance. This is where the influence of man may make or break sustainability of fish. Artificial stocking may supplement reduced populations when matters become desperate, but reared fish cannot really replace wild fish. Although they occupy the same situation they have not evolved to suit the locality. Nevertheless, most anglers would obviously prefer a pool of fish, which were stocked than a pool which is devoid of fish. As has been said, it is a matter of balance.

Loch Dusary, North Uist: Everywhere you look in the outer islands there are small lochs and tiny lochans.

The Life Cycle of Atlantic Salmon

The life cycle of some animals is truly unique; they occupy an ecological niche, which sets them apart from all others. The Atlantic salmon is especially remarkable. There are many prehistoric standing stones throughout Scotland with salmon carved upon them, marking the high regard primitive people had for the mighty fish. These hunter-gatherers would have noticed the annual patterns of ascending salmon. They would also have reaped the bounty of rich food, but none could have known the vast journeys that these remarkable fish had undertaken before arriving in the river.

Salmon live two lives. They are born in the higher parts of rivers, where they grow to maturity over two to three years as a wholly freshwater species. Then they become ready for a transformation as they swim downstream into the sea to become marine fish. The young salmon – called smolts – undertake a great journey to the rich feeding grounds of the North Atlantic off Greenland. Their food in the sea consists mainly of small fish species and crustaceans, sand eels, capelin and herring, and is supplemented by larger plankton. The abundance of food species allows the salmon to grow at a prodigious rate – they become sleek, powerful fish. As is the way with young adults, they start to feel the urge to reproduce. The instinct to return to spawn starts in some fish after a single winter in the sea. The returning salmon are called 'grilse' ('one-sea-winter' salmon). For others, it may take two or more years before they return.

Salmon also pick up a further description as 'spring', 'summer' or 'autumn' fish depending on the time of their arrival. Some Scottish rivers – the Tay, Spey and Tweed in particular – benefit from runs of fish from the start of each year. These early running salmon – called 'springers' – are superb fish. They are as fit as they can be – svelte and silver with each scale perfectly formed and aligned. An iridescent purplish-pink hue catches the light along their gleaming flanks. They are fin-perfect and powerful, fit for game angling, worthy to grace any table – undoubtedly a wonderful prize. Increasingly, anglers opt to return their springers to encourage greater numbers of these lovely fish in the future.

Summer salmon come when rain breaks the summer droughts, often coinciding with runs of grilse. This is from June to August. Autumn fish come in September and October with some rivers, like the Tweed, having 'back-end' runs through November into December. It is true to say that salmon arrive at the mouths of our rivers throughout the whole of the year, but discernible 'runs' are seasonal peaks of numbers.

Salmon are truly enigmatic. When they enter freshwater, it is almost invariably into the river where they were born. Research has shown that each river has its own 'odour' and this aids the salmon's homing instict. When they enter the river they cease feeding, and do not eat again until they return to salt water many months later. Not many of the post-spawning fish manage to return to the sea – there is a high mortality rate. For the few that do reach the lower river, it may be nearly a year before

The River Shin: Summoning huge reserves of energy, the Atlantic salmon accelerate in the lower parts of the pool below the fall then burst into a shimmering leap of many feet to clear the obstacle. Sometimes they gain the lighter flow at the top and get over the barrier, sometimes they fall back to try again.

they slip back into the estuary. They have eaten nothing, relying on body stores developed during their feeding in the ocean. Little wonder that a much-reduced number of post-spawning fish, known as 'kelts', survive and even fewer beat the odds and return to the sea.

Amhuinnsidhe Castle, Isle of Harris:
Salmon and sea trout wait in the sea loch for an increase in the river level which will encourage them to run upstream.

Atlantic salmon spawn in shallow nests called 'redds' scraped in the gravel in the closing weeks of the year. The female lays eggs (ova) amongst the gravel of the redd, while the male releases 'milt' over the eggs. Following fertilisation, the nest is re-covered with gravel and the ova mature for several weeks depending on temperature. A ten pound female salmon lays around 7000 eggs and as high a proportion as 90% of these hatch. Larger salmon may lay as many as 15,000 eggs. However, winter floods, interference by eels and birds and deposition of silt greatly influence the survival rate of fertilised ova.

In March to April, the eggs hatch out into small fish-shaped creatures (called alevins), which retain some of the egg yolk-sac. At about four weeks, the yolk-sac is absorbed and the fry feed independently on microscopic particles. At this stage the greatest mortality occurs and around 90% of all fry fail to thrive. Growth continues over one to two years until, in early summer, the largest parr take on silvery coloration and head towards the sea. This is normally two to three years after hatching. The 'smolts' are vulnerable to predation by fish-eating birds, but a proportion reach salt water, escape the seals and head off to the Northern Atlantic. Only 10% of smolts may return as adults, some coming back to the river of their birth after one full winter in the sea (grilse) and the remainder as multi-sea-winter salmon.

Atlantic salmon numbers and runs seem to vary cyclically – although this is hugely inconsistent. The late twentieth century saw a decline in numbers throughout the whole range. Exactly why this happened has yet to be determined, although there is evidence that sea temperature increases influence growth and return rates. Many factors undoubtedly affect salmon numbers including: predation by seals and fish-eating birds, netting at sea, shore and in-river netting, changes to spawning areas, inappropriate fish-farming practices, weather patterns and angling pressure. Each of these factors plays a part. It is gratifying to see the strong conservation measures that anglers take to protect salmon. These include releasing some or all salmon caught, improving the river environment and limiting the ways in which salmon are fished for.

It is easy to be pessimistic about the future of salmon in our rapidly-changing world, but there are excellent demonstrations of genuine success. Worthy of note is the River Kelvin, flowing through the heart of Glasgow into the River Clyde. The Kelvin was heavily polluted and uncared for. But clearing out the obstacles, and ensuring that the water ran clear and unpolluted, the river was returned to a healthy state. Salmon were introduced and a spawning population established. You can now stand in central Glasgow, look over a bridge, and see salmon. If it can happen in the heart of a modern European city, there should be valid grounds for optimism for our wild rivers; but concerted and effective action must be taken by all parties at sea and at home.

Top Salmon Flies

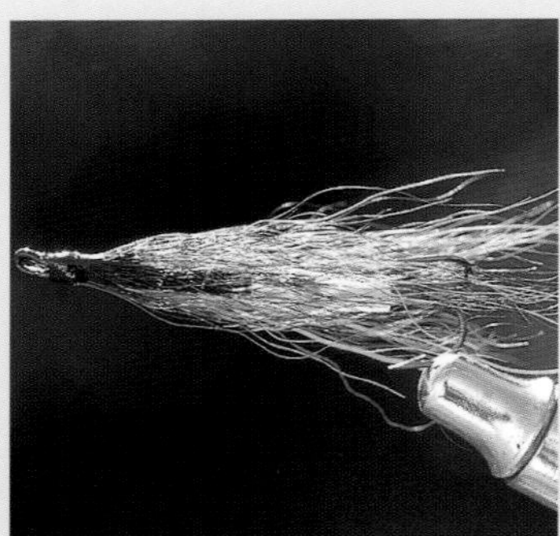
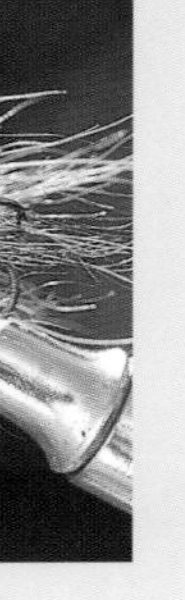

WILLIE GUNN

There are many patterns of salmon flies and my top ten selection comes from experience; you gain tremendous confidence if you have hooked a salmon or two on a particular pattern. You will disagree with some, if not all of my choices, but your choice will be based on your experiences, not mine. If you have yet to catch your first Scottish salmon, then believe me, the flies mentioned here will do the job extremely well.

WILLIE GUNN: the archetypal Scottish salmon fly; a staple pattern with many versions of its basic dressing but each version has most of the standard attributes including: a subtle blend of colour in the 'wing', dark contrast in the body and a glowing glint from the rib, which are all crucial elements in any successful pattern. The Willie Gunn is tied as a single hook or, using double or treble hooks, with long wings or short wings, on waddingtons and on tubes. It is a truly versatile fly and an essential addition to your fly box. Use versions with vibrant yellow and orange colours in the hair wing mix when the water is coloured, and smaller, more lightly-dressed versions when the river is low and clear. One of the best variants is the Golden Willie Gunn, which simply screams and begs for every salmon to take it!

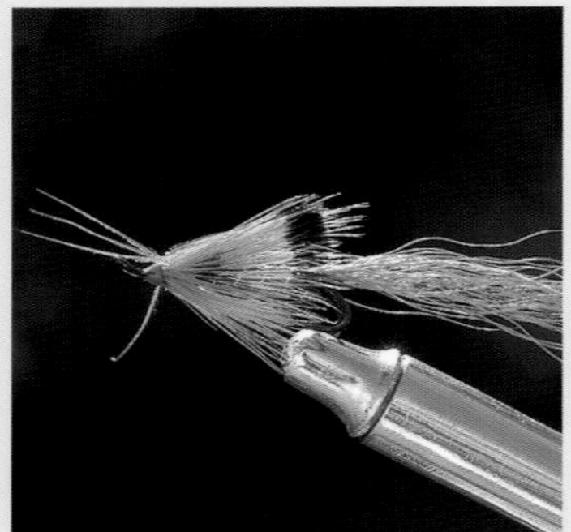

ALLY'S SHRIMP

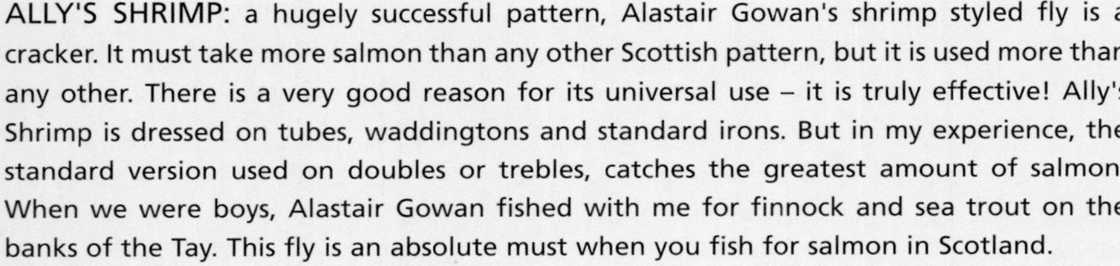

ALLY'S SHRIMP: a hugely successful pattern, Alastair Gowan's shrimp styled fly is a cracker. It must take more salmon than any other Scottish pattern, but it is used more than any other. There is a very good reason for its universal use – it is truly effective! Ally's Shrimp is dressed on tubes, waddingtons and standard irons. But in my experience, the standard version used on doubles or trebles, catches the greatest amount of salmon. When we were boys, Alastair Gowan fished with me for finnock and sea trout on the banks of the Tay. This fly is an absolute must when you fish for salmon in Scotland.

SILVER WILKINSON: a fancy, shiny pattern, which is particularly useful when the water is cloudy or coloured. It is in this situation that you benefit from the bright blue and magenta colours and the iridescent tinsel that gleams in the murky water. This pattern has a long history; first tied in the late 1850s by its originator, the Reverend P. S. Wilkinson, it was used on the Tweed with great effect, and still is 150 years later.

STOAT'S TAIL: after many years of fishing, I have come to the conclusion that some of the variants of fly dressings perform better than the originals. I believe this to be the case with the Stoat's Tail. Although, the original Stoat's Tail catches many fine salmon and grilse, I have found that the Jungle Silver Stoat's Tail, with jungle cock cheeks, is a much more effective salmon fly. The addition of jungle cock cheeks adds a further dimension, which increases the chance of a decent catch; the vibrant silver body almost guarantees a bite from a freshly-run grilse. An added bonus is that sea trout queue up to take it, which makes it an absolute essential for summertime river excursions.

HAIRY MARY

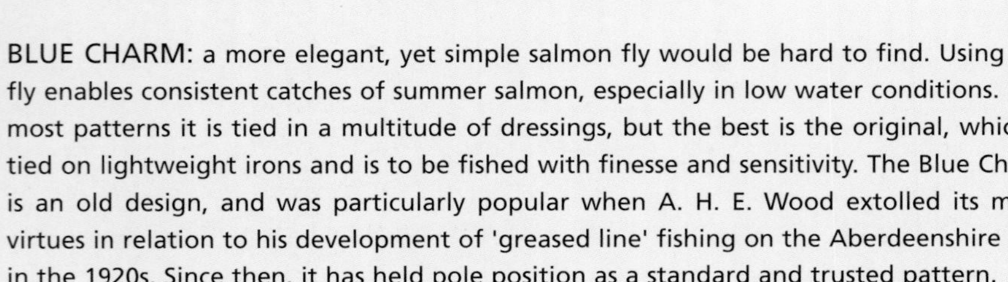

BLUE CHARM: a more elegant, yet simple salmon fly would be hard to find. Using this fly enables consistent catches of summer salmon, especially in low water conditions. Like most patterns it is tied in a multitude of dressings, but the best is the original, which is tied on lightweight irons and is to be fished with finesse and sensitivity. The Blue Charm is an old design, and was particularly popular when A. H. E. Wood extolled its many virtues in relation to his development of 'greased line' fishing on the Aberdeenshire Dee in the 1920s. Since then, it has held pole position as a standard and trusted pattern.

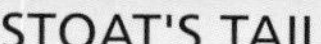

STOAT'S TAIL

TEMPLEDOG

JOCK SCOTT

GARRY DOG: invented by James Wright of the famous Sprouston Beat on the Tweed, who allegedly named it after his Golden Retriever 'Garry'. This pattern has embedded itself firmly into Scottish salmon fishing and is often used as a coloured water pattern, due to the contrasting red and yellow on the wing. The tying was one of the first to break away from fully-dressed patterns in favour of the slimmer and longer lasting hair-wing style. Small Garry Dogs also attract sea trout when the fly is tied on low-water irons. It is a versatile and effective pattern and a worthy addition to your collection.

MUNRO KILLER: this very successful Speyside pattern – derived from Munro's tackle shop in Aberlour, on the banks of the River Spey – was originally developed for use on the lovely Spey. Similarly to other salmon patterns, the Munro Killer has an attractive contrasting colour scheme, including the almost mandatory yellow underwing, which aids visibility in coloured water. Not everyone uses a dropper when fishing for salmon; some believe that it causes more problems than it catches fish – but there can be no better pattern to try than a small Munro when using a dropper.

HAIRY MARY: a grand summer pattern, especially in finer dressings, the Hairy swims through pools of salmon and draws many a cold-eyed glance, sometimes followed by a great surging run. Is it the hair-wing translucency, the gold-over-black contrast, or the cobalt blue throat hackle, which gives this pattern its life and resonance? Who knows? What is important is that the fly works, and does so consistently, in all Scottish rivers.

JOCK SCOTT: possibly the best known salmon fly in the world and emanating from Victorian times, when exotic plumage was 'busked' onto large irons, this pattern originated on the high seas. The pattern was fathered by John Scott, better known locally as Jock, who was retained as a ghillie by Lord Scott of Bemersyde, on the River Tweed. Lord Scott and his ghillie Jock were enduring a rough passage over the North Sea to Norway, and passed the time tying salmon flies for use in the great Scandinavian rivers. During the height of the storm, the fly now known as Jock Scott came into being and has enjoyed great success wherever it is offered to Atlantic salmon. This pattern does not suffer from over-tight prescription, almost anything goes in its tying recipe, although the yellow and black body provides lively contrast and the glowing mix of wing materials offers vibrant translucency. A grand fly.

TEMPLEDOG: sharing much more with the fully dressed flies of the past, the Templedog is not strictly a pattern in itself. Rather, it is a style of tying, a kind of 'concept' fly. Many different materials may be included, and the result tied on to single irons, or, as is more popular at present, on tubes. These tube flies are often weighted quite heavily in order to reach deep lying fish, and this is when they score best. The main feature of most Templedogs is the richness of their dressing; they glide through the pool like brilliant sparkling gems, emitting colourful hues designed to entice the most wary of salmon. The Templedog is not Scottish, it in fact comes from Scandinavia and is attributed to Swedish fly-tyer Hakan Norling. A truly effective design.

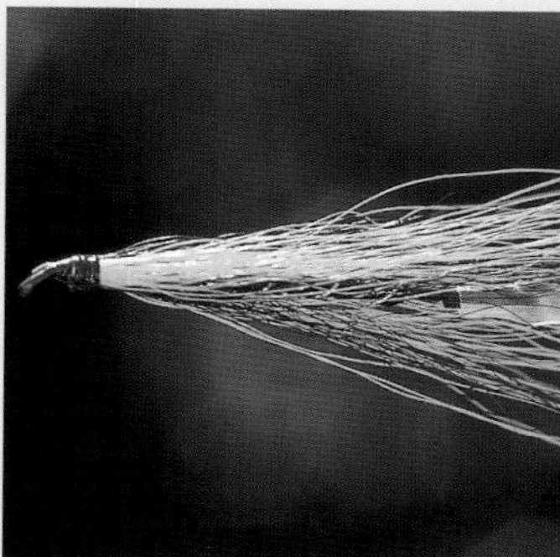

BLACK AND YELLOW

CASCADE

SILVER DOCTOR

Scotland's Geography

Loch Tollaidh, Wester Ross: The grandeur of the scenery surrounding most West Highland lochs may disturb your concentration on fishing.

Jutting out bravely into the eternal swell of the northern Atlantic provides Scotland with several major features which influence her fishing. The types of rock and ages of geological turmoil affect the topography of the land and, consequently, its aquatic environments; but other factors combine to make this region unique. These include the temperate oceanic climate and the persisting effects of the last Ice Age. The geological processes that shaped the landscape are still at work. The ancient rocks are still being ground away by the relentless effects of weather. Nothing stays the same, a fact that is obvious to the river angler who will often see the shape of his river changing as its course is reworked by winter floods.

Scotland has three main geological regions differentiated by their location and form. The first is the great expanse of the northern Highlands, which includes the Hebridean and Northern islands. It is a wild, mountainous area bounded in the south by the Highland Boundary Fault – the joining of two tectonic plates of the Earth's crust. The Highland Boundary Fault is marked along much of its length, by high ground to the north and low ground to the south. Some rivers tumble over the fault line, while others run through the great swathe of the low ground below. The valley of the River North Esk, near Edzell, presents a fine opportunity to stand astride the actual line of the Highland Fault, while the glens of the Rivers Tilt and Garry show where lava forced into the Fault's side cracks, to form igneous dykes over which the rivers tumble and foam.

The second region is the sweep of the Forth/Clyde valley known as the Central Lowlands. Here the rivers are wide and slow running. The River Forth meets the sea close to Scotland's capital city, Edinburgh, and the Clyde does the same near Glasgow. The greatest salmon river, the Tay, also runs through the central Lowland plain before it meets the North Sea. The third main geological region is the hilly Borders region known as the Southern Uplands. Here the rivers run through gentle valleys, many being tributaries of the mighty Tweed.

The rocks of the Highland north are mostly very ancient and metamorphic, with quartzes, gneisses and schists predominating, basalts and other igneous intrusions fill in the spaces. The Central Lowlands is a valley consisting of sandstones and other metamorphic conglomerates of younger age. The Southern Uplands are similar in geology to neighbouring north England, with folded and fractured metamorphic rocks showing the general north-east to south-west fault orientation. There are outcrops of various rocks in most areas, some with significant influence on fishing. A prime example being localised limestone of the far north and west, which brings richness to the aquatic environment.

Countless aeons of battering by oceanic waves and above-average rainfall have worn the west-coast into a deeply-etched system of fjordic sea lochs and islands. The west coast valleys carry spate rivers flowing mostly over bare rocks, and freshwater lochs where water is trapped in peaty glacial valleys. The effects of glaciation are visible everywhere. Smooth rocks polished by the ice sheets; deeply-cut glacial valleys show the tremendous sculpting power of the ice; and in many valleys there are raised beaches showing where seas once lapped at heights unimaginable today. In most valleys there are moraines – sediment deposited by glaciers – left behind following the melting of thousands of feet of ice at the end of the last Ice Age.

The east coast of Scotland is quite different from the west. Here the land tends to be much gentler in character with fewer, but longer rivers. Similarly, there are fewer lochs, perhaps due to lighter rainfall. The land slopes from the massif of the central Highland plateau towards the North Sea, and down this incline flow some of the most famous salmon rivers in the world including: the Tay, the Tweed, the Dee and the Spey.

For hundreds of years, major changes to Scotland's original landscape have occurred due to the impact of agriculture and forestry. The forests, which once stood throughout the country, were decimated for fuel or cleared for farming. The great Caledonian pine and oak forests are long gone, although you may still see the remaining vestiges on the island of a remote loch. There you may see red-trunked Scots pines providing a canopy over smaller hazels, birches, willows and alders. Birch forests have taken over where the great pine and oak trees once stood, but the planting of non-native conifers is the feature that most signals man's intervention through forestry. Many glens are flanked by mono-cultures of Sitka spruce and larch, although more-enlightened planting over recent years has seen the return of mixed deciduous trees. Many of our river banks have retained tracts of native species trees and are all the more attractive for this.

Man has also transformed the shape and course of many of the waters of Scotland. This process was

River Nith, South West Scotland:
The variety of landscape within Scotland is truly remarkable. One minute you are in a mountainous wilderness, the next you enjoy green rolling pastures and attractive old towns – and the fishing reflects this wonderful diversity.

River Lyon, Perthshire: Of all the glens in Scotland, Glen Lyon is held by some to be the most attractive.

at its height during the early part of the Industrial Revolution, where water power was essential for industry. Water, taken from dams, often comes from well below the surface of the impounded loch. The water may be cooler in high summer – an advantage – but may be less well-oxygenated – a temporary disadvantage – as the water should soon be aerated particularly if turbulent. Such water may also show variable chemical composition due to differential absorbance of nutrients at different temperatures and pressures in the dam above. On a practical level for anglers, keep in mind that the sudden onset of generation may create a very rapid, and potentially dangerous, increase in water height.

The impounding, the extraction, the creation of barriers and the rapidly changing river heights and flows all impact on fish feeding and migration patterns. The demand for a supply of potable water has resulted in an evident change to many of our river and loch systems too, although some have been very beneficial. For example the lochs of the Trossachs – the main source of Glasgow's drinking water – are very attractive and productive fisheries. Others have been less so where streams, prime areas for reproduction of fish, have been disrupted. Rivers have been channelled for road systems, dammed for industrial purposes and retained to lessen their impact on agricultural land. The canalisation of the rivers has made them prone to flooding, especially where flood plains have been drained and embanked.

Our attempts to improve salmon 'lies' may actually have resulted in damage. The 'croys' placed in rivers to make streams and pools more attractive to fish only do so for a few seasons, then their effectiveness fades. There are several layers of flow in rivers, which may help to explain this. There are surface currents and deeper currents of mid water, both of which are quite different from the surface layers. Deeper still, there are the bottom currents, which are slower as they drag along the roughness of river bed – they are extremely powerful. Finally there is the flow of silt, gravel and stones, which constantly sculpts the bed of the river into new shapes. Most fish like to adopt lies, which provide them with a supply of foodstuffs, adequate cover, if they have to hide, and a comfortable and even flow. To place obstructions in the path of flow, such as croys, often gives rise to turbulence. Therefore, it is evident that man's intervention tends to be 'against the grain' of the river, and having negative as well as positive consequences.

It is the sheer variety of Scotland's landscape – and her fishing opportunities – which attract people to the remoter parts of the country. Within a few miles, it is possible to fish for wild trout in the lochs of the 'machair', the coastal fringe of sand-dunes where the lochs are rich and productive, yet so close to the waves of the ocean; to fish in dark, peaty lochs amongst heather moors; to fish in one of the great lochs contained between high rocky peaks then fish for 'wee brownies' in a tumbling burn. What a wonderful, endless variety of fishing.

Scotland's Climate

It is easy to generalise about Scotland's weather; many agree that our climate is indeed 'temperate', just as defined by meteorologists. Scotland does not suffer extremes of weather. This however, does not present a wholly accurate picture because it fails to emphasise the variety of conditions, which makes our weather so diverse. The rapidity of these changes also contributes to our fascination with Scottish weather. There can be no doubt, our weather is capricious and inconsistent, but this adds to its attraction rather than detracts from it.

Temperatures are kept within a moderate range due to the effects of the Atlantic Ocean and North Sea balancing potential extremes of heat or cold. As a consequence, the land-mass is kept relatively warm during winter, and cool during summer. In addition, the Gulf Stream wafts warm currents onto the west coast, enhancing rainfall and impeding excessive winter cold. Additionally, the heat that builds up on the land during warm sunlit days creates cool on-shore breezes. These sea breezes can be quite strong at the coast and may penetrate thirty or forty miles inland but are often present only in the middle hours of a warm day. The mechanism for their formation consists of warm air rising several thousand feet in a thermal draught over the land which has been warmed by the sun, in turn drawing cool air in from the sea.

There is adequate rainfall to sustain rivers and stillwaters, especially in the west where mountains collect most of the available moisture from the damp air-stream. Cool northerly air from the Arctic blends with moisture-laden warm air from the mid-Atlantic and heads westwards across the Atlantic towards Scotland. It then literally collides into the higher hills of the western isles and mainland and cloud is generated. The rain then descends, sometimes not enough for anglers waiting for the rivers to rise sufficiently to excite salmon, and sometimes too much, causing the rivers to rise to high levels, an equally poor prospect for fishing.

It is no accident that anglers use the weather as a major excuse for their lack of success; even when conditions are perfect, they can change for the worse in a matter of minutes! Excuses such as "the wind is coming from the wrong direction", or "the light is too bright (or too dull)" are regularly heard on the beat. If it wasn't for the weather, anglers would have to blame their lack of success on their own lack of ability – not likely!

Rain comes in many forms in Scotland, from torrential, almost monsoon thunderstorm downpours, to light hill fogs, mists and east-coast

River Gruinard, Wester Ross:
Rattling through rocky rushes and deeper pots, the typical west coast river does not dally in its rush towards the Atlantic Ocean. The high ground of the western seaboard mountains drops steeply into the coastal shelf and the rivers dive down these steep glacial glens.

The River Nith, near Dumfries: There is a great difference between the precipitation of the wetter west and drier east coasts, and between the north west and south west. The high mountains of the north tend to draw rain. The south west is drier, and its flatter landscape results in slower sedate rivers.

'haars'. The greatest rainfall is in the north-west, where annual precipitation can reach 5000 mm (nearly 200 inches). In the drier east 500-600 mm (around 20 inches) may be expected each year. Most precipitation arrives in winter, but there are few days in Scotland when there is no chance of a shower somewhere.

Overall, Scotland's rainfall has increased by around 20% over the last decade due to the effects of global climate change. The extra water provides additional flow in our rivers which may have otherwise been depleted due to hydro-power generation and abstraction for agricultural irrigation. However, the extra rain often falls at less beneficial times when the river is high anyway, and any positive effect may be negated by damage to the river environment or its surrounds. Flash floods tend to bring additional solids, which 'silt up' the river. Substantial floods alter the bed and course of the river and disturb deposited ova when these are present in the river's substrate. We are warned that it is not only rainfall patterns which will increase, but we should expect winds to become stronger and from differing directions. Global climate change continues and presumably always will. It remains to be seen how, over the years, it will impact on our fishing.

Temperatures rarely reach the extremes of continental landmasses, although some high mountain plateaus of Scotland, such as The Cairngorms, are classified as sub-Arctic and the high tops are frozen for many months during the year. The snowfields are not permanent and increase the water flow as they melt through spring into summer. When summer droughts shrivel rivers to a trickle, their poorly-oxygenated flow may cause fish populations to suffer. These droughts, however, rarely last long and rainfall patterns during summer consist of short dry spells, interspersed with sudden downpours. This constantly-changing pattern results from the progression of anticyclones and depressions tracking in from the Atlantic Ocean. A few days of high pressure and fine weather is soon followed by the next low pressure depression with its associated cold fronts and rainfall.

Wind affects sport fishing greatly. Its direction alters fish behaviour, especially their feeding habits. Brown trout often take windblown insects in the shallows of the exposed 'lee shore'. Fishing close to the breaking waves often provides good results; in Scotland this is called 'fishing the foot o' the wind'. Rainbow trout, and to a lesser extent brown trout, may feed while swimming into oncoming wind. A further example of how wind presents food to the fish is when terrestrial insects are blown onto the water by off-shore wind and the fish gather to take advantage. Rainbows may gather at the 'upwind' end of a stillwater to take land-based insects as they fall, or to feed on hatching aquatic insects before they leave the surface. Brown trout also do this, but keep in mind that the 'foot o' the wind' offers concentrations of food items and is also worth fishing.

The wind also seriously affects how anglers are able to fish. Clearly, a force 7 or 8 gale is not the time to be afloat in a small boat on a loch or around our rocky seashore. However, strong winds also impair our ability to present lures and flies properly. Most anglers would state their preference of a light to moderate wind, especially if this happened to be under overcast skies. Whatever the weather, we must accept that we can do nothing to change it on the day – but at a macro-level we must act carefully to prevent major change. Speaking about climate change and the effects of global-warming, Professor Olav Orheim of The Norwegian Glacier Museum warns us:

'We are the first generation to influence global climate, and the last generation to escape the consequences.'

Fishing Seasons

Seasons significantly influence fishing activities in Scotland for several reasons. Firstly, the time of the year changes so much of how fish behave, and consequently how we fish for them. Secondly, the fish need to reproduce to sustain viable populations and we have introduced regulation in the form of 'close seasons' to avoid disturbing them at this vital time.

Fish are cold-blooded creatures. They are at the mercy of their environment, having no means of generating body warmth or getting rid of excess heat. The consequence of cold-bloodedness is that at the extremes of the Scottish temperature range, fish may find themselves in distress. Too cold, and they fall into a torpor, do not feed, and swim so slowly that they are prone to predators. At the other end of the temperature scale, the oxygen level in the water is depleted and as a result the fish struggle to intake a sufficient amount of oxygen. Another consequence is that unlike warm-blooded animals, they are unable to rid themselves of the heat of the surrounding water and perish due to heat exhaustion.

Each new season brings quite different behavioural activity in our fish. In Scotland, the winter cold causes ice to form on freshwater; the water in rivers and lochs becomes denser; and the metabolic processes of fish slow down to minimum levels. There is not much food available because insects are also cold-blooded and are not active in periods of penetrating cold. Curiously, it is not unusual to see upwing flies hatch from rivers in winter, but they are inconsistent and short-lived, with only a few insects surviving. These winter hatches are the exception, and the rule is that few flies come to the surface during cold spells. Due to limited feeding availability, fish feed on bottom-dwelling insects or species, but not as voraciously as they do in warmer conditions.

Pike feed during winter, but only for a short period on most days. They do not eat heavily because their sluggish metabolism requires low levels of energy input in cold conditions. Winter does not affect sea species to the same extent, due to the temperature buffering effect of coastal currents. They feed throughout the year, and winter offers excellent opportunities for cod fishing from our shores. This is often most successful at night and there is a hardy band of Scottish shore fishers who stay out through the dark winter nights on rocky promontories to fish for cod.

Spring brings relief from winter's deep chill and water temperatures rise in conjunction with lengthening warmer days. Food for freshwater fish is also more readily available, as insects and crustaceans become more active. Spring is a time of rejuvenation, and fish which have endured the winter months feed hard and freely. At this time of the year, after an enforced winter's fast they are at their most vulnerable to the angler – later into the summer they may be more fussy. There can be few more pleasant experiences than a spring day by the river or lochside with the birds singing, the cool

The River Tay, Murthly, Perthshire:
In the depths of January the frost can shrink the river to almost summer levels, but this is when the season opens and the chance of a 'springer' attracts many salmon anglers to test their tackle and cold-weather gear.

fresh air sweet and clear, and the trees in bright green bud marking a new season full of hope and promise.

During the summer months, lochs are layered, with warm water at the surface and cooler water below. Trout may opt to lie deeper to find cooler water with higher levels of oxygen content. For a period of weeks fish are active only at dusk and dawn when insect hatches reach their height. The 'evening rise' is a typical manifestation of this phenomenon.

The cool of autumn and its increased rainfall heralds spawning time for some species before the returning onset of winter cold. Species that spawn in late autumn and early winter feed avidly in preparation for their fast, taking advantage of the cool, fresh conditions. A Scottish autumn can be splendid. The air is still mild, the days are mellow and rich, the colours intense and glowing. The fishing is revitalised after the 'dog days' of high summer. Salmon enter the rivers in large numbers and trout are brightly-coloured and active with spawning ahead. It is a time of plenty with the prospect of winter ahead – a time for the angler to 'make the most of it' before winter closes in.

Salmon spawning patterns are reflected in the legislated fishing seasons. There are times, throughout the country, when salmon fishing is prohibited. Local fishery boards determine the specific start and finish dates for this period. Some river systems have salmon actively spawning by mid-October, although most fish start a few weeks later. Most salmon are at the height of their spawning activity in November to December. Some are considerably later however, which affects the finish date designated by the fishery board. The River Tweed and its tributaries are open until the end of November, when fresh fish are still entering the system in considerable numbers, but this is not the norm and most systems close the season during or at the end of October.

Trout tend to return to their place of spawning in the period from October to December. The fish are in poor quality in the early months of the year following the rigours of spawning and their winter fasting period. The opening of the trout season in Scotland is March 15th, but this is too early to expect fish to be in tiptop condition, especially at higher altitudes and in the far north. Realistically, trout fishing is at its best in May when they have had a chance to replenish themselves and regain full physical fitness.

The River Tweed, near Melrose: Summer brings its own delights. The river is alive, albeit at low water levels, and the landscape around it is green, lush, and pleasant. As the days lengthen, however, the fish become less ready to grab your offering and may be more likely to sulk during the warmer 'dog-days'.

Rivers, Lochs and Shores

The River Spey, Boat of Garten.
Scottish rivers: Some are spate rivers filled briefly by heavy showers tumbling through precipitous boulder-strewn river beds, where cascades of seething water froth and crash down mountain sides. Others are sedate streams meandering though wide valleys under mature trees and fringed by verdant banks.

What is it that makes Scottish rivers, lochs and shores so interesting? For some, the water may have a mystical attraction; for others a spiritual appeal. However, for most anglers the waterside is a crucial requirement in their everyday lives, they would be hopelessly lost without the sea or freshwater around them. They obviously have a great affinity with the water, which for others may be less well-developed, but for anglers it is paramount. Who amongst anglers can cross a bridge without leaning over the parapet to inspect the stream below, sometimes disappointed when it is a railway line lying there rather than a limpid pool, full of lively fish.

Rivers and lochs are expressive. Many anglers believe that they are are communicative, aiding their approach and technique. The perceptive angler is able to discern where fish are to be caught and how. But this predictive quality is not available to everyone – some miss out on the enchantment that it brings. Maybe this is why some people enjoy angling, while others are bored by it. The awareness exists in some people, but not all; it develops through experience and practice in the fortunate few who have it. The more you use it, the stronger it becomes.

Maybe it is a primitive trait, which modern life has overwhelmed. This form of natural awareness and consciousness is a residual element from our primeval past, a skill no longer needed for modern life, but still able to be revisited. It is that wonderful feeling of anticipation as you walk to the riverbank; or the strong sense of forthcoming success as the line sinks into the depths of the sea. It is the indescribable excitement that makes the hairs on the back of your neck bristle and pulses adrenalin to accelerate your heartbeat just before the fish takes.

Scottish waters are far more eloquent than waters elsewhere. This is due to the variety of their form and the climatic conditions in which they exist. The stillwaters are tremendously varied with small, dark, lochs high on wild heatherclad, moorland or at the other end of the scale, great lowland tracts of clear water, with scattered islands and sweeping bays. The communicative nature of these lochs are diverse. Rivers too are similarly varied in their form and expression. Some are spate rivers, filled briefly by heavy showers, tumbling down precipitous, boulder-strewn river-beds where cascades of seething water froth and crash down mountain sides. Others are sedate streams, meandering through wide valleys under mature trees and fringed by verdant banks. Each communicate in different ways to the receptive angler; each with a different story to tell.

A sun-lit loch, with gentle sparkling ripples

rhythmically sluicing onto the shore, can be transformed in minutes into a wild, dark place, when the clouds race in and the wind rises to send great waves to beat angrily against the land. The tranquil river pool on a summer evening, where bats flit after airborne insects and birds call quietly as they go home to roost, is a far cry from that same pool on a February morning, when a northerly gale blasts in from the Arctic to batter the bank with hail. The burnished surface of the sea in the sunlit bay of a July morning, with the raucous call of nesting seabirds on the cliffs, is a completely different place when the dark November gales drive huge breakers to pound the rocks. The diversity of each situation is reflected in the different messages conveyed. In essence, underlying our physical and scientific understanding of our aquatic environment, there is a mystical element that we cannot fully understand despite the fact that it often touches us when we venture to the waterside.

The Diversity of the Scottish Fishing Scene

There is a remarkable range of sport fishing available in Scottish waters. To categorise the individual types into sections, by species, venue or activity, may be a little misleading because some types of fishing fall into more than one description. For instance, you may bait fish for mullet in the sea, or fly-fish for them when they venture into the brackish water of an estuary, or even spin for them with tiny lures. Nevertheless, making a list serves to convey the width of interest and variety of Scottish sport fishing.

Sea Fishing: Around Scottish shores there are plenty sandy beaches to fish for flat-fish; there are cliffs which offer excellent rocky shelves for cod fishing; there are places exposed to the waves to enjoy surf fishing for silvery bass; there are off-shore wrecks for conger; there are wide bays which tend to accumulate mackerel, tope and spur-dog; there are sheltered estuarial areas which have a huge variety of species; there are warm-water outflows close to industrial plants and power stations where mullet congregate; there are deep-water ocean shelves where giant halibut and side-of-house skate swim in the clear green depths; and there are countless piers and jetties around our shores where youngsters cut their fishing teeth catching small fish – and the occasional larger one!

River Fishing: Rivers are, by their nature, wholly variable. No two pools are ever the same, and the volatility of conditions of water height and season create a constantly-changing riverine environment. But each river is also different from each of its brethern. There are the majestic sweeping pools of the great salmon rivers of Scottish east-coast rivers like the Tay and Tweed; there are the swift 'glide-to-pool-to-glide' of the classic medium-sized salmon rivers like the Spey and Dee; there are the highly acclaimed smaller salmon rivers like the Helmsdale, North Esk and Brora; in the west there are spate rivers which need rain to put the foaming flesh of flood water on their otherwise skeletal bones to encourage the fish to ascend the system; there are Highland 'freestone' rivers, rocky and tumbling, where small trout sport under the foam flecks; there are the sedate meandering ox-bows of the lowland streams where perch and pike join eels and roach; there are cascading burns and awe-inspiring floods, there are upper tributaries and wide brackish estuaries. What a wealth of river fishing!

Loch Fishing: When we consider Scottish stillwaters, the array of fishing and venues is just as stupendous and mind-boggling. There are literally thousands of tiny lochans – some tainted by the salt-tang of the sea – whilst others nestle in the sub-Alpine conditions of the highest corries of the Scottish mountains; there are carefully-managed small 'put-and-take' fisheries with unnaturally large, cultured, rainbow trout; there are remote lochs in the depths of genuine wilderness which have never had a fish put in them but where populations of charr and trout live in splendid isolation; there are highland lochs fringed with peat and rocks; there are lowland lochs with patchworks of fields dotted with tranquil cattle; there are high dams and deep reservoirs; there are small machair lochs beautifully fringed with beaches of pure white shells; there are rock-bound lochs as big as seas, dotted with islands, each of which benefit from the shade of native trees of great antiquity; there are tiny ponds with lily pads and bright-finned perch and voracious yellow-green camouflaged pike; there are lochs which salmon and sea trout run into; there are magical places tucked away from prying eyes where exotic species have been introduced. The list is as endless as your imagination – and you will need every ounce of your imagination, fitness and skill to be able to fish even a small proportion of them.

Biodiversity and Conservation

Mixed Bag of Salmon: It is not unusual to find a farmed fish amongst the wild ones which you catch. Here, one of the salmon is an 'escapee'.

All anglers, by virtue of regularly visiting the waterside, come into close contact with the natural environment. A successful angler must go beyond a simple awareness of their surroundings; instead they are obliged to appreciate and understand what is going on around them. In some ways people who go fishing cannot fail to notice things happening around them. This affinity with nature is a consequence of observing a wide range of animals, insects, birds, plants, and of course, the fish in their natural habitat. Anglers become naturalists, admittedly not always in a strictly academic sense, but they do appreciate natural processes and the relationship between some of these complex systems. Many anglers are very knowledgeable and contribute significantly to scientific work. There is no doubt that had it not been for anglers, wishing to enjoy natural rivers and lochs, the environment would not be as clean and productive as it is today. This is paticularly true in Scotland, but it applies throughout much of the world. It is part of a cycle: anglers require fish, fish require to have a well-balanced, sustainable aquatic environment and anglers increasingly fight to keep this part of our natural heritage in good condition.

For passionate anglers who wish to conserve their environment, there is no shortage of problems to be tackled. Ultimately, Man's activities will have an affect on the natural environment. Many will have a detrimental impact, such as the addition of pollutants to our waterways. Clearly the discharge of industrial waste is a threat to the environment because of the potentially highly toxic content,

Restocking Salmon, the River Carron: Catch-and-release is increasing considerably. This initiative is targeted at securing more fish in the river systems so that spawning may be at optimum levels, and the status of Atlantic Salmon should be secure for the future.

although some of the industrial waste contains soluble phosphates and nitrates, which enrich our waters. Many farmers utilise huge quantities of fertiliser to ensure maximum growth of crops; but a significant proportion of these chemicals dissolve in the run-off waters which fill our streams. Enrichment can cause many problems including: excessive weed growth, change to inter-relating bio-systems and an algal bloom, which, in extreme cases, may be toxic.

As a consequence of fish farming a huge quantity of soluble material in the form of nitrates and phosphates is released into the sea around the coast of Scotland. Fin-fish farms (as opposed to shell-fish farming) allow uneaten food, plus the faecal waste of the fish, to fall through the cages onto the sea floor, where it destroys the existing habitat. Added to this are the effects of the overuse of highly-toxic, anti-fouling chemicals, which are applied to keep the cages clear of weed and algae. The widespread use of prophylactic drug treatments to reduce disease in fish also has a detrimental effect on the ecology of the surrounding sea floor. Many freshwater systems have fish farms, which divert water from natural streams into ponds and tanks to raise juvenile fish. Such procedures inevitably increases the quantity of dissolved chemicals being released into the surrounding watercourse. Recent reports provide evidence that blooms of toxic algae are directly linked to the practices of fish farming.

Another implication of fish farming is the potential for the spread of disease. There are many diseases which afflict fish – some native and some more exotic in origin. In recent times, Infectious Salmon Anaemia (ISA) has hit the headlines. The disease spread rapidly through the fish farms of Scotland, via the transferal of juvenile salmon, and resulted in the mandatory cull of millions of pounds worth of stock. The threat of *Gyrodactylus salaris*, the salmon parasite which scourged Scandinavian rivers, hangs over Scottish rivers. Originating from fish farms, sea lice afflict native sea trout leading to their extinction from some river systems. They are often present in huge numbers around the cages.

Fish farms also suffer the problem of the escape of large numbers of fish. Sometimes, huge numbers of fish swamp the area, displacing native fish stock and even consuming them as food. The magnitude of the economic problem for the fish farmer is small compared to the impact of the escaped fish on the environment. Large numbers escape into the sea, particularly salmon, which rely on their innate sense to locate the local rivers. Some have been observed mating with wild fish, while others disturb the native stock, which affects the level of successful spawning. The hybridisation of native fish with farmed fish changes the genetic profile of the river population and may lead to loss of homing instinct in the progeny. Displacement and cross-breeding further harm salmon stocks, which are under other pressures throughout their range. In freshwater, most escapees are rainbow trout, which prey on juvenile wild fish, thus displacing native stock and damaging the natural environment. Many observers are very distressed by the burgeoning growth of aquaculture without the application of the appropriate 'precautionary principles' of control. It is encouraging that regulatory agencies are being forced to act to contain this threat to the cleanliness of our freshwater and coastal resources.

The effects of predation on native fish species are increasing. Sea fish and migratory salmonids are eaten, in considerable quantity, by the ever-growing population of seals throughout their north Atlantic range. Grey seal populations are increasing at an annual rate of 10 per cent, while common seals increase at around twice this rate. There are presently over 130,000 grey seals plus a further 35,000 common seals around UK shores; each of these seals may eat up to 2.4 metric tonnes of fish each year. If only one per cent of this total is salmon – an extremely conservative estimate – then at least 3960 metric tonnes of salmon are eaten by seals each year. If you compare this to the national annual aggregate of salmon caught by man, which has been as low as around 250 tonnes, the magnitude of the predation problem becomes clear.

However, it is not only seals that eat fish. Studies of the River North Esk in eastern Scotland showed that the merganser, a species of saw-billed, fish-eating duck, can account for huge quantities of juvenile salmon and sea trout during the period when the birds are fledging their young. In one study, twelve birds caught 8,000-15,000 juvenile fish during the smolt run; it was estimated that this constituted as much as 16 per cent of the total run of smolts.

Anglers play a large part in sustaining the dwindling populations of the native brown trout, sea trout, salmon and the coarse species that frequent Scotland's waterways. Replacement stocking is practised widely, especially in lochs, but also in some rivers, where there is heavy angling pressure. Not everyone looks kindly on introducing non-local stocks of fish. Most anglers prefer to retain the essential wildness of local fish. However, this may, in truth, be a rather wistful, romantic notion, for records show that most lochs and rivers have had introductions of fish from other waters at various times throughout their history. Nevertheless, a cautious approach to restocking is required if the best outcome is to be achieved.

Scottish anglers are progressive in both thought and technique. Increasingly, game anglers practise 'catch-and-release' following their coarse angling fellows. Current angling trends are moving away from the 'catch-and-kill-everything-that-swims'. Insead anglers are implementing techniques based upon the enlightened realisation that the future depends on moderation. Regulation is key; developing ways of retaining the pleasure of the pastime without negatively affecting the species on which it depends. Some river systems have adopted mandatory return of fish caught. Others adopt more gentle persuasion and education of their anglers. Whatever the method, anglers are increasingly becoming much more sensitive to the requirements to conserve and sustain their aquatic heritage and to leave a thriving legacy for those who follow us.

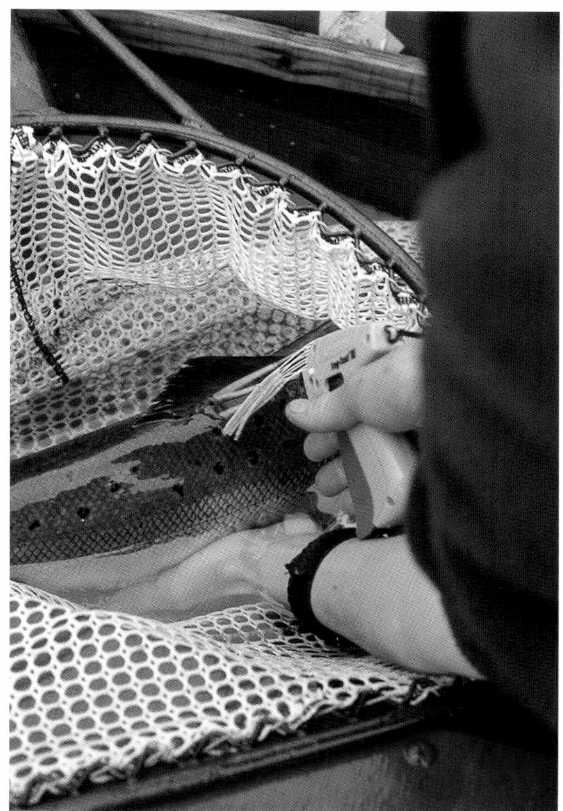

Tagging Salmon: Scientific data is necessary to show trends in salmon survival and their population dynamics. Tagging of fish can provide crucial information by showing where fish are at particular times, what they are doing and what their fate may be.

CHAPTER TWO

THE DEVELOPMENT OF FISHING IN SCOTLAND

Ghillie, River Spey.

Fishing is deeply embedded in Scotland's history and heritage. The importance of fishing to Scotland cannot really be overstated. It is enjoyed by the many, still owned by the few, brings vast revenue to the economy and is probably the subject of more argument than even football – Scotland's national game. There is an interesting unconfirmed statistic – no one knows exactly where it came from, stating that more people in Scotland fish, than play or watch football. Regardless of whether this is true or not, there is a significant proportion of the population enjoying our sporting asset. Sport fishing has been around for a long time – hopefully this will continue. It has also seen some fairly radical change over the recent past and will develop further in the years to come.

Since the advent of angling for sport, there has been a definite shift in focus from fishing for food. The key to angling in the twenty-first century is challenge. The intention to 'kill' is steadily disappearing. Anglers are fishing more demanding beats; skill and prowess is being put to the ultimate test. This change in emphasis is pivotal to the way in which sport fishing will develop further. As an angler, it is an intriguing task to try to predict the direction of the sport in the future.

The Rise of Sport Fishing

Exactly when the pursuit of fish for food turned into a sporting activity is unclear. It was almost certainly a gradual process over many centuries, and is still developing. People who caught fish purely for food, or to gain their livelihood through selling the fish they caught, must have gained great satisfaction and pleasure from their best catches. How this turned into the kind of sporting satisfaction that we enjoy today is complex and difficult to determine.

Fishing with hooks has been around for a long time. The forerunner of the bent and pointed hook was the 'gorge', which – when hidden inside bait – lodged in the throat of the fish. There are examples of Scottish Stone Age 'gorges' in the National Museum of Scotland, Edinburgh, along with other fishing artefacts like 'leisters' – barbaric pointed spears used to catch salmon.

Based on a wealth of archaeological findings in Pictish dwelling sites in Scotland, it has been determined that fish has been a staple part of man's diet since his arrival on these shores. The Picts carved relief images into their great standing stones – many of which were clear depictions of salmon. Whether this was a totem symbol or some kind of fertility invocation to induce runs of the great silver fish is not clear. But it is evident that the Atlantic salmon played an important part in the lives of 'the painted people'.

Fishing rods and barbed hooks were depicted in Egyptian hieroglyphic art from around 4000 years ago. We know from ancient Chinese literature that fishing with rod and line was a contemplative and pleasurable pursuit at least 2500 years ago. There are many references in European literature to fishing with rod and line, which suggests that the pursuit was well established in pre-Christian times.

References to sport angling with rod and line were first recorded in the Middle Ages. Later, in the seventeenth century, Izaac Walton wrote the famous *Compleat Angler* (1653). He recorded his ideas and understanding of fishing in England. Therefore, it is absolutely inconceivable that this form of angling was not also carried out in Scotland at that time. Before that, towards the close of the fifteenth century, the nun Dame Juliana Berners wrote about fly patterns in use at the time, including details about how to tie and use these creations.

It is clear, therefore, that fly-fishing was being practised in middle England over 500 years ago. But, did it constitute sport fishing? It certainly did in Walton's time, for he describes it in terms of a

River Tyne,
'Haddington 1757'.

The Victorian Fly-Fisher: 1840, by W Topham.

fish, and more than a few references to quarrels between local lairds about fishing rights. Again, it is notable how the dispute over ownership of fishing rights has caused so much heated argument throughout the centuries.

These ancient records are fascinating; they are even testament to the creation of new Latin words such as *salmunculus* – the young of salmon – and *salmonarius* – a salmon fisher.

It seems that sport fishing for trout and salmon came into its own – as we know it – in the mid-nineteenth century. During this period, Victorian Britain witnessed many rapid technological advancements, which, among other things, led to the development of the railway system and the growth of sporting estates as the countryside became more accessible. It was a time of tremendous change. Local fishers who had previously had the opportunity to take an odd fish or two for the pot, without incurring the wrath of the laird, were now displaced from the water in favour of fee-paying visitors. The lairds also encouraged the promulgation of new laws and introduced new staff whose primary aim was to keep poaching, and poachers, at bay.

These new developments had a tremendous impact on fishing. Fishing clubs were founded, whose main purpose was to organise visits to the rivers and lochs for the urban worker. In addition, an uneasy tension arose, which is still evident

pleasant pastime and not as a means of gathering food. There would have been a time of overlap, where anglers fished for food, and the aspect of pleasure developed simultaneously, until sporting ideals gained sway.

In the Exchequer roles of Scotland between 1264 and 1359 AD there are many references to salmon, but they relate to salmon as foodstuff. There are several records referring to the taxation of salmon and fishings, along with documented complaints of tax collectors concerning the inaccurate counting of fish for taxation. There are also references to the 'kippering' of salmon and its export to the European Low Countries (the Netherlands, Belgium and Luxembourg) as smoked

The Victorian Angler had far longer rods than modern practice dictates, but in this print, the battle seems excessively robust.

today, between the landed gentry and those who had previously had access to the waters and a 'right to fish'. In Scot's law there is no such right, except where gifted by decree and this is limited by area. Prime examples of the right to fish being bestowed on townspeople and local citizens are still applicable centuries after their origination. Residents of Perth have the right to fish within the boundaries of the town. In the south-west of Scotland, near Lockerbie, the Royal Four Towns Association still manages the fishing of part of the River Annan catchment area due to the actions of Robert the Bruce in the fourteenth century. As a gift, the King gave the area of water to the local people in appreciation of the support given to his war-mongering efforts against the English.

Clearly, fishing as a pleasurable sporting pastime has been enjoyed from times long before written records were kept. Even then there was a subtle distinction between catching fish for food and sporting activity. It is the aspects of enjoyment and challenge that differentiate anglers from fishermen. Most anglers will readily agree that fishing is much more than just catching fish – there is more to it than that. Few however, can tell you exactly what these pleasurable aspects are. What generates enjoyment for one angler may be quite different from another, but many would agree that one of the main elements is challenge. To enjoy fishing to the full, it is necessary to pit yourself against the natural elements and to outwit wily fish.

In the early days, anglers seem to go through various, recognisable stages until they reach a certain level of proficiency. The first stage is simply to catch a fish – any fish will do – and this is easily satisfied by the first exciting success. Who cannot remember their first decent trout or the surging run of their first salmon? It is an occasion indelibly marked in the memory and quite unforgettable.

The next stage consists of catching more fish – this time larger – which again is fairly easy to achieve. But after a while, the level of satisfaction begins to dwindle as larger and more plentiful catches become more frequent – the result of an increased level of skill.

The latter stages involve the pursuit of fish that are far more challenging to catch, even for an experienced angler. These stages do not have clear boundaries; they apply to each individual differently and at different times. All anglers constantly set themselves different challenges to gain their sporting pleasure.

The process of development may involve a narrow choice of species, or as is increasingly popular in the USA, a quest for purely wild fish. It may involve being highly selective about a choice of venue – some anglers take great pains to visit the remotest fisheries. It is likely to involve specific tactics and methods, with some anglers selecting a very narrow mode of fishing, often to the exclusion of other, equally successful, methods. A typical example is game anglers, who consistently choose fly-fishing. It is almost as though we place artificial barriers in our way to make our successes even more satisfactory when we achieve them.

There can be little doubt that catching fish with a net, gaff or trap – all methods largely excluded by law – must have provided their users with a satisfaction that went far beyond simply gathering food for the table. It was also highly challenging and it is within the realm of challenge that we must look for how sport fishing developed. The final aspect which fuels the process of development is that of pleasure.

It is hard to believe on a freezing January morning, when we are standing chest deep in a Scottish salmon river leaning into the gusts of a northerly Arctic blast, with icicles forming on your rod rings, when there is little real chance of hooking an elusive spring salmon, that this is all done in the pursuit of pleasure. On the other hand, a day on Speyside, in late May or early June with the freshness of spring in the air, the sound of singing birds in the trees and the evocative sound of a fishing reel's ratchet being drawn by a fine trout or salmon, is pure bliss for any genuine angler.

Abbotsford, on the River Tweed:
The home of Sir Walter Scott. The Tweed, in the mid nineteenth century, was the place of much angling development.

The Victorians

Fresh Water Fishers: Edinburgh Angling Club c1870s.

In Britain, the Victorians did much to shape our present-day fishing. It was wealthy Victorian families who first left their smoky city life in favour of their houses in the country, or the new hotels and lodges specifically built for shooting and fishing. This annual safari, which may have lasted throughout the entire summer, gave rise to country sports and the sporting estates that we are still familiar with today. Whole families hired ghillies to help them catch salmon and trout, or to take them into the hills to shoot grouse and deer.

Ghillies still exist on Scottish estates today, but any comparison with their forelock-tugging predecessors is entirely inapt because, far from being a humble servant, the modern ghillie is a highly skilled expert. In fact, many who now fish or shoot in Scotland rely entirely on the excellence of their ghillie for their success. Ghillies are highly competent, experienced, almost invariably good-humoured and great company. But we have the Victorians to thank for their development and for the estates on which they are now employed.

The estates were owned by the aristocracy, commonly referred to as 'lairds'. Traditionally, lairds passed the estates down to their offspring over many centuries and when intermarriage between wealthy, highborn families took place some amalgamation of land occurred. On the other hand, some estates were divided when sons inherited part of the family land. It was relatively uncommon to break up estates through inheritance until more recently when tax became a consideration. The first-born usually inherited the whole estate and the other sons were unlucky! Daughters, of course, were considered wholly unworthy of ownership of land. How things have changed. Some of the estates were huge; for example it is recorded that the fishing on the whole of the River Spey was in the hands of just six estates.

Bear in mind that this includes both banks of the river. This changed in more recent times when the great Speyside estates were broken into smaller land parcels, due primarily to taxation and inheritance policies. The effects of this system of ownership were far reaching. The law favoured the few, thus limiting access to Scottish waters for the majority of Scots. As a consequence, the masses were denied the pleasures of major tracts of the countryside and country pursuits.

During the Victorian era, ostentation was the order of the day. The upper classes expected favour and the best of country sports. This was in complete contrast to the humble artisan who, after a hard working week, took great pleasure from his precious days by the waterside. However, what united these widely different social groups was an enjoyment of fishing – the pursuit of relaxation and challenge. To get out into the country was their greatest joy.

The ostentatious nature of the Victorian age was reflected in their elaborate dress, architecture and etiquette, but it also influenced the development of fishing tactics and tackle throughout this period. The most appropriate demonstration of this was their artificial flies. Victorian salmon flies were large, multi-layered creations of brightly coloured feathers from exotic species of birds, tied with great artistry and skill. The fact that these flies were successful is bewildering, because they do not look like anything natural. Today these flies, made from the feathers of birds that are now protected, are collected for their art. They are not to be used, but simply admired for their colourful design and workmanship.

Like many things, there will always be trends within fishing. This is particularly true of artificial fly-design. Following the colourful fly designs of the Victorian era, during the early years of the twentieth century, there was a vogue for patterns of dull colour and more life-like shape. This was followed in the 1950s and 60s by the development of fluorescent lures of lurid colour, very similar to those of the Victorian era, as rainbow trout gained supremacy in stocked waters.

Many of the great tackle manufacturers were founded in the mid-nineteenth century, which is indicative of the rise in demand for quality fishing tackle in this period. Local shops employed their own craftsmen to make rods and reels, to tie fishing flies,

Kinlochbeg, c1896: Young Victorians enjoyed their fishing too.

The Ghillie.
It was in the Victorian era that the fishing ghillie came to the fore. He was his 'gentleman's gentleman', standing discreetly a pace or two behind, always ready with advice, and the net, of course.

and to work alongside the gunsmiths who lovingly made side-by-side shotguns and hunting rifles. Patents were taken on reel assemblies, fishing lures, nets and all sorts of tackle. Much of this tackle is collectable today and attracts high prices at auction. The mid-nineteenth-century Scottish tackle shop was the blueprint for a huge retail industry throughout the world. The sale of rods from wooden racks, the displays of lures and flies in glass-fronted cases, and the hangers filled with clothing items, frequently found in tackle shops today originate from the Victorian establishments of the nineteenth century.

The Victorians had a great impact on Scotland's physical landscape; in central Scotland, many Victorian reservoirs and fine fisheries still exist today.

The Victorian influence on fishing today is also present in the structure and organisation of our sport. In the nineteenth century, clubs and national organisations burgeoned. Victorian anglers went to extraordinary lengths for their fishing. On the 1st of July, 1880, the first trout fly-fishing competition took place at national level in Scotland. The venue was Loch Leven. What would later develop into the prestigious Scottish National Fly-fishing Championship was the precursor of all modern international, common-wealth and world events. Scotland has, over the years, played a huge part in the development of fly-fishing in so many ways, and continues to do so. At the seminal event, only seven angling clubs took part: the West of Scotland Angling Club; Kinross-shire Fishing Club; Perth Anglers Club; Stirling Fishing Club; Dundee Angling Club; Waverley Angling Club and Falkirk Fishing Club. The prizes were cash. The first prize was a hefty £15 – a remarkable sum for its day – which is in itself indicative of the sector of society that was taking part. This was not a competition for humble artisans, it was exclusively for those of substance.

It must have been a tremendous occasion with the anglers dressed in oiled-cloth coats, tall 'tile' hats and knee-high leather boots, their whiskers blowing about in the breeze as they stepped into the boats on Loch Leven. They wielded their heavy greenheart rods, with horse-hair lines and gut casts; the trusty boatmen strained on the oars to take the anglers to their favourite parts of the loch. At the end of the day the winner was Mr D. B. Macgregor of the West of Scotland Angling Club with 14 fish weighing 11 lb and 14 oz. In second place was Mr P. D. Malloch, a member of Perth Anglers Club. It is notable that Malloch went on to compete in no fewer than 29 nationals and won an amazing six times – a record not since beaten. He was also founder of the prominent tackle business, still in existence today, in the fair city of Perth.

Some of the older clubs in Scotland have records which show that they would hire a single carriage in a train – or even the whole train – to take their members near to a venue. This must have been an enjoyable way to travel to a day's fishing. You can imagine the mounting excitement amongst the members as the train pulled into each small station; they would be chattering about which fly to use, where to take the boat and what the weather was going to be like. They would probably be conducting business, for the members of these clubs were, on the whole, industrialists. From the train, members would transfer into horse-drawn coaches and be driven to the waterside. There they would hire their boatmen and were taken out onto the loch, the boat pulled all day by their trusty oarsmen. Their clothing, tackle, transport and tactics were a far cry from their modern equivalents, but this demonstrates how the foundations of club angling were laid down in Victorian Scotland. The development of the railway network in the middle of the nineteenth century opened up the possibility for city dwellers to gain ready access to the country. This, in turn, allowed sport fishing to burgeon. Long journeys by coach or horse were uncomfortable, which discouraged people from enduring such a journey just to go fishing. The ornate railway stations of Royal Deeside are confirmation of the central role that the new railway system played in the proliferation of sport fishing in Scotland.

During the nineteenth century, the expansion of the British Empire continued in areas such as the Far East, Africa, India and Australia. In many parts of the empire, the Victorians introduced fish from Scottish waters – particularly brown trout from Loch Leven. The Scottish brown trout were taken to the high streams of the Kashmir in India, the rivers that cut through the blue mountains of South Africa, the crystal lakes of New Zealand and Tasmania and various other corners of the globe where Victorian men were posted.

The journeys which had to be undertaken to take the fish to such faraway places were quite incredible. This was long before ships had engines or refrigeration. The ova were transported in thick wooden cases, which were 'iced' occasionally, and stored well below deck. The eggs themselves were carefully laid down on sphagnum moss, hatched out and grown in pools in their new country before being transported on horseback to their intended river or lake. The fact that eggs survived, trout hatched and a sustainable population was established is truly remarkable. And yet, there are many places in the world today where you may catch trout which are descended from those that swam in Loch Leven.

c1870, Clovenfords: Edinburgh Angling Club Members.

Lore and Tales

A Tweed Cauld, c1930s – with large salmon making their way upstream.

Wherever in the world there is fishing, there is also a richness of storytelling which, at the waterside, dissolves into a blend of fact, fantasy and fiction. Scotland has a storytelling tradition that has lasted for centuries. Although the mythical figures of Scotland's past are now confined to the history books, Scotland's oral tradition is continued in the guise of waterside lore. Besides the anglers themselves, the most important purveyors of this heritage are our fishing and shooting ghillies.

Ghillies are the most patient of people, but then they really have to be, because they are often obliged to help and advise those inexperienced anglers who really could not catch a fish to save themselves. They also have to bear those insufferable 'know-all anglers' who simply will not listen to genuine advice. Ghillies often have to put up with the worst of weather and sometimes company that they must tolerate, rather than enjoy. Their patience may wear a bit thin, and who can blame them, but the way in which this surfaces says much about the character of Scottish fishing ghillies.

One such instance is exemplified by the tale of a ghillie who had looked after a pair of visiting anglers for a full week. He had rowed them all over the loch; shown them the best salmon lies in the river; given them his favourite flies; put up their rods each day; and had generally been a great help. However, all of his efforts had mostly been unappreciated and had not resulted in any tangible success. In fairness, the weather during the week had not been good, and the gales and rain had relented for only very short spells. The river was now in full spate and thickly coloured so they resorted to the loch to try for a fresh-run sea trout or salmon as this was their last day.

The boat had collected a few inches of rainwater that day. The anglers gear lay in a sodden heap as the water swilled around the bilges. Everything was dripping wet, including the anglers. Now, where the rumour started has been lost in the mists of time, but there is a belief that ghillies quite like to savour a small measure of decent uisghe beatha from time to time – purely for medicinal purposes

A Run of Tweed Salmon Fishers gathered to take advantage of the great bonanza of a big run of fish coming into the river. This photograph was taken at Selkirk Cauld c1930.

'The Ghillies': At the height of the popularity of Highland angling holidays – from the late nineteenth century until the Great War, many hotels retained the services of their own group of ghillies. This group was photographed in 1911 at the Cuilfail Hotel, Kilmelford in Argyll.

you understand. However, the pair of visiting anglers managed to fill out a dram for themselves each day, but always missed out their faithful advisor. During a particularly heavy downpour one of the anglers seemed more than usually irritated by the relentless rain:

'Is there nowhere dry in this part of the world?' he enquired.

'Weel now sir' the ghillie replied, 'my tongue has been damper.'

Colourful visitors are an integral part of the Scottish angling scene. They bring richness in many ways – not solely in the thickness of their wallets – but also in their attitude to their pastime. A rich and voluble American happened to come to Scotland to fish for salmon. He was one of those anglers who had been everywhere; caught every conceivable species of fish; knew everything about everything, and did not hesitate to let anyone who would listen know how much he knew and how much he had done. He had booked a fortnight on a prime beat of a major salmon river. He had enlisted the help of the most experienced and capable ghillie in the area and had brought the very best tackle – everything was set for success. Despite his previous experience and knowledge, however, that wonderful first draw of a salmon as it takes the fly had eluded him. Day after day fish would leap around him, but paid scant attention to his bait. Eventually, it was the final day of his two weeks. It was nearing dusk on that final day, when a salmon did actually grab his fly and a vigorous battle commenced. The angler played the fish well and a grand salmon was eventually dragged onto the bank. As the angler and ghillie looked at the fine fish the visitor drawled:

'Do you know Angus, this fish cost me over six thousand dollars. It cost me two thousand dollars to fly to Scotland premier class. It cost me two thousand dollars for my hotel and the cost of this beat. It cost me two thousand dollars for my tackle and the rest of my expenses. Six thousand dollars this fish has cost me.'

The patient ghillie responded dryly:

'May the good Lord be thankit sir that ye didnae hae the misfortune tae catch anither yin!'

Everywhere the angler goes there are stories and folklore. Legends are born on the banks of rivers. The names of the pools on Scottish rivers each tell a story of people or past events. The names of bays, headlands and islands in lochs are surrounded by myths and stories of historical events. Many of these tales have evolved over the years, and always with an extra element added for dramatic effect.

Poaching

Poaching on the Tweed: Poaching with leisters and cleeks: these barbaric spears were once quite common. Modern poachers make use of agricultural poisons and mono-filament nets. Print by W. Scope, 'Days & Nights Fishing on the Tweed', c1843.

As much an integral part of the Scottish rural scene as the heather, hillsides, trees and fields, the poacher has a mystique and roguish charisma that is hard to define. He is a furtive figure often perceived as 'putting one over' on inflexible authority – a likeable villain, if even a villain at all. There are two quite distinct types of poachers. Firstly, there is the rustic rascal who nips out on the darkest night to put a pheasant in the pot for his hungry offspring, or extracts a single salmon from his local river. However, there are also groups of organised criminals who decimate the countryside for nothing other than greed. It is the rogue that will be explored in this section, the other type is not a suitable subject of a book about pleasure and sport.

Can it be pure hunger that encourages a poacher to break the law? Probably not, for most agree that it is the thrill of the chase and the pitting of self against the skills of the gamekeeper that makes the challenge fulfilling. It is not worth being fined or spending time in prison for one salmon, there simply has to be more to it than that. For those who participate it is a pleasure-providing activity; the fun of the chase animates the nocturnal pursuits of the average poacher.

Poaching methods have developed over a period of many years. Many salmon are still hooked illegally, meaning that they are caught with a hook without the fish taking it into its mouth. This ranges from using a conventional rod, line and terminal tackle but presenting the hook in such a way that it catches the fish across its back or on its underside, to the use of tackle, that no angler would ever use, which snares a fish by similarly foul-hooking it.

It is not all that unusual to accidentally foul-hook a salmon when fishing conventionally; there is even a rich vocabulary to describe this occurrence – 'catching a fish by the jersey' is a typical example. If you do happen to do this, the best course of action is to play the fish as quickly as possible and return it carefully with as little fuss as possible. On the other hand, the deliberate act of fishing with tackle or methods designed to foul-hook fish is called 'sniggering'.

Some poachers simply get into the water and catch the fish by hand; most children who grew up near rivers or burns greatly enjoyed the precursor to this, known in Scotland as 'guddling' or 'tickling' trout. To get a positive hold of a large fit salmon and get him ashore is far more difficult than it sounds, although there are tricks of the trade that make the task easier. One 'wee hint' here is that a fish is likely to lie much quieter if you turn it over onto its back – something that all anglers might bear in mind when they are handling fish. Getting close enough to a salmon in a pool without scaring it is difficult enough, never mind being able to grip it.

Fishing equipment of the past is often displayed in museums and private angling collections. Exhibits often include tools such as gaffs – a hook that is now outmoded – which were used a few decades ago to lift large salmon from the water once they had been played out. How fashions change, but in this case a change for the better because many salmon are now returned to the water and a great gaff hole in the side is hardly conducive to longevity.

'Cleeks' and 'leisters' of various design were also common – these were long-handled, barbed spears, which would be thrust into the fish so that they could be pulled from the pool. Snares of several types were also used, as were traps. A few years ago the local authority gardeners in a major Scottish city were dumbfounded by the regular theft of the wire-netting guards placed around their newly-planted trees in local parks. These tubular, galvanised structures were then found in nearby salmon rivers strategically placed to trap running salmon in a kind of lobster-pot alteration to the original assembly. Clever recycling of everyday materials without doubt, but not exactly consistent with the thrust to restore the sustainability of the Scottish salmon population.

Professional poaching is a different affair altogether. The use of chemicals like Cymag (a material sprayed onto potatoes once the tubers have ripened to burn off the green 'shaws') kills everything in the river. The sight of a river after a Cymag attack is horrifying – adult fish, belly-up, fall downstream with the current, but there are also small juvenile fish pitifully drifting downstream as stiff as boards. Such an act of irresponsible stupidity could be detrimental to fishing in the future. A few fish killed for greed in this way can hugely harm fish populations – and repeated poisoning simply wipes out the future.

The introduction of salmon farming was temporarily heralded as the solution to ending professional salmon poaching. Many believed that farmed salmon would bring the price down to a level that would make poaching non-viable. Paradoxically, the reverse happened. Although the price did drop dramatically over a short time span, the poachers simply took more fish to make up for the reduction in value, even going as far as buying refrigerated lorries to transport the increased quantities of fish to market. Fortunately, greater supervision and surveillance of potential poaching sites and a much more appropriate court sentencing policy has reduced this activity greatly.

The local worthy who catches the occasional salmon for the pot still slips through the net and takes a fish from time to time, just as his father, grandfather and those before them have done for years. Many would argue that such small-scale activity does not strictly harm the river, but it greatly depends on whether you accept that the small-time poacher is part of our heritage, or whether you hold the view that to take a fish illegally is always wrong. In the present climate of salmon conservation it is obviously inconsistent to condone non-professional poaching regardless of its colourful traditions.

One thing is for sure, the Scottish poacher possesses the richest vein of local river knowledge, and some of the best gamekeepers might tell a story or two about poaching and poachers if you pressed them sufficiently and bought them a dram or two!

Spearing Salmon in 1773: There is a long history of illegally taking fish from Scottish rivers. The use of lights and flaming brands, as shown in this print, was also made illegal. From Mclans 'Highlanders at Home'.

Changing Times

Now we are in the twenty-first century we must expect to see change in some aspects of our lives. Fishing will not escape this trend, regardless of how many anglers would love to retain its traditional values and practices. The last century saw fairly significant movements in the ethics and practices of our pastime, and progress will continue as long as we go down to the water to fish.

In Scotland – focusing on fly-fishing for the moment – the twentieth century saw the rise of the 'put-and-take' trout fishery, probably the most significant change to impact our sport. Medieval monks initiated the concept of put-and-take in Scotland when they stocked ponds with coarse fish, which would be caught later for the table. The stocking of brown trout in lochs to supplement the natural stock was widely practised in Victorian times. On the other hand, the introduction of a non-native species solely for sporting purposes was a novel initiative with huge repercussions.

It was the large water supply reservoirs in England that first took advantage of stocking with rapidly growing rainbow trout. Soon, there were smaller stillwaters doing the same; latterly, there has been an explosion of specially-dug ponds opening as small trout fisheries. The methods and

Spey Casting

There aren't many places in the world that are synonymous with a particular style or method of fishing; but there can be few salmon anglers who are not aware of, or aspire to be proficient at, Spey casting. There are two basic Spey casts – the single Spey cast and the double Spey cast. Both are roll casts, taking advantage of a loop of line to load the rod, rather than a back cast to transfer forward movement into the line. Spey casting comes into its own when there are strong winds, which could bring the fly dangerously close to the angler, or when banks or trees behind the casting position prevent a full overhead cast.

To execute a single Spey cast, the rod is drawn upstream to bring the fly and line to the surface of the water so that it lifts off easily. The fly should be made to sit a few feet upstream of the rod tip and a little beyond it. To do this you may have to shorten line by drawing it 'to hand' through the rings – it will be made to 'shoot' later. Don't overdo the retrieval of line – you need sufficient to load the rod properly. The aerialised loop of line may now be rolled forward in a continuous smooth, but firm casting action. This lifts the line off the water and propels it forward, rolling parallel to the surface. Sounds straightforward and it is, once you get your timing right.

The double Spey cast requires that the fly be placed downstream of the rod – if it isn't you will hook the line on casting. Similarly to the single Spey cast, the rod is raised to draw the fly and line to the surface, ready to be lifted off. Then you form a wide loop of line by drawing the rod across in front of you, starting low and lifting the rod tip progressively. This loop will load the rod when you now flex it against the loop's weight, rolling the line out and lifting the fly off the water to land many yards away.

Timing is of paramount importance. Cast too soon, and the rod has insufficient weight of line to load it fully and power is lost. Too late and the loop falls back into the water and the hook sinks, making the job of propelling it forward a lost cause. In these circumstances – try again, all is not lost. When it does roll out nicely, a Spey cast gives a warm tingle of pleasure. When the line then stops in its downstream travel and powerful tugging starts, the warm feeling is replaced by that of excitement.

Miss Ballantine and the 64-pound Tay Salmon

It was late afternoon on Saturday October 7th 1922, Miss Georgina Ballantine was fishing the Tay, near Caputh, with her ferryman father James. Earlier in the day she had caught three salmon – one of 25lbs, one of 21lbs and one of 17lbs. They were harling from the boat at the top end of the Boat Pool on the Glendelvine Beat, just as the sun dipped below the lovely Perthshire hills. As they came downstream just above the Bargie Stone, still a prominent marker in the Boat Pool today, a fish took on Georgina's rod. It immediately took a huge run of about 500 yards downstream, followed by the boat with James rowing with all his might.

The fish swam downstream under the piers of Caputh Brig, and they went ashore to fight the fish with more side-strain from the bank. The great fight continued into the deepening dusk. They were not able to bring the fish to shore so James and Georgina re-embarked in the dark and dropped back all the way down Sparrowmuir Pool. James insisted that greater and greater strain be put on the rod until at last the fish came closer. Eventually it came close enough to use the gaff, and drag it over the gunwale and into the boat. Mr Moir's 'Nabbie' – a priest – was used and the great fish went to meet its maker. It was 64 lbs in weight, a record which has not been exceeded as a rod-caught salmon in Scotland.

philosophies of the fly-fishing public have swung far away from the traditional values that existed for so long. The full impact of these changes could not have been foreseen.

It is the technical approaches to fly-fishing that indicate the impact of time. Once, we fished at a leisurely pace; now, things go faster and we follow blindly. Even the way in which we cast and retrieve flies changes over time. At one time casting and retrieving was a slow activity – we enticed the fish to come to the surface to accept the 'dibbled' fly. Now we cast huge distances and tear lures back at a rate of knots. There was a team of three anglers who fished Loch Leven together during the late 1990s. They were referred to by the other anglers as the 'Fiddlers Three' due to their upper arm movements. They were excellent casters, throwing a long straight line then pulling their flies back rapidly, their arms moving rhythmically as though playing the faster passages of Bruch's Violin Concerto!

Salmon fly-fishing has changed dramatically too, especially since the preserve of the rich, Scottish salmon rivers offered 'association water' fishing. These open beats were bequeathed by landowners, bought by forward-looking associations, or were leased from the estates. As a consequence, Scotland's wealth of salmon fishing was now available to the ordinary angler.

There were many examples of 'town water' fishing, where ancient rights had been established for local residents. However, the advent of associations, which owned or leased their own beat, opened up salmon fishing to everyone regardless of where they lived. The emancipation of the sport brought beneficial ideas and opportunities, but it also brought problems related to increased demand. However, on balance, salmon fishing is the better for it, even though, on occasion, the rivers are over-fished due to the popularity of the sport. It is customary to discuss salmon fishing with anglers from other parts of the globe – particularly from North America – where a system of national ownership exists rather than land ownership. They are surprised by both our antiquated system and our exploitation of salmon, as they release most of those they catch.

The development of different modes of transport throughout the twentieth century has also had a dramatic impact on fly-fishing. Today, we step into our cars and think nothing of driving to a prime fishing beat a few hours away and return home in the evening. Some of us even fly to more remote parts of the world to enjoy our fishing. Scottish fishing is now accessible to all.

The Introduction of Rainbow Trout

Coldingham Loch, Berwickshire: This attractive loch was the first in Scotland to have rainbow trout released into it. These magnificent fish are still stocked at Coldingham and it is a superb place to fish for them.

The native trout of Scotland are the brown trout and its wandering sibling the sea trout. Brownies are found in most of our rivers, streams and lochs and are an excellent traditional sporting quarry. Wild brown trout suffer from the fact that they take considerable time to grow to adult size and then, especially if the supply of feed is meagre, they mature into adults at a comparatively slow rate and attain only a modest size. They are also selective feeders and have a short season when they feed most actively. Their transatlantic cousin, the rainbow trout has several attributes which make it an appealing fish to stock in the trout fisheries throughout Scotland. As a consequence, the rainbow is established in a prominent place in Scottish game fishing.

The rainbow is a voracious feeder. It hunts food in a wider range of temperatures and throughout much more of its available life. It lives harder during a life span which is considerably shorter than that of a brownie. A brown trout may live for up to 20 years, whilst a rainbow lives for four to five years. Rainbows tend to eat anything that comes their way, making them comparatively easier to catch. (The word 'comparatively' is used here very carefully because they are occasionally extremely difficult to catch). Nevertheless, they feed more aggressively and are more likely to grab your fly than a wily old 'brownie'.

The fact that they may grow to maturity in fewer seasons than brownies, makes them a more cost-effective fish to stock – especially for put-and-take fisheries. This does not mean that rainbows are the only trout to be stocked in Scottish waters. Many supplement natural brown trout stocks with artificially reared brownies. However, rainbows have taken over where stocks of brown trout are less resilient to angling pressure, and where stocking with huge numbers of brown trout would be financially inappropriate.

Rainbows are fished for in different ways to the styles recognisable as 'traditional Scottish brown trout fishing'. There has been a revolution in tackle design and its use, specifically targeted at catching rainbows. Of course, traditional and modern methods overlap and each are effective given the right conditions. However, the emphasis on catching rainbows, particularly at depth, has driven the development of tackle, techniques and tactics away from 'top-of-the-water' short-lining in Scotland's lochs.

Brown trout used to be fished for in the surface layer of the water using floating lines. The artificial fly

Carron Valley Reservoir, near Denny:
One of an ever-decreasing number of lochs where rainbows are not stocked. Few lochs in the central area of Scotland still rely on stocking solely with Scotland's native brown trout.

patterns were mostly small and imitative – if a little fanciful as far as their representation of natural food items was concerned. A freely-drifting boat was used and the angler would cast a short line a length or two in front of the boat and work the flies on the surface to elicit a 'rise' from the brownies. This worked well while there was plenty of trout looking for food at the water's surface. More recently however, polluting elements on the surface of the water mean that native brownies now feed near the bottom. The quantity of food at the bottom has increased and the need to come to the surface to feed on hatching aquatic flies has diminished. The overall effect is that brownies tend to feed less at the surface than they used to do.

The movement away from traditional surface fly-fishing was almost inevitable. Rainbow trout are more likely to be encountered at depths below those normally involved in traditional fly fishing. Their feeding patterns and natural habits made rainbow trout fishing quite different from traditional loch-style fishing. The flies used by anglers tended to be larger, gaudy creations visible in the murky depths and more acceptable to the ever-hungry rainbows. However, there has been a change in recent seasons. Many anglers believe that the progressive movement away from huge lures towards a more imitative style is for the good of our sport. Many anglers now use small nymphs and dry fly techniques, especially 'buzzer' imitations. As most of the the stillwater trout diet is composed of chironomids, the use of 'buzzers' is obvious and effective. Buzzer fishing is both productive and fun, it requires careful skill and is easily learned – little wonder that it has caught on so widely.

The Scottish trout fishing season has changed due to the introduction of rainbow trout, if not legally, it has lengthened considerably in practice. Brown trout are protected by Scots law from being caught between the 6th October to the 15th March

Headshaw Loch, near Selkirk: The integration of browns and rainbows is not without its difficulties. Their vigorous feeding habit tend to encourage rainbows to succeed at the expense of native browns. Headshaw is one place where they co-exist well, providing varied and quality fishing.

each year. The law is designed to allow them to reproduce without disturbance. Rainbows are not covered by this legislation and many Scots now venture out to fly-fish for rainbows throughout every month of the year. The growth of small stillwater fisheries has encouraged the development of this longer season, thus providing great sport during the months when brownies are out of season.

The proliferation of small stillwater fisheries has wrought significant changes to many aspects of trout fishing. Some are clearly beneficial, some may be less so. The advantageous elements include the extension of the season and the availability of reasonably inexpensive, high-quality fly-fishing throughout most of the country. No longer is a day fishing an expedition; there is likely to be a rainbow fishery within a few miles of almost everyone. Access is superb; you can drive up to the side of the water, ideal for less-able anglers and for those who have no time to drive many miles into the country. However, the ethos of instantaneous availability and access have brought with them a change in ethic and philosophy.

Previously, most anglers went to the river or loch for a day away from their ordinary routine – a day out in the country. Now they go to the fishery with the specific intention to catch fish. The distinction is not subtle; the emphasis on catching fish has grown, while the enjoyment of a rare visit to a wild and beautiful part of the country may have diminished. The quality of the fish has to be much higher than previously, and this has created a belief in many anglers that small, natural brown trout are not worthy of their pursuit. These anglers are wanting to catch fish of a greater size, rather than enjoying the challenge offered by wild and wily natural creatures.

Catching big rainbows is fun – of course it is. Rainbows are extremely vigorous when hooked. They leap about and pull violently. But catching wild brownies in a remote loch or burn has wonderful attractions, and often offers greater challenge. It is horses for courses; if you have only a short time and want a guaranteed catch, then the small stillwater is definitely the place to visit. However, if you don't mind a walk along a rocky shore to the next sheltered bay, or over the rough banks of a tumbling river, then you will enjoy wider horizons. We are so lucky in Scotland to have different types of fishing that suit the requirements of a variety of anglers.

One rather disappointing repercussion of the popularity of small stillwater rainbow trout fisheries is their negative effect on angling clubs. It is possible to visit these fisheries and socialise only very little. Sometimes, even approaching an angler just along the bank, is overtly unwelcome – you may be intruding into his space. This is not always true of course, but the sharing of a day with an angling friend is not always the way in which small fishery ethics have developed. The traditional angling club, where members would spend a day together enjoying each others company in a boat, putting the world to rights over the tip of their fly rods, seems to be in decline. This is very regrettable for the quality and reputation of many of the larger lochs is due to the regular visits made to them by angling clubs.

There is something quite unique about membership of a decent angling club. There is the enjoyment of light-hearted competition, the sharing of successful methods and tackle, the sharing of the latest jokes and stories, and the commiseration when failure prevails over success. However, there is the much greater enjoyment of meeting and discussing our sport with other like-minded people.

The steady decline of the angling clubs may be because the length of time that an outing normally requires is too long for many younger anglers. It may also be due to the fact that most Scottish angling clubs are mostly composed of members who are middle-aged or older, rather than those in their teens and twenties, which is likely to deter younger anglers from going out with the 'old wrinklies'!

The need to join an angling club to gain access to some of Scotland's prime waters has diminished – most now offer private bookings to all comers. It would be inappropriate to claim that the introduction of rainbow trout is the sole cause of any decline in the Scottish angling clubs scene. Nevertheless, it is clear that the instant availability of large, fit, rainbow trout in small fisheries, where they are relatively easy to catch, has definitely had an impact on the popularity of club fishing. It would be such a great pity if the fine tradition of belonging to a good angling club was no longer available to future Scots.

Beecraigs Loch near Edinburgh: One of Scotland's big-fish waters. Here, giant rainbows are common – and the small fishery is extremely popular.

Coarse Angling

Pike Fishing:
There is something special about fishing for pike. They may lurk without any visible trace for hours or even days, then they all come on the feed together, providing sport that is fast and furious.

There is no doubt that game fishing in Scotland occupies a prime place in popularity – a reflection of its quality. Nevertheless, fishing for 'coarse' species is developing rapidly and has always had its dedicated adherents. Probably because game fishing is so good, the quality of Scotland's coarse fishing has been masked, but it is equally as good as game fishing generally, and exceptionally good in places.

There are distinct types of coarse fishing available. There is an active group of pike enthusiasts fishing large and small lochs for the beautiful green and gold 'freshwater shark'. There is also a growing body of anglers who buy or lease small lochs and stock them with tench, bream, rudd, carp (common, mirror and crucian), perch and roach and, at their leisure, enjoy the fishing for these species.

Non-native species have been introduced (accidentally and deliberately) into various waters and have established breeding populations; a typical example is the barbel, which can now be caught in some reaches of the River Clyde. Barbel are at the margin of their natural range in northerly waters, but recent mild winters have allowed them to flourish; it remains to be seen whether they are able to survive more severe and prolonged winters. Large chub are found in the rivers of the south-west and Solway coast providing anglers with significant opportunities to enjoy varied coarse fishing in Scotland.

Some commercial fisheries have realised that visiting anglers, plus the growing number of Scots, will pay for coarse fishing, and as a result they have established quality facilities catering for their pleasure. The world is becoming a smaller place and as it shrinks, fishing becomes more heterogeneous – we all gain from the cross fertilisation of ideas.

Using fine terminal tackle for perch, roach and chub is a far cry from heavier pike gear, but each has its individual attractions. There can be fewer pleasures quite so evocative on a frosty winter's morning, than the crackle of bacon frying in the pan on a brightly-glowing fire at the waterside, with the smell of fresh coffee wafting through the crisp clear air, then the rapid click of a reel's ratchet as a large pike runs with the bait – superb!

Coarse fishing is technical. The methods are highly developed and the baits and tactics are complex. Fly-fishing is seen by many as an intellectual pursuit, somehow exceeding coarse fishing in its practicalities and skills, but this is definitely not the case. To succeed well in coarse fishing requires skill and an advanced knowledge of the quarry, the tackle and how it may be applied. Coarse fishing is as demanding and challenging as any other form of fishing.

Because the population is densest and the climate slightly warmer, the majority of coarse fishing is situated in the southern part of Scotland. That is not to suggest that there are not lochs with large pike north of the Highland Boundary fault – there are, and some are quite spectacular – but the fact remains that most of the coarse fishing is done in central and southern areas. Fife has a dynamic coarse angling fraternity who have their own small waters – typical of the active groups all round the country.

There are plenty of small dams, ponds, lochs and even a few canals, in the south-central counties that support coarse fish. The larger lochs of the Trossachs also have healthy pike stocks. The rivers do contain coarse fish, but most of Scotland's coarse anglers tend to fish stillwaters. Coarse fishing attracts young fishers, as much as it does older enthusiasts, and it is a great way of drawing young people into angling. Let's face it, angling needs the constant infusion of young people to secure it's future – if it was left to us older ones the pastime would just fade away.

To safeguard the fish, which may be slightly more vulnerable at the extremes of their natural range, most Scottish coarse anglers invariably use barbless hooks. For the same reason, they tend not to use keep-nets unless they are participating in major competitions. Ledgering for large carp, dead baiting for huge pike, float fishing for roach and perch each have their special attractions.

There can be fewer more relaxing ways of spending a sunny summer afternoon than watching a float for that telltale dip. The variety of baits provides huge interest – are the carp taking luncheon meat today or are they on boillies? Is a maggot fished under a waggler float in mid-water going to take a bream or will it be silvery roach that take it? Should I spin a small, jointed plug close to these lily pads to see if that huge pike will take the bait? Too many questions, too few answers. But this is one of the great attractions of Scottish coarse fishing. If you haven't yet tried it, give it a go, you will not be disappointed.

A large pike from the margins of a reed bed: Scottish pike, in common with their counterparts in other countries, favour protected lies – wherever there are weedy bays, reed-beds, fallen trees etc. – that's where to hunt 'Old Lucius'.

Antique Tackle

Brass Fly Reels:
Established in 1860, John R Gow Ltd made reels until the middle of the twentieth century.

If you were to peer excitedly into the storage drawers, shelves, cupboards, or on a grander scale, the tackle rooms of most anglers, it is highly likely that you would find copious quantities of tackle from the past. We love to hoard equipment. Many harbour the belief that they may have a use for a particular item in the future. Anglers certainly do not like to throw items away. For others the propensity to retain or acquire tackle is much more, and becomes a separate interest in its own right. Collecting antique fishing tackle has become very popular.

Some collectors narrow down the range of tackle items they collect, focusing on specific items. Reels are a popular choice. The reason for this is straightforward – you can easily exhibit a collection of reels, whereas a display of rods is much more difficult. Collectors may even select a single manufacturer to collect – Hardy Brothers reels are popular for example.

House of Hardy reels have long been associated with high quality and their extensive range of reels has been around since Victorian times. However, it is not only reels that attract the interest of collectors. Spinning lures, creels, gaffs, line-winders and books are all sought after. Scotland has a rich vein of collectable fishing tackle due to the wide range of people who enjoyed fishing. Consequently, there is a high probability of coming across a fine old reel or some other antique item in a sale room or at a car boot sale.

The quality of antique reels enhance their appeal. The materials used were much more lavish than they are today. No lightweight plastic and cheap alloy here. Instead you will see dark ebony wood, smooth creamy ivory and time-burnished brass. The patina of long use increases their value and appeal. Similarly, rods were crafted from natural materials, adding to their attractiveness.

Solid wood rods of greenheart and the more complex, hexagonally-built rods made of Tonkin bamboo cane are a far cry from the later coldness of fibre glass, although it must be said that the present-day carbon fibre rod is a delight of design and practicability in comparison to its heavy antique counterpart. Nevertheless, old rods and reels possess something that modern kit is still too young to have accumulated – they have a history.

Fine Brass Salmon Reels:
The forerunner of the modern lightweight alloy reel, these grand reels had tremendous capacity and a ratchet which made the most evocative click as line paid out – no finer sound is there than the click of a decent reel responding to the draw of a large fish.

They carry reminiscences of fish caught, days of fun by a loch or river and disappointments suffered.

The collection of old fishing flies is a popular pastime amongst modern anglers too. The colourful creations of Victorian times make attractive displays. But it is more than simple artistry that makes them desirable, for an extensive collection will demonstrate how the various developments in fly design took shape. Initially, flies were fairly simple affairs, imitating genuine insects or other natural food items.

Gradually, they became much more complex and extravagant, reflecting the Victorian propensity to travel, because it was only through visiting foreign parts that the plumage of exotic birds could be obtained for fancy fly-tying.

Later still, the design of flies – trout flies in particular – reverted to more direct imitation of natural food items. Like many aspects of fashion, the tying of flies has enjoyed cycles.

In the nineteenth century, the manufacture of fishing tackle was a thriving industry in Scotland. Each of the major cities had tackle makers who sold the items they made in their own retail shops. In Aberdeen, William Garden made reels from 1869; Charles Playfair patented the first fly rod made up of spliced sections (fly rods previously had been one-piece). In Glasgow, William Robertson started making and selling tackle in 1885; while Alex Martin established himself as long ago as 1838, but later expanded opening shops in Edinburgh and Aberdeen.

The city of Perth had tackle manufacturers who supplied the anglers on the great River Tay – McNab's of Perth patented the first fly reel to have a ratchet in 1842. Previously, fly reels simply held the horse-hair line; they did not have the mechanism to brake against the run of a fish. McLeish's of Perth came into existence in 1880, and the famous P. D. Malloch's of Perth traded from the mid 1870s and is still in existence today. In Edinburgh, A & G Wilson, founded around 1846, were approved by Prince Albert as tackle makers to the royal family. In Dundee, John R. Gow Ltd was established in 1860 and made quality fishing tackle and guns until well into the twentieth century.

Not every modern tackle design is novel – if you look at the reels of the past you will see ideas of design and production which came and went, only to re-appear later as though they were an entirely new concept.

A Wooden 'Pirn' c1800: This is a type of antique reel is peculiar solely to Scotland. Note the hole for the rod to pass through and the antique lures of contemporary use.

Modern Tackle

The twentieth century was an age of technological advancement. As a consequence, you would think that the fishing tackle of today would be of vastly different design and construction from that of the past, but when you examine antique tackle it becomes apparent that there are many recurring themes. But most fishing tackle, whether old or new, serves fairly basic functions.

Rods flex under the strain of a casting weight, or fly-line and, hopefully, under the tension of a fish. In other words, they are 'loaded' by an optimum weight. Regardless of whether they are made from solid wood, sections of bamboo cane, fibre glass or carbon fibre, they are simply tensile springs that carry the line.

Reels on the other hand are receptacles for the line; they are likely to possess some mechanism for resisting the pull of a fish in the form of a drag mechanism, but their main function is simply to contain the line. For spinning reels there is clearly a need for them to allow line to run free off the spool and to retrieve it at various selected speeds. There are many different designs and variations of reel. Some involve complex gearing which speeds up the retrieval of line; some are very basic. An examination of antique reels reveals the fact that many modern reels are simply a variation of a pre-existing concept, they are not really new at all, except in the materials from which they are made.

A Modern 'Multiplier' Reel.
The sophistication of modern tackle makes it light, strong and incredibly effective.

The one exception to the uniformity of tackle over the years is the manufacture of fishing lines. Various types of fishing line have changed in several major ways over the years. The main contributor to this change has been the use of modern materials, particularly man-made fibres and plastics.

Probably the most notable line, which in name still exists today, was 'gut'. As the name suggests it was made from animal tissue, although the use of intestines was uncommon. People still talk of 'gut', although they are now referring to monofilament line. Other lines were made of silk, linen and other natural fibres including horses hair.

Modern monofilament is a single-strand of man-made polymer (plastic) material, most often nylon, extruded from a spinning machine, polished by rollers and wound onto spools. It is strong, light, consistent and not very visible to fish – just what is needed from a fishing line. Monofilament nýlon lines are used in freshwater and in the sea – they are even used to make nets. It is true to say that nylon revolutionised fishing line manufacture.

Braided Dacron, a type of polyester, also found favour, particularly amongst the sea fishing fraternity due to its strength, suppleness and its resistance to wear. Metals have also been used with good reason and effect. Copper and lead were included in braided leaders to make them sink, and steel traces are common for heavy sea fishing and to protect running line in pike fishing. Fine lengths of steel wire are used in a variety of situations, especially by tropical sea anglers.

One of the latest monofilament lines to hit the tackle shop shelves is made from fluorocarbon and has several advantages over conventional nylon. It is resistant to ultra violet light (making it last longer), it is slightly denser than water and as a consequence, sinks rather than snaking about in a highly visible way on the surface of the water. It has a refractive index very close to water, becoming almost invisible when submerged. Fluorocarbon leader tends not to absorb water in the same way as nylon does, staying stronger. Too few anglers appreciate that nylon line absorbs water over the first few hours of its use and may lose up to 30% of its strength.

Fly-line design has also become very high-tech in recent years. Modern lines replaced those made of silk during the mid-twentieth century. Braided silk lines were pleasant and easy to use, but needed to be treated with grease to make them float, however, when the grease dispersed they became prone to sinking again. The use of plastics penetrated fly-line manufacture, as it did throughout most aspects of modern life, and technology has created modern lines which are superb to use.

Not only are modern fly-lines made of modern plastics with slick coatings and excellent suppleness and strength, they also have a shape that would have been impossible to achieve consistently with past materials. Most use a profile which is termed 'weight forward' referring to the thicker torpedo-shaped portion near the tip of the line which narrows to the finer 'running line' behind it. This offers smooth and almost effortless casting to tremendous distances. The core of modern fly-lines are immensely strong and their coating is supple and smooth. In a range of floating or sinking rates to suit every occasion, there is little question that they are highly effective at presenting flies to salmon and trout and are a joy to use.

Flies:
There are more fly patterns today by many orders of magnitude than there were a few decades ago. The proliferation seems endless. Some innovations die unknown, while others establish themselves as firm and effective favourites.

A.H.E. Wood – The Floating Line

In the twentieth century, salmon fishing benefited hugely from the novel initiatives of A.H.E. Wood of Glassel, whose modernising influence on fly-fishing still inspires our fly-fishing thoughts.

Wood fished almost exclusively on the lovely Cairnton Beat of the River Dee in Aberdeenshire. He concluded after much experimentation that when the water was warmer, different tactics needed to be used when fly-fishing for salmon. By today's standards, this was not a radical concept, but for early twentieth century anglers it was a brilliant breakthrough. Rather than using large flies and sinking the line, Wood believed that salmon anglers should float their line and use smaller flies nearer the surface. By carefully controlling the direction of the line as it tracked across the stream, he believed anglers would be able to fish more effectively. Testing his new method, Wood fished near the surface on his 'greased line' using lightly dressed 'Blue Charms', a fraction of the length of the conventional flies of the period. It was a highly effective technique which brought him many fine salmon.

Wood's challenge to convention and his innovative observation revitalised a weary, dogmatic and dull way of salmon fishing. Salmon fly-fishing today is built upon the foundations laid down by A.H.E. Wood on the River Dee.

Fly-tying

Megan Boyd: One of Scotland's renowned fly-tyers. So many wonderful flies came from her creative hands in her workshop in Sutherland, that she became a legend in fly-tying and angling circles

There can be fewer more apt indicators of a nation's involvement in game angling than its history of artificial fly design and production. Scotland is the most advanced country in the world in this respect, due to its long-held position as a leader in the development of game angling. Modern practices come and go, innovations arise all around the world, but the foundations of modern fly-fishing and fly-tying were firmly laid in the rivers and lochs of Scotland. Evidence of Scotland's influence on fly-tying is plain to see. Just look at the basic design and patterns of most of the 'families' of fishing flies and you will see that the modern flies were, on the whole, first used or popularised on the banks of Scottish waters.

Curiously, given the tremendous role in its development, fly-tying did not originate in Scotland. Various commentators have cited Roman literature as the earliest references to using 'flies'. In the third century, by the rushing mountain streams of Macedonia, red wool and feathers were tied to hooks in the attempt to catch 'speckled fish' – presumably trout. Even in light of this, Scotland's unique influence on the development of the artificial fly is undeniable.

From the ancient days of millennia past, throughout medieval times when rods were simple affairs cut from riverside willows or ash, to the designs of rods which we are familiar with today, the use of hooks with some form of 'dressing' has always been a constant theme. These hooks were originally meant to represent the natural flies that fish rose to the surface to feed on, although they may not show all that much in common with flying insects.

There are four main types of artificial fly. The first is the lure, which is designed to entice fish to accept it, not necessarily by close imitation, but by charm, seduction and temptation. Lures are designed to replicate the natural prey of fish. Although brightly coloured, lures usually resemble a small fish and are used as an attractor, rather than an imitator. Salmon 'flies' are almost invariably lures.

Ian Moutter of Edinburgh: puts the finishing touches to a fully-dressed salmon fly in the comfortable surroundings of the Tweed Valley Hotel, overlooking the mighty river.

On the whole, the other three types of artificial fly *do* represent the life stages of insects, and are used to catch trout and grayling. The first of these broad types is the nymph,which represent the larval stage of aquatic flies. The next is the wet fly, designed to simulate insects or fish fry that exist nearer the surface than the bottom-dwelling nymph. The final distinct type is the dry-fly, which, as its name suggests, is fished on top of the water or within the surface film. Although patterns frequently overlap, these broad categories help beginners to unravel the mysterious intricacies of artificial flies.

Scanning through the lists of artificial flies in present use reveals the extent of Scotland's influence. Flies such as Jock Scott, Munro Killer, Mar Lodge, Dunkeld and Ally's Shrimp are standard salmon patterns, whereas Loch Ordie, Clan Chief and Malloch's Favourite are frequently used trout patterns. This list is just the tip of a very large iceberg and does not include the thousands of variants of traditional patterns and the fancier modern patterns, which have been developed for every application. Scottish fly patterns come from every corner of our country. From Orkney and the Shetland Isles in the far north to the rivers of the Borders, the variety of flies represent a full and fine tradition of innovation and ability and are a fitting tribute to Scottish ingenuity and craft

What is it that makes the art of tying flies so intriguing and absorbing? And why should it be so advanced in Scotland? There are as many answers to these questions as there are patterns of flies, but it has much to do with the variety of places and the diversity of conditions that the Scottish angler encounters. Our sport is infinitely varied, so there is a constant demand for flies to suit every occasion.

During the darkest of winter nights when Arctic gales howl like fiends around the chimney breast, and the television is predictably dire, an angler's mind may light up with a creative idea – a new fly pattern is being conceptualised. Several prototypes later, a refill from the decanter to gently lubricate the thought processes, and a new fly is born. It sits proudly in the vice, sparkling and unblemished, every fibre true, each twist of tinsel twinkling, its translucent hues exactly as its creator envisaged. It is ready for that special day on the

Fly-tying is open to young and old:
The art should be encouraged – for it adds extra dimensions to fishing which simply do not exist with shop-bought flies.

water's edge. With a complex mixture of pride, anticipation and a little nervous excitement because this might just be 'the one', the fly is placed in the safety of a fly box to nestle amongst the others. It will be many weeks or even months before it first flies through the air onto the water. Then, as if lifted from the depths by some mystical force, a huge salmon rises in the middle of the stream to take it firmly. Ah, what it is to dream...

There are active Fly Tiers Guild clubs throughout Scotland, meeting on a regular basis to share ideas and materials, and to extend the skills of the participants. This is an excellent way to improve fly-tying ability. In a relaxed and friendly group, the chatter is about fish that have been caught, fish yet to catch, fly patterns that have done well and those that will undoubtedly do well in the future. There is an optimistic ambience that is highly-enjoyable and genuinely practical.

The other driving force which enlivens fly-tying in Scotland is the enthusiasm of the club competition scene. Like-minded fly-tiers get together to test out new trout patterns both individually and in teams. The constant quest for a pattern or two that will secure a competitive edge powers the development of fly patterns. Competitors are always on the look-out for a special combination of form and colour that will make their new fly irresistible and puts them in an advantageous position. Once a pattern shows its effectiveness however, the word soon gets out and everyone else uses the new design. It is great fun, as long as it does not become too serious.

The recent trend in salmon fly design is to make longer, and less-complicated, patterns. Feather wings gave way to hair wings for many conventional patterns in the latter part of the twentieth century. Even simple patterns like Blue Charm and Garry Dog are an example of this trend.

The new designs feature long trailing tails and wings and are made using extremely ductile material like Arctic Fox fur, synthetic 'hair' and holographic tinsels. The Collie Dog (with three to five inches of trailing hair, and very little else) and the various 'Tadpole' patterns are examplers of longer flies and are probably taken for sand eels. These long-material patterns are usually grabbed ferociously by the salmon as though there isn't a moment to lose – just like catching a sand eel in the sea before it evades being eaten. Who knows how pattern design will evolve and develop – just as long as it does – for it is a dynamic part of fishing and offers great satisfaction.

Although many flies are designed to closely represent living insects, they are, in truth, fairly poor imitations. For one thing, there is always a great metallic hook hanging down between the artificial pattern's legs. We would dearly love to believe that our carefully crafted fly closely resembles a genuine natural organism and entices the fish to bite.

However, it is more likely that the fish sees something appear in its line of vision, wonders what it is, and takes it into its mouth to see if it is a tasty morsel. Colour, translucency and shape are all important factors when trying to gauge the success of a fly. Movement is of paramount importance when trying to attract a fish. Sometimes flies are painfully slow-moving, at other times far faster than any living creature could possibly swim.

KATE MCLAREN

KATE MCLAREN: invented by Charles McLaren and named in honour of his wife, this fly is the archetypal black midge, but possesses a tail that also gives it an 'upwing fly' dimension. It has several of the elements that many successful modern flies possess – the attraction of a black body ribbed with silver is undeniable. Fish this fly with confidence on the bob especially if the dressing is bushy, or lower down in a lighter dressing. It catches rainbows and brownies and is a great Scottish export to all parts of the world.

KE-HE: an Orcadian pattern invented in the 1930s, the 'Ke-He' is a fly that will successfully catch trout anywhere. I have used it in Australia and in Scandinavia as well as in countless lochs in Scotland. I find that it works well as a point fly or as a bob-fly when it is nice and fluffy. Although it is a bit of a nondescript pattern, based on ancient patterns, it is none the worse for this because the Ke-he has proven to be highly effective, on many occasions.

BROWN KE-HE

LOCH ORDIE: in the rolling heathery hills above Dunkeld another top fly was designed for use in Perthshire. The Loch Ordie fly is used as a dapping pattern and as a bob fly, usually with great success. Older tyings for dapping had a 'flying treble' hook, but this elaboration is missing from standard wet fly dressings.

LOCH ORDIE

CLAN CHIEF

GREENWELLS GLORY

INVICTA

Top Trout Traditional-Style Flies

CLAN CHIEF: the Clan Chief deserves its noble name but if Captain John Kennedy had known just how successful his creation would become, he might have been justified in calling it the Ard Righ – the gaelic title for the King of Scotland. The Clan Chief was originally designed for use in the machair lochs of the Western Isles, especially South Uist. However, in recent years it has become a firm favourite on all rainbow and brown trout waters. The amalgamation of black and claret colours, with silver ribbing and the brightly coloured tail, attracts trout marvellously. A bushily tied pattern is the ideal bob-fly. This is a relatively recent pattern, but one which has established itself within the ranks of traditionally-styled patterns due to its remarkable effectiveness.

GROUSE AND CLARET: the quintessential Scottish fly pattern that catches trout wherever it is used. Overall, the Grouse and Claret is used to represent flies from each of the main aquatic fly orders but its imitativeness really does not matter, for it is taken by trout as avidly as any other traditional pattern. Its near cousin, the 'Mallard and Claret', is almost as successful but in Scotland the wing feathers of the Highland grouse are used to create the fly pattern.

SILVER INVICTA: this is a classic fly by any standard and probably represents small fry or sticklebacks. It may also represent the film of silvery air bubbles which exudes from the hatching pupae of many aquatic flies as they ascend to the surface to eclose. Whatever the reason for its effectiveness, it is a fly that Scottish anglers should never be without. It makes the best middle-placed fly on a three (or four) fly cast. Brownies will readily accept Silver Invictas, providing they are the right size, smaller as the season progresses, but bigger on dark, windy days. Sea trout and rainbows are attracted to the Silver Invicta.

DUNKELD: on the banks of the River Tay stands the lovely small town of Dunkeld. Trout and salmon swim in its waters; the popular golden-orange 'Dunkeld' can be used successfully here. It is not an imitative pattern – there are few flies with a golden body and hot orange legs – but it is an effective attractor. Fish it anywhere on bright days in clear water, following the rule 'bright day – bright fly'. Also fish it on dark days and when the water is less clear, for it shines like a beacon, and trout will only chase what they can see.

ALEXANDRA: an old but effective point fly, the Alexandra provides flash and colour contrast. It has accounted for innumerable sea trout and brownies, and is yet to be fully exploited as a pattern for rainbows.

MCLEOD'S OLIVE: very similar to the most well-known fly, Canon Greenwell's Glory, McLeod's Olive is an old Scottish pattern. Designed to imitate the upwing natural flies, known by anglers as olives, McLeod's Olive should be used on the point, or middle position, in the cast and will work best when there are natural olives in the vicinity. It also works well when there are sedges hatching, especially if you are using a thicker version. In normal use, keep the dressing as slim and uncluttered as possible and you will have a genuine, traditional fish taker.

ZULU: the Zulu, or one of its many variations, is an essential inclusion in your traditional fly box. The standard Zulu is a great disturbance pattern when fished on the bob, but it works very well further down the cast (but remember to dress it slightly less densely). It successfully attracts rainbows and brownies and seems to benefit from a fore-hackle of light blue (the 'Blue Zulu') when used for sea trout.

WICKHAM'S FANCY

GROUSE AND CLARET

BLACK ZULU

CHAPTER THREE

THE MODERN ANGLER

The River Findhorn: A charming river and one of Scotland's many gems.

The modern fishing world is a different place to that of times gone by. Change is an inevitability; sometimes it has a negative effect, but it is mostly beneficial. Sport fishing in Scotland is no exception and has also been touched by change. Nevertheless, there is an unhealthy trait in some anglers to harp back to the good old days. They say "We've seen the best of it, it'll never be the same again", but this is strictly untrue and an unhelpful attitude.

There are more fish caught in Scotland now than ever before. Scottish fish are larger and better cared for; there are more fisheries; facilities have been improved greatly and this attention to comfort and access continues apace. Access is more open than it ever was, despite the view of a small minority that regulation somehow prevents them from enjoying their sport. More people now enjoy angling than ever before, so why is there a feeling that the position is not as good than it once was?

There are major problems of course. There has been a worldwide reduction in the number of salmon, and technologically enhanced net fishing has impacted heavily on the marine species around our coasts. There are still pollution problems to be countered, and the negative effects of fish farming need to be rectified. Nevertheless, our fishing is still excellent in comparison to most countries. It is only when you visit other parts of the world that you realise just how good Scotland's fishing really is. It is very, very special.

Modern methods are great fun and very effective. The sound basis of traditional angling, capitalised upon by novel innovations, has made Scottish sport fishing widely variable, technically challenging and immensely enjoyable.

Small Water Methods

The growth of small fisheries throughout the UK, and Scotland in particular, has led to the development of new methods of trout angling. Most of these fisheries are 'fly-only', although a number also include facilities for bait anglers. This, however, is a relatively recent occurence, because it was once believed that fishing with bait was somehow a lesser pursuit than fly-fishing – but gladly, these days are fading. If you wish to fish with bait, and it is within the regulations, do so. If you wish to fish with fly, do so. Do not criticise one or the other. The world is large enough for everyone to enjoy their own pastime as long as it does not impinge on the enjoyment of others.

To define what constitutes a small stillwater fishery is difficult because everyone's idea of what is 'small' will be different. Perhaps a better description would be 'purpose-built' as the great majority of small trout fisheries are natural waters, which have been modified. It is the methods and tactics which are of greatest interest here, and these have moved away dramatically from the traditional styles of fly-fishing in Scotland.

New tactics have evolved because, in small waters, trout behave differently. Trout in larger lochs, particularly brown trout, tend to hold station at a chosen depth contour. Often this is just deep enough for them to feel safe, while still enjoying the benefits of abundant shoreside (shallow) feeding. In other words, they congregate in predictable areas of lochs. This may change due to wind speed, direction, time of year, temperature and all the other factors that influence fish behaviour, but as a general rule the 'certain depth' concept holds. This, however, is not the case in small stillwaters – or at least, not to the same extent. The reasons for this are fairly logical.

Almost invariably, small stillwaters contain rainbow trout. These waters are frequently stocked; a system of 'put-and-take' is usually implemented meaning that each fish caught is replaced, thus maintaining a designated level of stock. Several issues arise from this. The first is that stock fish often swim in shoals as they did in their breeding ponds. This is similar behaviour to big cats in zoo cages – they tend to pace around constantly following a predictable route round their enclosure.

The second issue is that they feed in a conditioned way. When one fish swirls at a food item, the others recognise the activity and act similarly. Feeding in their rearing cage may have been done by hand with pelleted food thrown into the water at particular times of the day. As a consequence the fish have learned to expect food – a memory that persists long after their release into the fishery. Alternatively, they may have been fed from hoppers which were controlled by timers, but the net result is the same – when one fish chases food it stimulates the others to do the same.

To a great extent, behavioural traits such as shoal swimming and feeding patterns influence small stillwater fishing. Because the fish are swimming in compact groups, it is highly likely that there is an opportunity to catch more than one fish. In this situation it would be advisable, after you

Smaller Stillwaters: The advantage of smaller fisheries is that larger fish may be stocked in densities far greater that would be the norm in the wild.

Buzzer Fishing on Headshaw Loch, Near Selkirk: Buzzer fishing encompasses the use of flies tied to imitate the three distinct stages of the chironomid's life – bloodworms, midge pupa, and adult midge.

have hooked your first fish, to go back to the same place, with the same fly as soon as possible. Don't stop to admire the first fish; there are plenty of others to catch! See if you can predict the sequence of fish as they pass by. The route that they take will be very much the same each time. By observing carefully, you may be able to foretell when the shoal comes into your casting area or get into a position to exploit the shoaling activity. This shows a distinct movement away from the 'prospecting' type of fishing, which was traditionally the norm in Scotland.

As newly-stocked fish gradually break away from their shoaling habit, they become more interested in natural feeding practices. They do not expect regular pellet meals – the realisation that they must fend for themselves presumably dawns on them. They then start to look for things to eat. They mostly feed on midge species, for anything larger will have been rooted out and consumed long ago. Small stillwaters tend to have a limited range of aquatic organisms. There are large numbers, but few species. There are often a few species of upwing ephemerid flies, a population of water boatmen beetles, plus the ubiquitous chironomid midges 'buzzers'. The use of midge imitation has transformed much of stillwater fishing and this has transferred from the small stillwaters to larger lochs.

Buzzer fishing encompasses the use of flies tied to imitate the three distinct stages of the chironomid's life: bloodworm, midge pupa and adult midge. The pupal stage tends to be the most popular. Bloodworms are the larval stage of chironomid midges, which as their name suggests, describes their legless, red, worm-like form. These tiny creatures are small, measuring from 1-2 mm, to a maximum of 7-8 mm. They live in the mud on the bottom, feeding on vegetation and other organic detritus. Trout sometimes 'fossick about', stirring up the mud to disturb bloodworms, but it is the next stage of the midge's lifecycle that offers the greatest food potential and artificial fly pattern imitation.

The larval bloodworm is the longest living stage of a midge's life (some for a whole year, most for many months). The next stage, the pupa, normally only exists for 36 to 72 hours. The pupa is the intermediate stage between the bottom-dwelling larva and the sexually-mature flying adult. The size, shape and colour of pupae vary with species, but resemble each other broadly. The head and wing cases are visible, although they are sheathed inside the outer casing. The body is segmented and

Beecraigs Loch, near Edinburgh: A small heavily-stocked and highly-productive water with some huge trout amongst the population of above average weight fish.

slightly curved; there are light-coloured tracheal gills at the head, and light-coloured appendages at the tail end of the body, which aid propulsion.

Imitative pupae flies have developed over the years. Most fly-tiers simulate the curved shape by tying the body well around the hook shank or even using curved-shanked hooks, and use a ribbing effect to suggest body segmentation. The majority of tiers find some way of imitating the thicker thoracic area and the tracheal gills. Although it is evident that there has been a clear advancement in fly design, the way in which they are fished is key to the greatest change in trout fishing.

The most obvious changes are the use of unconventional materials and the tactic of fishing the fly without movement. Anglers hang the flies in the surface film, simulating the behaviour of hatching pupae. At this point, movement of the artificial fly would be distinctly counterproductive. Anglers also use surface indicators that reveal when a fish has accepted the fly some way below the surface and employ various kinds of sighting cues like highly visible tufts of coloured wool, little plastic floats or dry flies. The fact that anglers use such accessories is suggestive of a need to watch the wily rainbows that take the bait. Conventional nylon monofilament needs to be very fine if it is to avoid detection by finicky rainbows, especially when they have so much time to inspect the static fly, so the use of fluorocarbon has become widespread.

The fly patterns themselves have evolved in several ways. Firstly there are emerger patterns, which imitate the pupa hatching out into an adult fly at the point of breaking through the surface film. Pupae swim to the surface, hang with their gills poking up into the surface film, then turn upwards into a horizontal position before their sheath breaks open and the adult clambers out onto the water's surface. Emergers are semi-dry flies. They are hugely effective when trout are at, or near, the surface mopping up hatching midges. Artificial patters use plastic foam beads or the CDC feathers from the preen gland of ducks – 'cul-de-canard' – to keep them suspended in the surface film.

Midge pupae are imitated as widely as any other type of artificial fly. Recently, the patterns have become simplified representations, rather than fussy imitations, using modern materials to simulate the natural size, colour and form. A coating of epoxy resin provides a shiny, sheath-like finish, which aids the fly's passage through the surface film to the correct depth. The use of small metal beads has become popular with 'goldhead' patterns and are very effective.

Buzzer fishing has transformed small stillwater angling. It works best with rainbow trout, although it is a reasonably successful bait when fishing for brown trout. The slow, or better still, static presentation of the fly has moved away from rapid retrieval of lures and small wet flies, and adds a new and fascinating dimension to our sport.

The Use of Modern Tackle

The tackle of today is designed to enhance a day's fishing; there can be no doubt that it is highly effective, in fact, it is a wonder that there are any fish left to be caught when one reads the marketing blurb about new rods and reel lines! Probably the single most important advantage that has been brought into play is lightness. Modern materials are immensely strong for their weight: rods, reels and lines are very durable and lightweight. This allows longer casting – the increased strength being gained without the tackle being too heavy. It also brings lightness of touch, so that the faintest indication that a fish has taken the bait or fly can be registered.

The wide range of plastic materials has infiltrated almost every part of fishing – from floats and swim feeders to fly-tying materials. A look at the materials used in modern artificial flies reveals all. Artificial hairs and simulated furs are used to enhance long-dressed salmon flies, and holographic tinsels, which sparkle like gem stones, bring an attractive quality to any creation. The range is enormous and surpasses the natural materials that conventional fly-tiers were bound to just a few years ago.

So how has the introduction of these materials and designs brought change to actual fishing practice? The main elements are fineness and delicacy. Very fine leaders are used in fly-fishing that are almost invisible. In fact, some of the new fluorocarbon leader materials have a refractive index that is the same as water. This means that in the water light passes straight through the leader, thus making it undetectable. Using fine materials makes it easy to fool fish, or at least that is the theory.

The salmon pools of Scotland, which were once only accessible to the highly-skilled, are now fished by moderately-skilled casters who are now able to achieve the distances necessary to place the fly over all the lies. As a result, salmon are vunerable to a higher proportion of anglers. Trout fly-fishing has changed from surface dibbling of the fly, following a short cast, to throwing most of a 35 yard fly-line, allowing it to reach the required depth, then retrieving the fly from where the fish are lying.

Airing the Gear.

Previously, only the best casters had these skills, but now they are available to a wide range of anglers. However, similarly to Scotland's salmon population, a greater amount of trout are susceptible to the angler's hook.

Technology has touched coarse angling too. Pike anglers now set up their gear with electronic bite indicators. These invaluable gadgets make a loud signal if line is pulled through them, signalling the 'run' of a pike when it takes a bait. In this way, pike may be hooked more quickly and effectively than when the angler relied on watching for a take. New materials are also being employed by sea anglers; tackle is now much lighter making the catching of fish a much more pleasurable task.

Even trout flies are designed using modern materials to make them act in specific ways. The use of epoxy coatings on the body of buzzer imitations has beneficial effects. The tiny fly sinks to the required depth better with a hard coat of epoxy; it

Fishing Paraphernalia: Modern anglers carry much more kit than their predecessors – but enjoy the excellence that their modern tackle offers.

has good translucency imitating the natural closely, and has the extra advantage of being very resistant to wear. But how do you present these tiny lightweight morsels? New materials provide some answers. A floating fly-line may be used with terminal tackle, which takes the fly to the correct depth – either by the use of long fine leaders or by making use of poly-leaders or braided leaders, fished under a bite indicator. These leaders aid presentation when casting and have sink-rates designed to take the fly to the selected depth. By fishing these under the bite indicator – a tiny brightly-coloured and highly visible float – any take from a shy rainbow will be registered.

There is not an area of fishing that has not been touched by modern technology. When sea trout fishing, we use xenon-bulbs in our torches, generating brilliant light when old tungsten filaments merely glowed; the batteries which generate that power last much longer, and the small torch is now waterproofed up to a depth of 1000 feet. We put silent running electric outboards on our boats, a replacement for the leaking, misfiring engines of the past. We may even use portable sonar fish finders to locate fish at depths, where they once were safe.

More and more anglers are enjoying the advantages of using modern tackle and accessories, and long will the trend continue as the beneficial effects of new technology are realised.

The constant development of new ideas, and the reappearance of old ones in novel guises, is a fundamental part of fishing. In Scotland, we benefit from having a wonderfully strong base which

Sea Fishing from the Shore: Most sea anglers now use tackle which is much lighter than was used previously.

supports these new introductions. Innovation is what keeps our sport fresh and interesting.

Coarse fishing has long been practised in our country but this has primarily been as an adjunct to the more popular game fishing. Coarse angling techniques and practices in Scotland have, in the past, been somewhat archaic. It is normal to fish with dead baits for pike or to spin with small spinning lures for perch – methods which have been in use for centuries. However, angling for pike has developed momentously over the last decade or two. Not only has there been a dramatic increase in its popularity, but pike fishing techniques, tackle and tactics have become much more advanced.

The use of float tubes in pike fishing is an ideal example. There is a growing number of anglers who venture out onto the great expanses of Scottish lochs to fish for pike from float tubes. This has been described as fishing from an inflatable settee or sitting in a tractor tyre waiting for the inevitable puncture when a pike's jaw closes on the rubber! It is not just the methods of getting afloat that are changing. Anglers are also pushing back the frontiers by using lightweight fly-rods and specially-dressed lures, rather than the conventional baits of the past. That they enjoy this new way of catching pike is irrefutable – it is direct, highly-effective, physically-challenging, and more importantly, great fun.

The same is true of several aspects of sea fishing. Gone are the days of heavy gear. Light rods, fine tackle and more sensitive techniques are the order of the the day. New technologies have enabled the development of new tactics, which have opened up new possibilities for sea anglers. Bass anglers enjoy much more success in Scotland's surf when using light gear; fly-fishers are able to catch cod and pollack from the rocks at the bottom of our cliffs; specialists now venture out in small boats to fly-fish for sharks and dogfish in our sandy bays.

Everywhere anglers are testing the capabilities of the new tackle, trying to discover new dimensions to our sport.

Fly Selection:
Fly selection is everything – you need to have confidence in the creation which you are offering to the fish.

The River Dee:
Summer conditions require 'fine and far-off' fishing. Lightweight tackle and fine terminal gear offer far better chances than over-heavy equipment.

Catch-and-Release

Murthly, River Tay: Returning a spring salmon. Miss Ballantine's cottage is situated on the opposite bank.

Although game fishing originated in Scotland's lochs and rivers, it quickly became popular in North America. As a result, practices developed on the other side of the Atlantic returned to Scotland. 'Catch-and-release' is prime among these. Catch-and-release is the standard elsewhere in the world, but it has not yet established a following amongst Scottish anglers.

The reasons for this are based in the Scottish anglers' 'mind set'. We have long held the belief that we catch fish to kill, then eat. We have held the view that fishing was not solely for enjoyment, but that it was primarily a necessity; the trout or salmon caught at the waterside was for the table. Now this was true elsewhere in the world, of course, but in Scotland the traditional reason for fishing is to obtain 'something for the pot'. Elsewhere, the purpose of going fishing began to drift progressively towards enjoyment, and this was enhanced by the need to conserve vulnerable fish stocks. In some ways, we have fallen behind the rest of the world in relation to catch-and-release.

Until fairly recently, Scottish fish stocks had been sufficiently secure to avoid radical conservation measures; but in the last few years, our native fish stocks have shown significant decline. As a consequence anglers have become acutely aware of the growing need to conserve. However, Scots have not wholeheartedly adopted catch-and-release, at least, not yet. Certainly, there are more fish now caught and returned, as more Scots are convinced of the need to retain sustainable numbers of adult fish. Nevertheless, there is, among many anglers, still a degree of reservation. These misgivings are a product of a system of beliefs passed down through the generations.

Some hold an almost religious view that to deliberately introduce a wire hook into a fish's mouth, then stress it by 'playing it', only to let it go, is a violation of an animal's right to freedom from persecution. For them, it is more acceptable to catch that fish with the main aim of using it for food, even though this clearly involves deliberately killing it. To repeatedly hook, play, and release a fish is less acceptable in a philosophical sense, than to catch it and kill it as humanely as possible.

It is a matter of extent. For most, to return fish which are undersized or in poor condition is not a difficult decision; it presents no moral dilemma whatsoever. Where the problem arises is when the fundamental objective is to deliberately catch-and-release. It is the aim rather than the activity that is the issue. The problem is solved, however, when the decision is left entirely to the angler – it is not compulsory to return a fish, nor is it mandatory to kill it – it is a matter of personal choice. But this in turn leads to huge problems with regulation and control.

Scottish coarse anglers, and their sea angling counterparts, have adopted the practice of catch-and-release without any apparent problems. So why is it that most Scottish game anglers have such difficulty with it? One reason is that coarse fishing and sea angling do not have such a high price tag; some game anglers feel almost obliged to catch and kill something to partially justify and recoup the cost of the permit. Others feel there is a problem with returning salmon, for when they carefully release a fish it may swim into the next beat and be killed by the next angler who catches it. It seems to make no sense for them to put it back if it is to be captured again and killed. In this instance, they ignore the fact that each angler may return a proportion of the fish they catch and therefore in practice it does not matter which fish are returned, just as long as they are returned in good condition.

However, if you are going to release the fish there is absolutely no point in releasing it if it has been fatally damaged. If we are to return a fish, the less it is handled the more likely it is to survive. This means that, if possible, we should not touch the fish, because we remove some of its protective slime coating through handling. This allows bacteria to penetrate its protective barriers and infections to gain a foothold. Do not net the fish, as this also results in the removal of slime and scales. It is better to get a hold of the line and try to gently remove the hook, while the fish is still in the water. This is straightforward if the barbs have been removed or if barb-less hooks are used. Take great care not to damage the gills, they are fragile and prone to bleeding if roughly handled.

When releasing a fish we must treat it in a humane and sensitive way. We must be firm, to bring the release quickly to hand, but gentle as though we were handling something very fragile and precious, and the reason is that we are.

River Spey Salmon: Perceived wisdom has moved away from taking several salmon in one day, as this older photograph shows. Now, most anglers practise 'catch-and-release'.

River Tweed: The ghillie holds the boat while the fisher casts over a likely lie.

The Impact of 'Reservoir Style' Fly-Fishing

Traditional Scottish 'loch-style' fly-fishing, from free-drifting boats, has changed and continues to change with each passing season. This is not solely a Scottish phenomenon; new ideas and practices are also evolving in Ireland where there are similar conditions and fly-fishing tactics. Some of the reasons for the trend are clear, others a little more complex, but the overall effect is that the classical conventions of trout fly-fishing in lochs are rapidly changing. Some rue this loss of part of our rich fishing heritage; whereas most are cheerfully optimistic about what is happening and accept that it is probably inevitable.

Loch-style refers to the long-established traditional way of fishing for brown trout, in front of a free-drifting boat, (ie. downwind, with the breeze at your back). Loch-style fishing is mostly on, or near the surface, using a team of three or four small imitative or attractor fly patterns and the retrieval speed is quite slow. This does not involve casting huge distances, because, if you do, the boat overtakes the line before you are able to retrieve it. Most experienced anglers cast only a rod length or two in front of the boat.

Loch Style at Loch Lee, Angus:
Scottish lochs had a style of top-of-the-water fly-fishing which is miles away from the tactics and techniques used in rainbow-stocked reservoirs.

The aim is to bring the trout onto the surface to elicit the taking response. Dibbling the bob-fly in the surface film attracts the fish although they may take one of the flies lower down the cast. This is an absorbing and pleasant way of fishing, practised throughout the country, and is at its best in the wild lochs of the far north and west where the trout are hungry and fed at the surface. So, what has changed?

Probably the most important change is the introduction of rainbow trout. Rainbows are able to adjust and survive in a variety of environments unlike their cousins, the native brownie. They also feed differently. Rainbows feed at a greater depth than brownies; they search the bottom of the loch, feeding primarily on larval stage bloodworms. At other times, they drop to lower levels to find cooler, more comfortable conditions, where the oxygen content in the water is higher. The dissimiliar behavioural patterns of rainbow trout have prompted anglers to modify their tactics; many anglers now fish imitation and attractor flies at greater depths. This is not to suggest that rainbows do not feed at the surface – they most certainly do – but, unlike brownies, they also feed at a wider range of depths and roam around to find suitable feeding locations.

Brown trout tend to favour shallower areas of stillwaters and mostly feed when insects emerge from the bed of the loch and rise to the surface to emerge as adult flies. This explains why the 'evening rise' occurs – that wonderful period of intense feeding activity when it seems that every fish in the loch is at the surface consuming hatching flies. Brown trout take the opportunity to feed intensively at the water surface when the hatching activity takes place.

As a direct result of rainbow trout feeding at a wider range of depths, techniques have changed dramatically. The new approach to fly-fishing is known as 'reservoir-style' – a style that incorporates the use of fast-sinking lines that place the fly close to fish lying at deeper levels. It has also resulted in the development of the fly-fishing 'lure' – where larger than life-sized flies are created, often in very lurid colours that are designed to tempt fish swimming in the murky depths. These lures frequently represent the fry of small fish, which rainbow trout take more voraciously than brown trout.

One of the other impacts to propel the change

is the eutrophication of many lochs. This process of enrichment comes from many sources. As a consequence of inappropriate agricultural practices, fertilisers and other chemicals leach through the land and into the watercourses. Eutrophication may also result from in-river fish farming, where the effluent from uneaten food, treatment chemicals and faecal matter from closely-packed fish populations is released into the watercourse. In direct response to a shift in the chemical composition of the water, the habits of food chain species change. The feeding trout, therefore, must adapt their feeding behaviour accordingly. In the past, trout spent most of their time feeding on hatching flies at the surface, but now they feed at or near the bottom where food is more abundant.

Reservoir-style fishing relates to fishing at depth. Due to the high chemical content of England's lowland reservoirs and the fact that they are relatively shallow – there being few very deep valleys for impoundment in the mid-part of England – rainbows swim the entire area of the reservoir in search food. However, in the deeper Scottish waters, fish stocks tend to be concentrated in the shallower parts where food items are more abundant and accessible.

Not too many English reservoirs stock with expensive-to-rear brownies – most introduce cheaper rainbows. These rainbows feed well and flourish in the warm, rich water. When introduced, they feed on a variety of food items, sometimes taking surface flies, but also accepting sub-surface insects, daphnia and juvenile coarse fish.

As a consequence, fly-fishing has changed from a top-of-the-water pastime to a sunk-line activity. Anglers have, therefore, modified their tackle methods and tactics accordingly when reservoir fishing. No longer do we see free-drifting boats with anglers short-line fishing with small flies. Instead, anglers anchor where fish congregate, and fish with deep sunk lines and large lures or small static buzzer imitations. This must not be seen to be negative in any way, it is just different and it is highly effective.

Competitions have changed the ideology of traditional loch-style fishing too. Many competitions require the participants to fish at depth from free-drifting boats, but this requires the use of fast sinking lines that are able to get the flies down to the fish, then back, before the boat drifts over them. Long casting is the order of the day.

The flies that are used today have changed too. Gone, for the most part, are the traditional feather-winged patterns, which are steadily being superseded by the marabou and tinsel attractors of modern rainbow fishing. These attractor patterns may not have to be large, in fact, they are limited in size for many competitions, but they may have to be brightly coloured to be visible at all in the gloomy depths of the reservoir.

Popular trout fly-fishing magazines have been instrumental in change to some degree too. Their readership is high in England, and many of the articles feature reservoir fishing for rainbows. This is entirely proper of course, but it clearly emphasises the role of the rainbow and the placing of reservoir fishing to those that read the magazines. Not very much is written about truly traditional brown trout methods, and there is an obvious bias towards reservoir fishing.

What of the future? Will reservoir techniques completely take over from traditional styles? It is unlikely, especially in the more remote lochs where the trout are wild and the anglers wilder! Brown trout populations will continue to be natural and thrive where conditions favour.

Rainbows are a great boon to stillwater fishing, but they need not be applied to every water. There is scope for each species, and the great variety of fishing styles that they each encompass.

Loch Awe: One of the many lochs in Scotland which has a mix of native browns and released rainbows. 'Loch-style' and more-modern methods both work here.

Sea Fishing

In common with almost every pursuit and sport, sea fishing has become much more sophisticated and technically-oriented. In the past, sea anglers would persistently use one bait, one set of very conventional tackle and one general tactic, but now they enjoy a width of techniques and strategies far beyond those in use a decade or two ago. The main factor fuelling this change is the greater discrimination of anglers; they now have different aspirations about what they catch, and the methods by which they wish to catch their fish. An obvious symptom of this evolution is the proportion of fish returned. Gone are the days of huge catches and carcass counts. On the whole, sea fishing has become a more caring, environmentally aware pursuit.

Tackle development has also been influential in this movement towards finer fishing; sea anglers now use much more sensitive tackle than ever before. Lightweight carbon-fibre rods and modern lines of huge strength, but fine diameter, have transformed sea fishing. Sea anglers also have a finer approach to the whole sport, and this includes their philosophy, ethics and conservation awareness just as much as their tactics and tackle.

To some degree, practices must follow the development of suitable tackle; it is only possible to consider some angling practices if your kit will perform the intended function. On the other hand, it is only through the creativity of innovative anglers requesting tackle manufacturers to develop kit to suit new purposes that evolution may occur. The changes in sea angling advance almost daily. Many anglers are fly-fishing in the sea around Scottish shores, something that would have attracted scorn and ridicule just a few years ago. Yet these enterprising anglers enjoy fresh challenges and remarkable results.

Fly-fishing in salt water has been around for many years, especially in river estuaries and the voes of the Northern Isles where sea trout were, and still are, the target species. However, there has been a

The Pier at Gardenstown, Banffshire:
Scotland has many wonderful piers where fishing can be unusually good. Many young anglers gain the first angling experience on these piers then progress to other types of fishing, but their love of pier fishing always stays with them.

marked change in relation to the species targeted by fly-fishers. Around the south-west coast, there are fly-fishing anglers who catch cod, pollack and saithe using deep sunk lures pulled through the inshore pot-holes along rocky shores. In the warm water outflows around power stations and large water-cooled industrial plants, mullet are the target of fly-fishing specialists. Sharks and dogfish are fished for with fly. Bass are another species targeted by a small band of keen anglers who are trying to develop fly-fishing techniques specifically for this superb sea fish. New tactics and practices continue to be developed by enterprising anglers who are constantly trying to extend the capacity for fishing around Scottish shores.

Most European coasts have been intensively fished by commercial fishing boats in recent years – Scottish waters have suffered more than most. Populations of haddock and cod have significantly declined in many areas. There are existing boundaries along Scottish shorelines where trawlers do not venture. There is excellent shore-fishing available in these areas, but sea anglers are exercising great restraint not to over-exploit them. Catch-and-release has become an accepted norm. Scotland's shoreline fishing is a huge asset and should be protected from inappropriate exploitation through commercial fishing by Scottish and foreign vessels, and by anglers alike. It is salutory to note the lead taken by our sea anglers. It should be expected that the authorities will follow this example by establishing 'no-go areas' for commercial fishing and retain this vital part of Scotland's rich heritage.

It was not unusual a few years ago to see sharks and dogfish brought ashore after sea fishing excursions. These catches were then photographed alongside their captors on the pier-side. Nowadays, this is a rare sight; instead most sharks are tagged and returned when they are caught. There is some very good shark fishing around Scotland's south-west shores, and boats may be chartered to take you to catch tope, dogfish and rays.

The north-west coast offers some spectacular fishing for big flatfish. Halibut and skate, which put up a fight, can be found at depth off the Northern shores. To locate these fish you will need the services of a knowledgeable skipper. Heavy-weight tackle and a strong arm are also required for these big 'flatties' are feisty fish.

There can be few better sea fishing excursions than putting out from one of Scotland's north-west harbours in the bright, salt-tanged, coolness of a summer morning, bristling with excitement over the possibility of a great halibut or skate. The rolling waves calm the excitement until the skipper shouts that the boat is over the mark, and adrenalin races once more. Down the lines go. The deep, clear green water holds many mysteries, but will it hold a great halibut today?

Bass Rock, Firth of Forth: Success on Scotland's east coast.

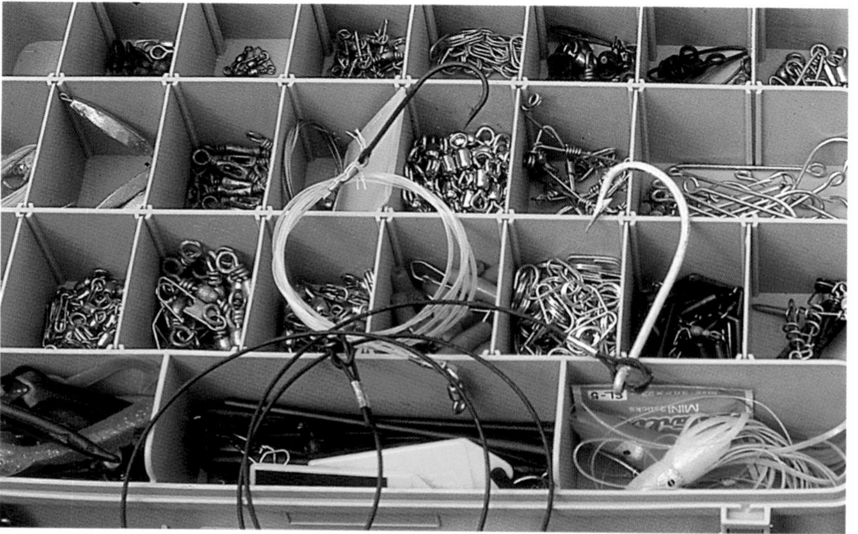

Sea Angler's Tackle Box: The complexity of modern sea fishing tackle increases almost daily. To attract a huge skate, cod or halibut, you need to place the right bait, in front of the right fish, at exactly the right time.

River Fishing Changes

In river fishing, there have been several fairly consequential changes in recent years in Scotland. Many of these trends are associated with the introduction of new items of tackle; others are developed based on fishing tactics from overseas. For example, when river trout fishing the use of gold-beaded flies has brought into play a new concept of fly-fishing, where the artificial fly is presented to the fish just above the stones on the bottom of the river.

Central Europe has gifted Scottish fly-fishing another innovative variation in fly-pattern design: the woven nymph. Using materials which can be wrapped into a weave, and weighting with lead wire within the dressing to make them sink rapidly, small imitative artificials were developed in Czechoslovakia and Poland and these have been used in the UK, and Scotland in particular, with devastating effect. By roll-casting a single woven nymph using a very short line, the angler fishes at depths in pools which otherwise would be very difficult to attain. Grayling and trout, and the occasional salmon, will take these small offerings when conventional approaches would mostly fail.

Fly patterns designed by Roman Moser, originally developed for the fast-flowing glacial streams of the Austrian Alps, are used by Scottish anglers fishing for trout and grayling. Using gold-plated brass beads, or even the heavier, more expensive tungsten beads in the dressing, these imitative flies – designed to represent the crawling stages of river caddis fly larvae – are very successful. Known as 'Peeping Tom' patterns – because they imitate the natural caddis larva's outer case of sticks, particles of sand and small stones, with the head of the caddis grub poking out at the front – they are extremely effective when fishing for trout or grayling near the river bed.

A further apparently minor change is the introduction of the use of 'polyleader' or 'braided leader' extensions to fly lines. By using different sink-rated leaders at the end of floating lines, fly-fishing becomes a much more versatile pursuit. The short sections of sinking line offer the angler the opportunity to fish the fly at any chosen depth, without necessarily having to change the main part of his line each time to attain the required length. By simply replacing the leader tip by 'loop-to-loop' connection, lines are adjusted to fish at any chosen depth with excellent effect.

Science and education has also changed many of the ways in which river anglers fish. It is now commonplace to hear anglers talk at length about aquatic ecology. Previously, many anglers had a limited knowledge of insect species; some were able to recognise the major families of insects that hatched from the pools in front of them; others were able to vaguely identify flies in a broader context, using their popular names such as 'olives' or 'March Browns'. Today anglers now have access to huge banks of knowledge from superb entomology books and ecology programmes on television, to magazine articles and websites on the Internet.

Anglers are able to use this new found awareness to their advantage. Many have moved into new fields of imitative fly-fishing. For example, anglers are now aware that a trout's diet consists of chironomid insects – a fact that was not truly taken into account in the past when tying and selecting artificial flies. This is a welcome and refreshing trend, one that should make anglers even more aware of the aquatic environment around them.

Tweed Flow:
Fishing swift-flowing rivers is a joy. But it does require care.

River Tweed:
The Famous Junction Pool where long and glorious tradition meets modern concepts and techniques.

Competitive Angling

Loch Leven, Before the Match:
Anyone who has been party to an international match will vouch for the great spirit of friendship that exists.

There is probably nothing quite so contentious as the element of competition in our sport. Some revel in the pitting of self against others, while others detest competition in fishing. Love it or hate it, the reality is that competition is here, and here to stay.

So what are the pros and cons of competitive fishing? Pro-competition anglers claim that it adds that certain edge to a day by the waterside. Anti-competition anglers argue that fishing is about pitting yourself against wily fish, not the skills or luck of other anglers. Regrettably, it is from ignorance that most criticism comes. Angling competitions bring out fraternity in the participants. Anyone who has been party to an international match will vouch for the great spirit of friendship and sharing that exists after the occasion. Before the match, tactics and techniques tend to be kept under wraps!

It is obvious that not everyone can win, so elements of challenge and enjoyment must be evident or participation will fade away. It is satisfying to win competitions, but there is no dishonour in losing. After all, fishing is not a sport where the harder you try the better your result may be. It is a combination of knowledge, technical skill, dedication, intelligence, the capacity to reason logically, and, perhaps most importantly, a certain amount of innate ability.

So what are the beneficial and negative effects of competition on our pastime? There can be no doubt that the technical development of angling would not have progressed so fast, nor advanced so far, had it not been for competitive fishing. The quest for the 'competitive edge' has encouraged novel design and creative innovation, which the traditional angler simply would not have considered. Furthermore, the development of effective conservation measures is often supported by competitive associations and federations who work hard to implement workable and effective rules. Some competitions are now wholly catch-and-release, while others apply very strict rules to prevent unsporting behaviour.

On the other hand, competitive angling puts severe pressure on fisheries and fish stocks. Of this there can be little real doubt. Competitive anglers do like to win, and to do so requires that they fish hard, almost certainly harder than the purely recreational, non-competitive angler. But competition is a part of day-to-day life; it is an integral part of the Scottish fishing scene and will be for a long time to come. It causes people from all walks of life to come together in friendly rivalry and to share a sport that is all about enjoyment.

Fly-fishing competitions originated in Scotland.

The Harbour at Loch Leven: The home of the national and international fly-fishing competition.

Loch Leven has long been the home of the competitive fly-fishing event for many clubs and associations. The Scottish National Angling Clubs Association (SNACA) – the governing body for competitive clubs formed in 1880 – declares in its Constitution that it aims to '… promote friendship amongst anglers'. Surely, there was never a better ambition. The SNACA amalgamated with The Scottish Anglers Association (SAA) to form the present governing body for game fishing in Scotland – The Scottish Anglers National Association (SANA). This excellent, national organisation co-ordinates national and international fly-fishing events. It also provides superb services such as coaching, environmental consultancy, legal advice and technical expertise, to name but a few.

What does Scottish competitive angling offer? Firstly, it provides challenge, as if it is not challenging enough trying to catch a cunning trout. There is no more exciting sport for those who enjoy the thrill of the hunt. Scottish fisheries and scenery, added to the quality of Scottish anglers, makes the competition scene vibrant and dynamic. If you wish to succeed, you will have to be on form, be able to use technical expertise and be very familiar with your chosen venue. You may also wish for a little good fortune – this never goes amiss! You will meet with a tremendous bunch of like-minded people, totally absorbed in their pastime. They are artists; to watch them prepare for a major event is like seeing the dedication of top-level athletes readying themselves for the Olympics. On the water, they know where the fish will be, what they will take, when the fish will come to the surface, when they will be at depth, and when to move to the next 'hot spot'. They are totally 'in tune' with their environment. They show superb artistry when they cast long lines, work the team of flies just right, and fool the wiliest of fish into accepting their precious offering. It is simple to state – just a man with a rod in search of a fish or two – but it is more, much, much more!

Coaching and Tuition

River Laxford, Sutherland: Just the place to learn the basics, under the tutor-ship of a seasoned angler.

Not everyone holds extensive skills in fishing or feels that they are sufficiently well prepared to catch the wonderful fish that they would like to. Many anglers – both locals and visitors alike – require the expertise of tutors, who help to extend their angling ability. We are very fortunate in Scotland to have teachers of the highest calibre who are willing to help anglers of all abilities.

The essential elements of an angling coach are patience, well developed individual skill and genuine experience, plus that crucial ability to implant angling skills in others. Not all successful anglers make good tutors – indeed the reverse may be true where relatively unsuccessful anglers make very good coaches.

There are numerous fisheries throughout Scotland that have a resident angling instructor. This is especially true of game fishing stillwaters. On rivers, most ghillies are very able and are ready to help the beginner, while at a regional level there are instructors who are accredited through their national bodies. There are also freelance coaches and instructors and some clubs have members who can tutor if required.

The main game angling bodies in Scotland who hold details of instructors are: the Scottish Anglers National Association, whose accredited instructors hold the Scottish Game Angling Instructor's Certificate (SGAIC); the Salmon and Trout Association, who offer STANIC certification to anglers who can demonstrate a wide local knowledge and teaching ability; and members of the Association of Professional Game Angling Instructors (who hold APGAI accreditation). It is important to locate an instructor who has undergone some form of accreditation.

The Scottish Federation of Coarse Anglers (SFCA) provides tuition and assistance through its excellent services. This association is developing coarse angling throughout Scotland, and follows the basic tenet that helping young people to understand and appreciate fishing will consolidate their future interest, and the fortunes of the sport in years to come.

The Scottish National Federation of Sea Anglers has a very good system of regional instructors who are pleased to show you where, when and how to catch fish around our shores.

By and large, you get what you pay for. A well-qualified instructor offers excellence in his or her teaching skills. You should see yourself progress in recognisable stages towards your goal and feel confident that you are receiving value for your

A lesson on the River Helmsdale.

money. Individual teaching in any skill can be expensive but you should improve your skills if you apply yourself. If you feel that you are not progressing you may need to change your instructor. As with most skills, different styles of tuition suit different people – it may be that you have to try more than one instructor before you find one on the right wavelength.

Game angling instructors have to undergo extensive accreditation. This includes testing of their individual ability to cast properly and, more importantly, to convey this skill to others. They are also assessed on a wide-range of knowledge based skills such as: insect recognition and imitation; fly-tying; tackle acquisition, preparation and use; first-aid; sports psychology and safety matters. The testing is carried out by senior coaches who have experience in running coaching systems and who have been accredited for a considerable amount of time. This rigorous system of testing ensures that all accredited instructors are well-prepared and able to pass on his or her skills and knowledge in an effective and enjoyable way. This help is absolutely invaluable to the novice.

Different instructors favour different methods. Some take beginners directly to the waterside, while others prefer to teach casting on level grass, then progress to the water. Some instructors prefer to sit down with the beginner and explain the background to the sport and how to carry out practical skills, whilst others favour a more direct hands-on approach. It is important that novices understand the basics of fishing as soon as possible in their learning experience. This avoids the pitfalls that may lie ahead, like falling foul of the law by fishing in the wrong place, using an illegal method or fishing out of season.

For a beginner, it also helps to know exactly what you are trying to do before you do it. This sounds like basic common sense, but many potential anglers give up simply because of an initial lack of success. Instructors are there for a good reason – use them.

Tackle Shops

John R Gow Ltd, Dundee: Scottish Tackle Shops. The best by far are the traditional shops where you find all manner of interesting items.

Regardless of where and how an angler plies his or her craft, there will always be the need to obtain suitable tackle. Nowadays there are several methods of buying what you need: visit your local shop, use mail order through magazine advertisements, or log on and browse the Internet.

Tackle shops are slightly different every time you visit them. There is always something new to investigate; they are a temple to the fervent fanatics – a magical mystery tour of tackle and equipment. They all have individuality. Each shop contains an array of items carefully selected by the owner – a bit of the proprietor is often revealed in their choice of stock. Maybe it is a bit like the author of a book divulging a little of himself within his characters. Of course, all shops sell a range of standard, staple stock items – invaluable items that no angler should be without.

The best, by far, are the traditional shops where you will find all manner of interesting items – not necessarily what you went in for originally, or even what you felt you needed! Lingering in these older shops are the evocative scents of oiled silk lines, wicker creels, leatherwork, and the naphthalene mothballs that are used to keep fly-tying materials safe from insects. There is something redolent about the place – a tackle shop is a great place to spent time browsing. Although traditional, they are not outdated, for the stock and service is an effective blend of the traditional with the modern – just what is needed to whet the angler's appetite and keep interest refreshed.

Similarly to when anglers are walking over a bridge they are compulsively drawn to look over the parapet to see if there are fish below, the same thing is true of fishing tackle shops. You are drawn to the shop window, then propelled by some invisible force towards the door, and lured inside. The Aladdin's cave waiting for you has an almost mystical attraction, your eyes widen and your undivided interest is aroused. The clothing, footwear, racks of rods, displays of gleaming reels, glass-fronted cabinets, drawers full of tempting flies and lures, notices, packets of sundries and the miscellaneous bits and pieces that may be used in the pursuit of fish are attractive beyond the contents of any other shop. When you visit strange towns – or even venture overseas – tackle shops always hold that special delight and are frequently the first to be visited.

There are some truly superb tackle shops in Scotland, especially those close to the major fishing areas that are traditional in nature. As you might expect, the largest fishing store is in the largest city. Glasgow Angling Centre is very modern and well-stocked. Also in Glasgow is the more traditional William Robertson's shop. To the south-west of Glasgow, Brian Peterson's shop in Greenock is notable for its comprehensive stock, angling awareness and value. To the east, in the capital city Edinburgh, are the excellent Mike's Tackle Shop in Portobello, the aptly-named Country Life, and Dicksons just off Princes Street in the city centre.

John R. Gow Limited, in Dundee, was established in 1860 and still treasures its first-class reputation for the best tackle, friendly service and knowledgeable advice. P. D. Malloch's shop in Perth is of a similar pedigree and provides an excellent service. The Mallochs have been a prominent family in many sections of Scottish game angling over the years. Graham's tackle shop sets high standards in Inverness, while McLeod's in Tain is highly convenient for anglers in Easter Ross, and the Sutherland Rivers Carron, Oykel, Cassley and the Helmsdale a few miles further north. On lovely Speyside, Munro's tackle shop in Aberlour and Mortimer's in Grantown-on-Spey are self-evident and conspicuous leaders. If you are in Orkney, Billy Sinclair's shop is an essential visit for up-to-date information and tackle. At the other end of the country, on the banks of the Tweed, you really should call into Tweedside Tackle in Kelso where a full range of angling products and helpful advice are always at hand.

It is not just dedicated country pursuit shops that sell fishing tackle in Scotland. Many ghillies on the larger beats of Scottish salmon rivers offer tackle to their guests, as do the skippers of sea fishing charter craft. Hotels, tourist offices, and countless rural post offices have a tray or two of locally tied flies, which are suitable for nearby fisheries. Even the local hairdresser may have a display of special flies. It is not unusual, in some of Scotland's more rustic pubs, to order your fly patterns along with your pint of beer.

There is also a long history of individual rod making in Scotland. These one-man businesses make rods to your individual specification. Sometimes these craftsmen work full-time, while some make superb rods as a hobby. The range of stock, type of service, location, history, traditional courtesy and tremendous local knowledge make Scotland's tackle outlets a rich study in themselves.

The Scottish tackle shop is also a meeting place. It is where the up-to-date statistics and information change hands with every customer. Most shops offer permits and recommend tackle and tactics for the local fisheries. Most of the proprietors are anglers themselves who readily share their fishing related experience of a region with visitors. Some offer tuition, others offer guiding services. Scottish tackle shops reach far beyond simply selling items of tackle, they are part of our sporting heritage. Curiously, our trans-Atlantic counterparts would love to have the older shops that exist in this country, for most of their tackle retailing industry is in the form of supermarkets and lacks individual character. They find the traditional tackle shop far more attractive.

Unfortunately, a number of these traditional shops are closing. This is due to a lack of support by local anglers, who would rather order their tackle through mail order advertisements and the Internet rather than using their local shops. It is a misconception that local shops are more expensive; the reality is that many of the traditional shops opt to match mail order prices. It would be a very sad if all the high street tackle shops were to disappear, so it is essential that we spread our buying across the whole range of suppliers. If we do not, we will lose another part of the character that makes Scotland so special.

Mike's Tackle Shop, Portobello, Edinburgh: Selecting tackle from the display of one of Scotland's premier tackle stockists.

The Law

Preparing for the day on the River South Esk.

Scottish fishing is regulated by a complex system of national and local laws. Individual fisheries, fishing clubs and associations collectively help to enforce the rules relating to when certain types of fishing are permitted. In law, methods used, species caught and size are also carefully defined.

Some of Scottish fishing laws are ancient and relate primarily to salmon. An excellent example is the regulation dating back to the thirteenth century in the reign of King Alexander the Second, which defined the gap that had to be left when building cruives (narrow fish traps) in Scottish rivers. The law required that a well-fed three-year-old pig must be able to be placed *'in sic ane manner that nather his gunzie, nor his tail tuich ony of the sides of the cruives'*. Imagine if this law was ever put to the test – the squealing pig being dropped into the swirling current, and the contesting parties arguing about whether his grunzie (snout) or his tail touched the sides.

However, regulation was introduced for sound legal reasons. Legal entitlement to the fish themselves, and the water in which they lived, had to be established to avoid conflict of ownership. This was often granted by the sovereign and, even today, people resident in a royal burgh hold permanent rights to take fish from their local river. Then came the legal protection of the fish themselves, laws frequently flaunted by a shadowy character – the poacher.

In Scots law, the right to fish for salmon confers the lesser right to fish for other freshwater fishes. So if you have a permit to fish for salmon you may opt to fish for trout quite legally. However, the reverse is not legal. To fish for salmon requires that you hold the permission of the legal owner, which should technically be in writing, although in many cases the practicality of permission is usually more informal.

There is no right to fish for native trout in Scotland. The law is quite clear about this. A belief may persist that there is such a right, but this is definitely not the case. Fishing is part of ownership and is a heritable asset in law.

Legal fishing seasons are sometimes a little difficult to follow, as each area may be different. In the north, rivers open their salmon season early in

Lunchtime on the River Ettrick, Borders.

the year – around the 11th and 12th of January. The notable exception is the River Brora which opens on the 1st of February. Next in line comes the mighty River Tay with its opening ceremony at Kenmore on the 15th of January (or on the 16th if the 15th falls on a Sunday when no salmon fishing will take place). Almost all the other river systems in Scotland open between the middle of January and the 1st of February with the Angus rivers, North Esk and South Esk, following on in mid-February. Closing dates reflect the timing of the opening date, with most finishing at the end of September. Some, like the Tay, end the season in mid-October, but the River Tweed and River Nith are latest of all, closing at the end of November.

The brown trout season applies nationally and is fixed from the 15th March until the 6th October (both dates inclusive). With reference to rainbow trout, there is a slight complication. They do not have a defined closed season, and are treated as non-native species. You may fish for rainbow trout throughout the year, but beware of catching or attempting to catch their native cousins outside the brown trout season.

There are legislative regulations that cover all aspects of fishing, including the size and condition of the fish caught. For example, brown trout measuring less than seven inches must be returned to the water and the same rules apply to salmon and sea trout kelts. The law also dictates fishing methods; netting methods are carefully described and rod and line activities are strictly controlled.

River Thurso, Caithness: Some angling huts are palatial, while some are slightly less so.

Not everyone appreciates just how severe the punishments may be for breaking laws relating to fishing. Significant fines are the norm, although, on occasion, terms of imprisonment have been enforced. Also, the courts may impound all the tackle used to perpetrate the offence, which includes all your equipment, clothing and even your vehicle. So beware, the implications of going fishing in the wrong place at the wrong time could be disastrous.

The antiquated portrayal of the poacher as a clever rustic who sets out at dusk on a moonless evening to take a salmon from his local pool, and 'put one over' on the laird, is an attractive one. It is, however, strictly an outmoded and inaccurate picture. The reality now is that the overall climate has changed and bona fide anglers despise poaching because they recognise it for what it is – simple theft. Many see it as aggravated theft because the fish stocks that are poisoned by modern poachers, or damaged in their nets, are part of Scotland's fragile natural heritage and should be carefully conserved by all.

Lunch Time, River Spey: The fishers gather to have a pre-meal dram and to talk and eat.

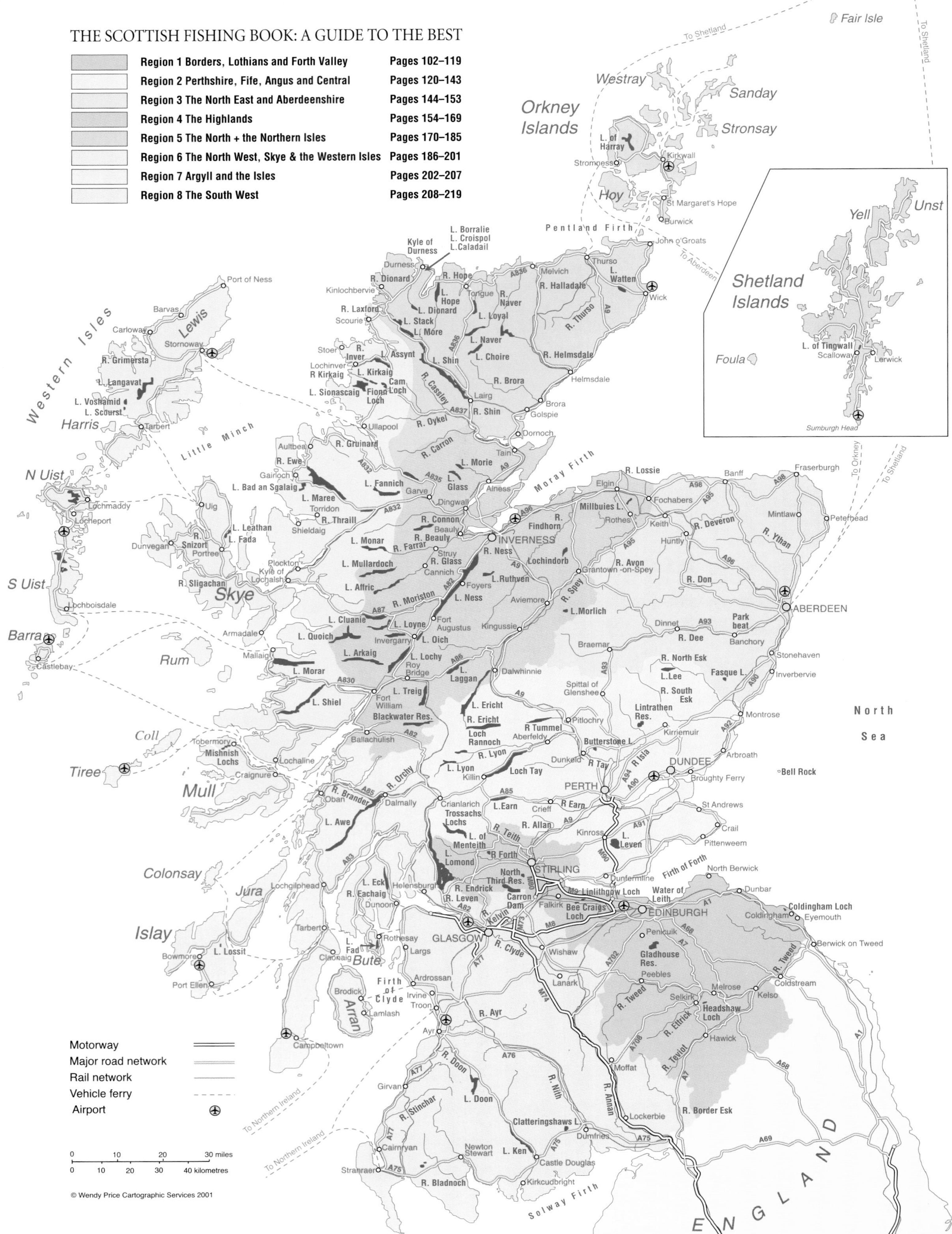
THE SCOTTISH FISHING BOOK: A GUIDE TO THE BEST
Region 1 Borders, Lothians and Forth Valley Pages 102–119
Region 2 Perthshire, Fife, Angus and Central Pages 120–143
Region 3 The North East and Aberdeenshire Pages 144–153
Region 4 The Highlands Pages 154–169
Region 5 The North + the Northern Isles Pages 170–185
Region 6 The North West, Skye & the Western Isles Pages 186–201
Region 7 Argyll and the Isles Pages 202–207
Region 8 The South West Pages 208–219
Fair Isle
To Shetland
Westray
Sanday
Stronsay
Orkney Islands
L. of Harray
Kirkwall
Stromness
Hoy
St Margaret's Hope
Burwick
Pentland Firth
John o'Groats
To Aberdeen
Shetland Islands
Yell
Unst
Foula
L. of Tingwall
Scalloway
Lerwick
Sumburgh Head
L. Borralie
L. Croispol
L.Caladail
Kyle of Durness
Durness
R. Dionard
Kinlochbervie
R. Hope
L. Hope
Tongue
R. Naver
L. Dionard
R. Laxford
Scourie
L. Stack
L. More
L. Loyal
L. Naver
L. Choire
Melvich
R. Halladale
Thurso
L. Watten
Wick
R. Thurso
R. Helmsdale
Helmsdale
R. Brora
Brora
Golspie
Dornoch
Stoer
R. Inver
L. Assynt
Lochinver
R Kirkaig
L. Kirkaig
L. Shin
L. Sionascaig
Fionn Loch
Cam Loch
R. Cassley
Lairg
R. Shin
Ullapool
R. Oykel
Port of Ness
Barvas
Carloway
Lewis
Stornoway
R. Grimersta
L. Langavat
L. Voshamid
L. Scourst
Western Isles
Harris
Tarbert
Little Minch
Aultbea
R. Gruinard
R. Ewe
Gairloch
L. Bad an Sgalaig
L. Maree
Torridon
R. Carron
L. Morie
Tain
L. Fannich
L. Glass
Garve
Alness
Moray Firth
Dingwall
R. Thraill
Shieldaig
N Uist
Lochmaddy
Locheport
Uig
L. Leathan
L. Fada
R. Snizort
Portree
Dunvegan
L. Monar
R. Connon
Beauly
R. Beauly
R. Farrar
INVERNESS
R. Ness
Struy
R. Glass
Cannich
Plockton
Kyle of Lochalsh
L. Mullardoch
L. Affric
R. Sligachan
Skye
S Uist
Lochboisdale
Foyers
L. Ruthven
L. Ness
R. Moriston
Aviemore
Fort Augustus
L. Cluanie
L. Loyne
L. Oich
Invergarry
Armadale
Barra
Castlebay
L. Quoich
Mallaig
L. Arkaig
L. Lochy
Roy Bridge
L. Morar
Rum
A830
L. Shiel
Fort William
L. Treig
Blackwater Res.
L. Laggan
Dalwhinnie
Kingussie
L. Ericht
R. Ericht
Loch Rannoch
Ballachulish
Coll
Tobermory
Mishnish Lochs
Lochaline
Tiree
Craignure
Mull
Oban
R. Brander
R. Orchy
Dalmally
L. Awe
Colonsay
Jura
Lochgilphead
Islay
Bowmore
L. Lossit
Port Ellen
Tarbert
R. Lossie
Elgin
Banff
Fraserburgh
Fochabers
Millbuies L.
Rothes
Keith
R. Deveron
Mintlaw
Peterhead
Huntly
R. Ythan
Findhorn
R. Findhorn
Lochindorb
R. Avon
Grantown-on-Spey
R. Spey
R. Don
L.Morlich
ABERDEEN
Dinnet
R. Dee
Park beat
Banchory
Braemar
Stonehaven
R. North Esk
Fasque L.
Inverbervie
L.Lee
R. South Esk
Spittal of Glenshee
Lintrathen Res.
Kirriemuir
Montrose
Pitlochry
R Tummel
Aberfeldy
Butterstone L.
North Sea
Arbroath
DUNDEE
Dunkeld
R Tay
R Isla
Broughty Ferry
Bell Rock
R. Lyon
L. Lyon
Killin
Loch Tay
PERTH
Crianlarich
Trossachs Lochs
L.Earn
Crieff
R Earn
St Andrews
R. Allan
R. Teith
L. of Menteith
Kinross
L. Leven
Crail
Pittenweem
L. Lomond
R Forth
STIRLING
North Third Res.
Dunfermline
Firth of Forth
North Berwick
Dunbar
L. Eck
R. Eachaig
Helensburgh
R. Endrick
R. Leven
Carron Dam
Linlithgow Loch
Water of Leith
Dunoon
Falkirk
Bee Craigs Loch
EDINBURGH
Coldingham Loch
Coldingham
Eyemouth
Penicuik
R. Kelvin
GLASGOW
R. Clyde
L. Fad
Rothesay
Bute
Claonaig
Largs
Wishaw
Gladhouse Res.
Berwick on Tweed
R. Tweed
Peebles
Lanark
Ardrossan
Brodick
Firth of Clyde
Irvine
Troon
Arran
Lamlash
Melrose
Selkirk
Kelso
Coldstream
Headshaw Loch
R. Ettrick
Hawick
R. Ayr
Ayr
Campbeltown
R. Doon
Moffat
R. Teviot
R. Nith
R. Annan
Girvan
L. Doon
R. Stinchar
To Northern Ireland
Lockerbie
R. Border Esk
Clatteringshaws L.
Dumfries
Cairnryan
Newton Stewart
L. Ken
Castle Douglas
Stranraer
R. Bladnoch
Kirkcudbright
Solway Firth
ENGLAND
Motorway
Major road network
Rail network
Vehicle ferry
Airport
0 10 20 30 miles
0 10 20 30 40 kilometres
© Wendy Price Cartographic Services 2001

CHAPTER FOUR

SCOTTISH FISHING: A GUIDE TO THE BEST

The main questions facing anglers who live in Scotland, or those who are visiting our country, are 'where should I go to fish?' and, 'what should I do when I get there?' This part of The Scottish Fishing Book attempts to provide some help in these directions. Scotland has so many fascinating places to visit that the problem is not what to include, but what to miss out. Those included in the following pages each have something special – something that places them above the rest.

On matters of how to fish, this must be a personal choice based on experience. Once again, each suggested water has something special that should be tried – something which may augment your normal practice and enjoyment.

There are around 150 places to choose from in the following pages. Some are where huge fish may be encountered, some are the most scenic, some are free, and some very expensive – but what links them together is their sheer variety. If you have the fortune to visit several of these places, you will appreciate how diverse Scotland's fishing really is. A further advantage is that many of the places listed are sufficiently large to warrant more than one visit. Keep in mind that they change dramatically throughout the seasons and under differing weather conditions, so visiting the same place will not result in boring repetition. Realistically, fisheries cannot be expected to offer optimum conditions at all times and each location must inevitably be mixed. The trick is to enjoy what you find, and not long for something else. Try to be as content as the subject of Izaac Walton's famous words: 'No life so happy and so pleasant as the life of the well-governed angler'.

THE BORDERS, LOTHIANS AND FORTH VALLEY

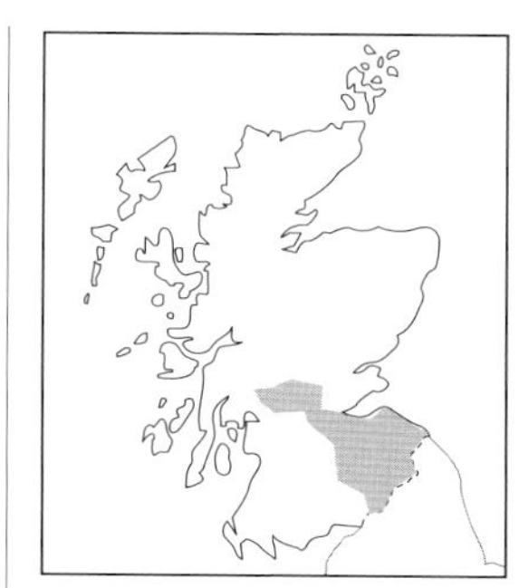

River Tweed: Temple Pool, just above Coldstream Bridge. A grand place to swim a traditional Tweed pattern like a Jock Scott or a Garry Dog over the salmon lying in the tail of the run.

The south-east corner of Scotland, from the border with England northwards to the central belt, has a large population and many enjoy the challenge of the region's varied fishing. Parts of the region are fortunate to have a hilly backbone which tends to hide the many fisheries and make them seem remote and well away from the pressures of contemporary Scottish life. These fishing venues are the respite for countless anglers who greatly enjoy their day in the country, sometimes only minutes from their home in one of the larger towns.

The Borders hills are not populous. Their great rolling lift draws rain down into the valleys to fill the Tweed and its tributaries, which are tremendous fisheries of world-wide renown.

To satisfy the demand for angling facilities in the region, there has been a development of many small fisheries stocked with rainbow trout. These fisheries and the rainbow trout that they hold have moved traditional Scottish fishing aside and established quite different methods, tactics and philosophies. There is an instantaneous feel to them; they provide 'fishing by the hour,' rather than whole-day excursions to more remote lochs and rivers. The trout are easy to catch and much larger than would normally be expected in such small waters.

Fortunately, there are plenty of places to fish within the Borders, Lothians and Forth Valley, and their variety is such that there is something for everyone. The coarse fishing is amongst the best in Scotland and there is sea fishing along the coast from Edinburgh southwards, but it is the region's excellent game fishing that attracts most anglers.

Lochs of the Borders, Lothians & Forth Valley

Gladhouse Reservoir: Highly attractive and productive. Try around the island with small flies and floating lines in fine conditions, and in the deeper parts with lures, especially earlier in the season.

Beecraigs Reservoir: Book early to avoid disappointment. This is the place to catch a real specimen. Big fish and big lures are the anticipated order of the day, but trying a smaller pattern often draws a positive response when your larger flies fail. Beecraigs is a small loch – but has superb fish.

BORDER LOCHS

It is inevitable that the small number of stillwaters in the Borders causes their importance to fade somewhat in comparison with the splendour of the region's excellent rivers. However these lochs which sit so peacefully in the lovely valleys are quite superb and should not be overlooked. Most of these waters are small lochans – there are none of the huge sheets of water common elsewhere in Scotland – nevertheless, they are important fisheries and enjoy popular and fully-merited renown.

Possibly the most well-known Borders stillwater is Coldingham Loch near St Abbs Head, within yards of the sea coast between Edinburgh and Berwick. The loch was the first in Scotland to benefit from the introduction of rainbows and still holds a prominent place in any top ten listing of fisheries which must be visited. It is a delightful place set high on the eastern edge of the land, with the boom and crash of North Sea breakers plainly heard on the rocky beach beneath the cliffs.

Fishing is from boat and bank, and the rainbows and brownies are simply superb. Buzzer fishing has reached a peak here, although traditional methods entice fish effectively too. Watch the kittiwakes swoop overhead, breathe in the salty tang of seaweed from the beach below, and the soft scents of the wild flowers clinging to the grassy cliffs, and listen to the steady slurp of trout feeding on surface flies. This is really an idyllic place to spend your fishing time.

Amongst the other popular Borders lochs which should be given a cast are the remote Fruid and Talla Reservoirs tucked in the hills close to Tweedsmuir, and Headshaw Loch, a few miles south of Selkirk. A warm welcome is a feature of the area – Borders people may be a little shy to begin with,

GLADHOUSE RESERVOIR

Location Details
Close to Edinburgh, Gladhouse Reservoir is near Howgate.

Type of Fishery
Boat fly-fishing only.

Description
Water supply reservoir, Gladhouse Reservoir is 400 acres.

Species
Stocked Rainbow and Brown Trout Stillwater.

Season Details
Opens in April to October 6th.

Permit Contact(s)
East of Scotland Water, 55 Buckstone Terrace, Edinburgh. Tel 0131 445 6462 (permits available for other local reservoirs).

Favourite Flies & Baits
Buzzers and hoppers when fish are rising. Small lures (especially muddlers) and conventional traditional patterns when no fish are seen on the surface. Try small (12-14s) tinsel-bodies patterns – Silver Invicta, Dunkeld.

How to Fish
Fish the shorelines. Gladhouse is not deep, but is most productive in its shallower parts. Keep clear of bird sanctuary.

Linlithgow Loch: Dramatic, historic and challenging for the fly-fisher. At last light, the trout gather in the margins to feed on the prolific insects. Try hoppers and 'cul-de-canard', buzzers fished to rising fish or 'pulling flies' when they are just below the surface.

but they are utterly genuine and sound in their advice.

St Mary's Loch and the nearby Megget Water should be on your list, as should some of the small commercial fisheries like Clerklands, not far from Selkirk. There is an increasing number of small commercial fisheries opening in the area and each of these provide typical facilities for the few hours that many of us have available. They may not be the 'whole day expedition' type of water, but when you would like to straighten a line, then feel a plump rainbow tug your string, they are absolutely fine. The Borders region is highly attractive and very accessible. The region's lochs are well-stocked and thoroughly worth fishing and provide an especially welcome back up when the rivers are in full flood or stricken with drought.

LOCHS OF LOTHIAN

Scotland's capital attracts many visitors from every corner of the world. Edinburgh is a wonderful city, rich in culture, architecture, history and humming with a vibrancy which reflects its capital position. Fewer of the people who enjoy Edinburgh's dynamism are aware of the fine angling facilities which lie within a few minutes drive from the city centre – in fact, some of these fisheries are in line of sight of Edinburgh's immediately recognisable skyline.

Several of these fisheries are water supply reservoirs, set in the hills to the south of the city, and still benefiting from the expert work of Victorian water engineers. Their legacy lasts to this day in the form of fine stone building and attractive lochs which have blended naturally into the picturesque countryside. These are not the concrete bowl reservoirs common in the south, but are fine buildings with superb design and execution – but it is their fishing that we are most interested in!

If you would like to fish in a natural loch with a truly historic backdrop there can be few places better than Linlithgow Loch. Just a few metres from the waterside, the Palace of Linlithgow towers six and seven storeys skyward in the most dramatic of settings. The Palace was a royal residence from the middle of the 12th century until it was destroyed by fire in 1746 and was the birthplace of Mary Queen of Scots in 1542.

As your boat drifts quietly down Linlithgow Loch, you may well picture all the regal goings-on which must have occurred in this splendid setting but then your reverie will be broken by the take of a fine trout! Linlithgow is a most interesting place to fish and well worth visiting.

Nearby, Bowden Springs is a small fishery with an excellent reputation for hard-fighting rainbows, and if you wish to catch a glass-case specimen you have a better than average chance at Beecraigs Loch

Coldingham Loch, near St Abbs: The loch was the first in Scotland to benefit from the introduction of rainbows, and still holds a prominent place in any top ten listing of fisheries which must be visited.

on the outskirts of Linlithgow town. If you are attracted to wilder scenes and more traditional brown trout fishing, then Gladhouse Reservoir is amongst the best in the area. With rolling hills, partially-wooded shores, and tree-clad islands it is a nature reserve and home to wildlife. Gladhouse is highly attractive and productive, and is a great place to catch fine brownies.

Other reservoirs worth fishing include Clubbiedean just off the City Bypass; Harperrigg, Harlaw and Threipmuir near Currie, to the south west of the city; and the Whiteadder Reservoir near Gifford, to the south east of the city. Commercial fisheries like Markle near East Linton, and Portmore, just south of Penicuik, are also highly rated by locals and visitors alike.

LOCHS OF FORTH VALLEY

Further to the east lies Carron Valley Dam in the Fintry Hills near Denny. This is a large reservoir with first class amenities for trout fishing. It is a mark of its stature that various national competitions are staged here. Nearer Stirling is Gartmorn Dam, ever-growing in popularity as a bank and boat brown trout water. Also near Stirling is North Third Reservoir which offers excellent fishing for decent-sized rainbows from bank and boat.

COLDINGHAM LOCH

Location Details
Near St Abbs, signposted from the A1.

Type of Fishery
Boat and bank fly-fishing only.

Description
22 acre loch set high on cliff edge above North Sea. Mature and well maintained – a very fine fishery.

Species Stocked
Rainbow and brown stillwater trout.

Season Details
Commences 15th March, rainbow trout fishing until 30th October. (Brown trout standard season ends 6th October).

Permit Contact(s)
Douglas Aitken, West Loch House, Coldingham, Berwickshire.
Tel 01890 771270. Fax 01890 771991.

Favourite Flies & Baits
Great buzzer water, plus hoppers and dries when conditions favour. Otherwise, 'pulling flies' and small lures. Claret bodied flies excite fish, and try bright flies on bright days.

How to Fish
There are some quite large fish in Coldingham, so fish carefully. Traditional tactics do well – free drifting boats fishing at its best.

Carron Valley Reservoir, near Denny:
A larger loch than most of its close neighbours, Carron Dam is simply magical on a balmy June evening. Fish rise all around you and take your best patterns fished on a floating line.

CARRON DAM (CARRON VALLEY RESERVOIR)

Location Details
Near Fintry (sign-posted from the B818, towards Denny).

Type of Fishery
A water-supply reservoir for Central Scotland Region, this is a boat fishery (no bank angling) and it is fly-only.

Description
Over 900 acres of water set in rolling hilly country. Attractive, but can be exposed in high winds. Good boats and facilities.

Species
Brown trout stocked in good numbers and condition. Trout average 'around the pound'. Generous bag limit.

Season Details
Opening in mid-April each year, closes at end of brown trout season – October 6th.

Permit Contact(s)
East of Scotland Water, St Ninian's Road, Stirling. 01786 458705. Booking 'Helpline': 01342 823698.

Favourite Flies & Baits
Black flies do best – especially early, when black midges hatch. Kate McLaren – a justified favourite. 'Buzzers' effective in calm conditions. Silver and gold-bodied flies (try Silver Invicta and Dunkeld). Size 12-14, unless very calm, when 16s can be effective, or when choppy, use bushy bob flies size 10. In really robust conditions, a Muddler is deadly. Small 'goldheads' worth trying.

How to Fish
The south shore provides consistent sport, but like most upland waters, it is the shallower areas that excel. Traditional 'drifting boat' fishing. If there is no surface activity, try an intermediate or medium sinking line with a team of small flies. Vary the retrieve speed.

Lake of Mentieth

The Lake of Mentieth, near Aberfoyle:
One of the sparkling jewels in the crown of Scottish fishing. 'The Lake' offers superb fishing using the widest range of tactics from deep sunk lure stripping, to tiny dry-fly techniques, in very attractive, historic surroundings.

Conveniently set close to the central populous part of Scotland, the Lake of Mentieth is a must on any visiting fishers list. Brown trout and rainbows are stocked regularly and with generous density, while the locally grown-on rainbows are plentiful, and fine sporting fish. There are 'hot spots' of course, but recently, the practice of releasing the fish all around the lake has meant that fish are encountered anywhere and everywhere.

Some of the most incandescent of the 'hot spots' are International Bay, part of the tree-lined Rednock Shore; Lochend Bay, in front of the chalets and large house; the reedy area known as 'the Butts' in Otter Bay; the Heronry, westward to the shallows of the Malling Shore; around past Dog Island, particularly close to the golden reed beds on the north shore; Stable Point and Gateside Bay; the Rookery then eastwards into Hotel Bay. It is also well worth fishing the shallows around Inch Talla island, and close to the overhanging trees along the shorelines of Inchmahome.

THE LAKE OF MENTIETH

Location Details
Near Aberfoyle, fishery access at Port of Mentieth.

Type of Fishery
Stocked stillwater which is fished from boats only. Fly-only.

Description
Reputed to be Scotland's only lake – although there are others which may contest this, the water is 700 acres with several islands and wide bays. Mostly quite shallow - and therefore productive. Unquestionably one of Scotland's premier trout fisheries. Well appointed fishery lodge and boats (outboard engines for hire). Disabled facilities. Generous bag limits. Fine wildlife. Site of Special Scientific Interest (SSSI).

Species
Mostly rainbow trout, but also stocked with good brown trout, shoals of wild perch and some quite large pike too. Rainbows average well over a pound and a half with many much larger.

Season Details
From 1st April to end of October.

Permit Contact(s)
Lake of Mentieth Fishery, 'Ryeyards', Port of Mentieth, Stirling FK8 3RA. Tel 01877 385664.

Favourite Flies & Baits
The whole range of rainbow trout lures like Cat's Whisker, Rainbow Warrior and Humungous very popular. The use of dry fly tactics increasing – CDCs, Hoppers and emerger patterns. Buzzer fishing also becoming highly popular (deservedly) with goldhead and epoxy patterns highly effective. 'Booby' patterns work tremendously well when little surface activity is present.

How to Fish
Fish where you are recommended to by the excellent fishery staff – they know the water better than anyone. Hotspots are the Rookery, The Heronry, Dog Island, Stable Point/Gateside Bay, Hotel Bay, Lochend Bay, International Bay. Intermediate lines as a standard approach, with deep-sunk lines for boobies, and floating lines for shallow water/ top-of-the-water tactics. Vary speed and depth of retrieve until you determine how the rainbows would like their offerings today.

Rivers of the Borders, Lothians & Forth Valley

RIVERS OF LOTHIAN

The Lothian region does not have many large or small rivers, but those that do exist are fine streams. They suffered from industry and mining in the past but have been restored through the hard work and dedicated care of local enthusiasts. Maybe it is the lower than average rainfall of the area which keeps the streams small. Most were worked very hard for many decades after the onset of the industrial revolution by mills and other enterprises taking water and power from the dams and weirs which harnessed the streams. Some of these impoundments still exist although many of those which impede migratory fish have been removed.

The Water of Leith is a typical example. A small stream, it runs around twenty miles from Harperrigg Reservoir in the Pentland Hills, deep into the heart of the city of Edinburgh, through the housing schemes and commercial areas, then finally meets its destiny in the salty water of the estuary of the River Forth amidst the docks at Leith. The local authority led the way in cleaning up the Water of Leith and now the river hosts a sustainable population of brown trout and provides quite good fishing. It must be said that these trout see a lot of anglers and are consequentially not easy to fool. But if you would like to fish for wily broonies in the historic capital city of Scotland, then the Water of Leith is definitely the river of choice.

Joining several other River Esks around the east coast of Scotland is the Lothian River Esk which flows from the Pentland Hills to the ancient and royal burgh of Musselburgh on the coast a few miles to the east of Edinburgh. The (Lothian) Esk runs through industrial sites but holds trout and the odd salmon and sea trout. Although not the bonniest River Esk in Scotland it's well worth wetting a line if you are in the area. Just as there is more than one River Esk, there is also more than one River Tyne – the Scottish River Tyne rises in the bare heights of the Lammermuir Hills and meets the North Sea near Dunbar at Tyninghame. Tyne trout are wild and wily so fine tackle and stealthy tactics are the order of a fishing day there.

Curiously, there is yet another duplicated name in the Lothian's River Almond which shares its title with a River Tay tributary in Perthshire. This Almond runs to Cramond amongst lands previously heavily mined but now restored to attractive state for the most part. In other places the river is entirely natural and the rocky sections are very picturesque. A few salmon and sea trout augment the population of natural brownies and make the river a fine prospect.

THE WATER OF LEITH

Location Details
The Water of Leith runs through the great city of Edinburgh itself.

Type of Fishery
Small river. Stocked with brown trout.

Description
Remarkable examples of an urban stream which has been cleaned up so that wildlife thrives within a truly city environment.

Species
Brown trout, with very, very occasional salmon and sea trout (very rare).

Season Details
Standard brown trout season – March 15th until October 6th.

Permit Contact(s)
Edinburgh City Council, Waterloo Place, Edinburgh. Tel 0131 229 9292.
Water of Leith Conservation Trust, Lanark Road, Slateford, Edinburgh. Tel 0131 455 7367.

Favourite Flies & Baits
Imitative ephemerid nymphs and dries – Gold-ribbed Hare's Ear, Iron Blue Dun, Light Olives and Dark Olives, Greenwells Glory.

How to Fish
This is a small river. It is fairly hard-fished and the trout are consequently not easy to fool. Outside the city there are parts which are more natural with heavy bank-side vegetation and overhanging trees – quite a challenge. Fish upstream dries for trout when conditions favour. Conventional tactics otherwise.

RIVERS OF THE FORTH VALLEY

The fishing rivers of Central Scotland are mostly tributaries of the east-flowing River Forth or form parts of watersheds which flow to

River Forth, at Stirling: Taken from the historic Wallace Monument, this picture shows the winding pools of the lower river. Besides being a fine river for fishing, the banks of the Forth are steeped in history. When you fish here you walk in the footsteps of armies and tread through battlefields.

the west through the Trossachs lochs. They are not typically Highland spate-rivers nor are they slow Lowland rivers either – they are intermediate rivers – with rocky, swift-flowing sections and slower meandering pools. All carry wild trout and most carry varying runs of migratory fish.

The Forth itself is a large river when it opens out into its estuary below Stirling. This estuary runs wide and open for around forty miles to the North Sea at North Berwick. Runs of salmon and sea trout inch along the shores guided upstream by the freshwater taste of the rivers of their birth.

THE RIVER FORTH AND MAIN TRIBUTARIES: THE RIVER TEITH AND ALLAN WATER

Location Details
The Teith/Forth system runs from the lovely Trossachs (sources in Loch Katrine and Loch Ard) then, by winding turns, through historic Flanders Moss (battle site) towards the equally historic town of Stirling, then to the great swathe of the estuary guarded over by the majestic Forth Rail Bridge and the suspended span of the Forth Road Bridge.

Type of Fishery
Conventional river fishing – some spinning and bait fishing in deeper pools but most fishing with fly. Some expensive salmon beats; a number of easily accessed reaches of modest cost.

Description
Mainly highland rivers (rocky and swift) in upper reaches transforming into typically lowland characteristics (slow winding loops) as they near the sea.

Species
Salmon and sea trout as migratory fish, wild brown trout, and escaped rainbows from fish farms, occasionally. Coarse fish in the lower reaches.

Season Details
Brown trout 15th March to 6th October, migratory species from 1st February to 30th October.

Permit Contact(s)
County Pursuits, 46, Henderson Street, Bridge of Allan. Tel 01786 834495.
CKD Finlayson Hughes, Barossa Place, Perth. Tel 01738 630926.
Visitor Centre, Queen Elizabeth Forest Park, Aberfoyle. Tel 01877 382265.
Stirling District Council, St Ninians Road, Stirling. Tel 01786 432348.
James Bayne, Main Street, Callander, Perthshire. Tel 01877 330218.

Favourite Flies & Baits
Salmon: Shrimp patterns, Munro Killer, Garry Dog, plus spinning with devons, rapalas, flying Cs and tobies.
Sea Trout: Stoat's Tail, Teal, Blue and Silver, small devons.
Trout: Ephemerid imitations – olive nymphs and dry flies.

How to Fish
Conventional game fishing. Best after rise in water height.

River Teith, near Doune: Downstream from Callander, the River Teith becomes an impressive necklace of fine pools and swift glides. This is fine, readily accessible fishing. Good trout water co-existing with fine salmon pools, the Teith is too often under-rated.

They accelerate as they run from saline water into brackish water then, losing the salt tang completely, ascend the runs and glides to lie in deep pools of the rivers.

Above Stirling, the main stem of the River Forth is joined by the Allan Water and the River Teith while below Stirling, the River Devon cuts through Clackmannanshire to add its contribution to the flow. The River Forth originates in the trout lochs in Queen Elizabeth Forest Park near Aberfoyle. The embryonic river flows through a mixed landscape of agricultural, forestry and wild ground draining a wide area of moorland and hill pasture. Salmon ascend right up to this head water, taking full use of all spawning and juvenile growth areas.

The Duchray Burn and Kelty Waters are joined by the Goodie Burn as these tributaries increment the flow, although the pace slackens downstream of the Goodie confluence. Now the river runs in relatively slow, winding, ox-bows towards the estuary. The fishing is average for brown trout and adequate for salmon and sea trout, although sea trout seem to have increased in recent years, bucking the national trend.

It is the River Teith that draws the best of the migratory fish runs into the Forth system. The upper part of the Forth-Teith system is formed by the River Leny, a tumbling, small, spate river which carries a good head of salmon – some quite huge for the size of river. Like other rivers of the region the Leny benefits from, and is disadvantaged by, the lochs which they drain from. In the case of the River Leny, it is Loch Venacher which helps or hinders it. Some of these lochs help by providing flow when drought afflicts the region, while at other times, abstraction for supply purposes diminishes their flow. The Leny is nevertheless an excellent river, highly attractive and proportionally very productive.

From Callander downstream, the River Teith becomes an impressive necklace of fine pools and swift glides, providing the finest of salmon fishing water. There are also good populations of brownies and fishing the dry-fly in high summer here can be as productive as anywhere in the country. Sea trout ascend the Teith earlier than they seem to on other east coast rivers, although there has been a recent trend for early running generally.

There are plenty of outlets for permits for the Teith – the river runs through many estates each offering day and weekly tickets to visiting anglers. There can be few parts of a populous area better served by fine rivers than this central region – lovely landscapes fine rivers and superb lochs – who could ask for more?

Above: The River Tweed near Dryburgh. This wonderful river runs through some of the loveliest landscapes in the Borders. Hills, trees, sloping banks and glistening pools – and fish everywhere.

Top right: The River Tweed; Bemersyde. One of the finest beats of Tweed to fish, known as Scott's View.

River Tweed

THE RIVER TWEED

Location Details

The great Tweed runs through the Borders hills and vales towards the sea at Berwick.

Type of Fishery

An outstanding salmon and sea trout river with a justified reputation for quality brown trout and grayling.

Description

Upper Tweed is clearly smaller than the river once it has gained the contributions of her many tributaries. It takes migratory fish some time to reach these upper pools and glides especially in the cold water of spring. Upper Tweed is a great trout water.

The middle river is wide and full, and is prime salmon water throughout the whole year. Brown trout and grayling fishing here is simply superb.

The lower river is large and swift in places. Wading can be less comfortable. Migratory fish enter the river over the whole year.

Species

Salmon in excellent numbers, sea trout (some very large), fine brown trout and good grayling, a few rainbow trout 'escapees'. Coarse fish include eels, dace, gudgeon, roach, perch and pike.

Season Details

Salmon February 1st to the end of November, brown trout from March 15th to October 6th.

Permit Contact(s)

The Factor, Mertoun Estate, St Boswells, Borders. Tel 01835 823236.
James H Leeming, Stichill House, Kelso TD5 7TB. Tel 01573 470280.
For Bemersyde, Boleside, Edenfoot, Fairnielee, Hendersyde, Junction, Ladykirk, Learmouth, Pedwell, Tweedhill, Traquair and Sprouston beats E. McCorquodale, Crossflat Farm, St Boswells. Tel 01835 823700.
For Maxton Beat and Lower Mertoun beats Tweed Valley Hotel, Walkerburn, Peebles. Tel 01896 870636.
Galashiels Angling Association, J & A Turnbull, 30 Bank Street, Galashiels. Tel 01896 753191.
Selkirk & District Angling Assocn., Tel 01750 721571.
Peebles Town Water: Tweed-dale District Council, Dovecot Depot, Peebles. Tel 01721 723354.
Kelso Angling Association, 33 Tweedsyde Park, Kelso. Tel 01573 225279.
Peebles Angling School (Andy Dickinson proprietor), 10 Dean Park, Peebles. Tel 01721 720331.

Favourite Flies & Baits

Salmon flies: Munro Killer, Ally's Shrimp, Willie Gunn (and 'Golden Gunn'), Comet, Jock Scott, Silver Wilkinson.
Sea Trout Flies: Teal, Blue and Silver, Stoat's Tail.
Trout: Greenwell's Glory (developed for Tweed).
Spinning lures: Devons, Tobies, Rapalas.

How to Fish

Conventional salmon fly-fishing and spinning in high water (where permitted). 'Harling' from boats on some beats.
Trout: dry fly-fishing and 'down-and-across' nymph fishing.
Deep nymphs for grayling.

SALMON POOLS OF THE RIVER TWEED

The Middle Tweed

The middle beats are undoubtedly the most sylvan and idyllic parts of an extraordinary river. Mature trees lounge over the sedate pools and swift glides, as the river winds in loops through the comely Border hills. This is fishing in a class of its own, and so famous that they need no real introduction. Bemersyde, Mertoun, Rutherford, Floors, Junction, Hendersyde, Sprouston; names that are deeply etched in Scottish fishing heritage.

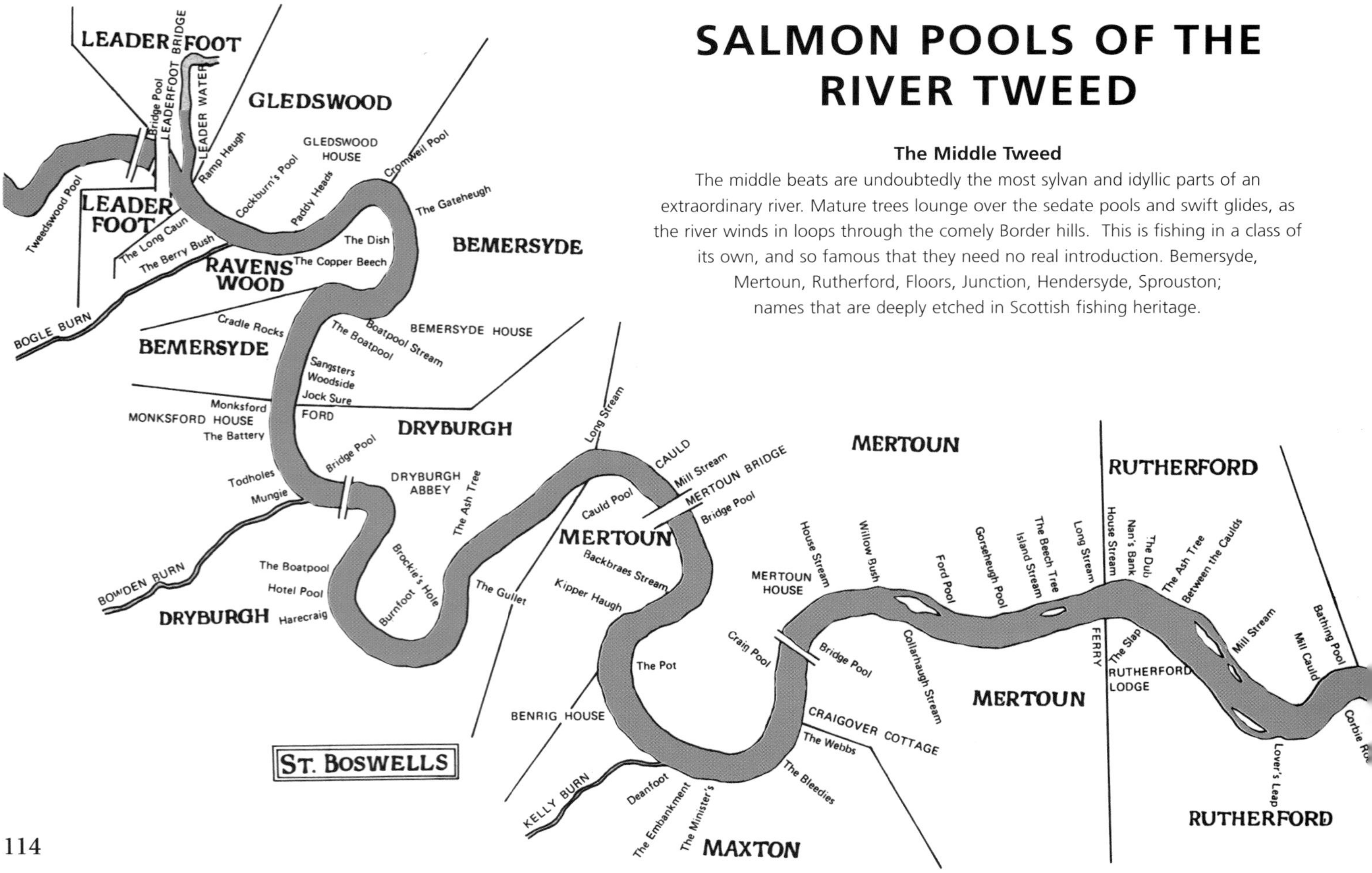

The entire Borders region is punctuated by historic castles and fortified houses, each set in lovely country and often beside a river or stream which now provide peaceful angling delight. The River Tweed provides a natural boundary between Scotland and England and is one of the most prolific trout and salmon rivers in the world. Running nearly one hundred miles from its birth at Tweed's Well near Moffat to its outflow into the North Sea at Berwick-upon-Tweed, the Tweed flows east through the rolling Border hills collecting many tributaries, each of which are fine fisheries. The trout fishing in the upper tributaries such as Lyne Water, Leithen Water, Megget Water, Yarrow Water, Gala Water and Leader Water is very good, as it is in the main river throughout its entire length.

Excellent runs of sea trout enter the lower tributaries like the Whiteadder, Blackadder and Till and significant numbers of large sea trout are caught each year in the main stem of the Tweed itself. The river and tributaries have excellent stocks of fine grayling while the slower tributaries like the Till have pike and perch.

Left: The Famous Junction Pool on Tweed, at Kelso. This is where the River Teviot joins the main stem of the Tweed. The epitome of Tweed fishing – rich, abundant and with a designer-styled price tag. Floors Castle looks over the angler as he or she casts over the pool, where so many great salmon have been landed.

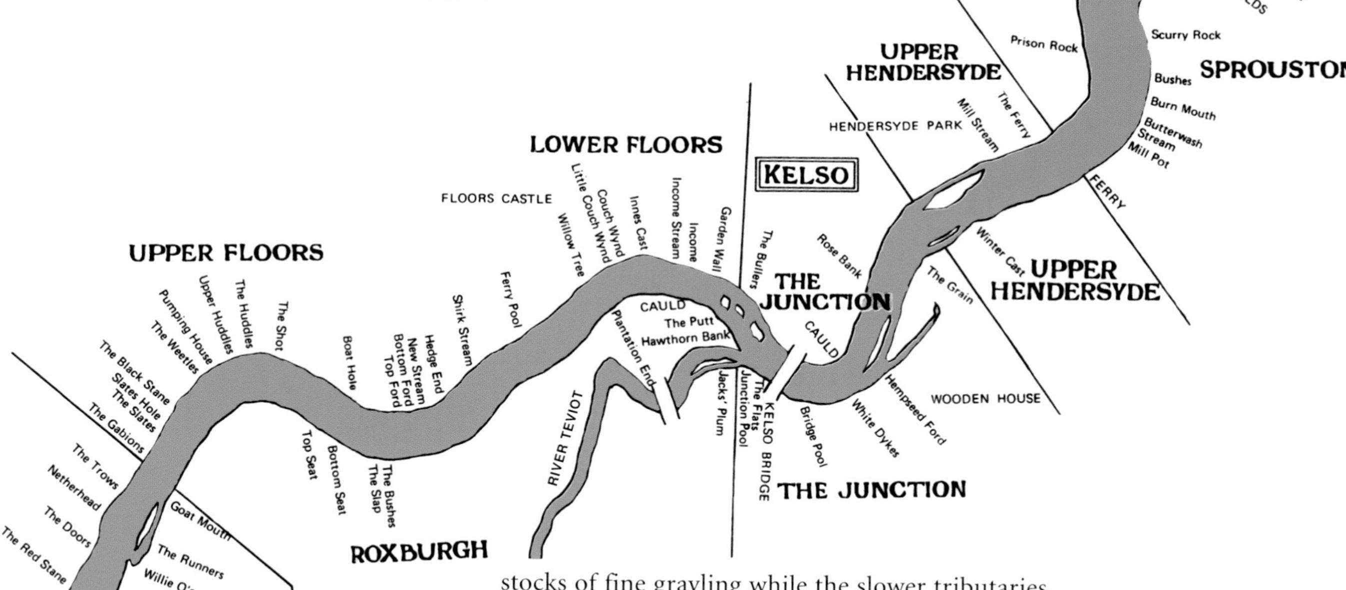

The most notable salmon fishing in spring and autumn is arguably in the middle river between its junctions with the Rivers Ettrick and Teviot, for here are a number of famous salmon beats like Pavilion, Mertoun, Makerstoun, Bemersyde and Floors. The beats below the uniting of the Tweed and Teviot at Kelso's Junction Pool are also widely famed for earliest spring and summer fishing. The runs of grilse and summer salmon tend to hold to

Opposite: The River Tweed, near Melrose. Using a boat, aided by the services of a trusty ghillie to cover the lies effectively, is a traditional way to fly-fish on the Tweed. When a salmon is hooked, the boat is brought to the shore and the angler plays the fish out on the bank.

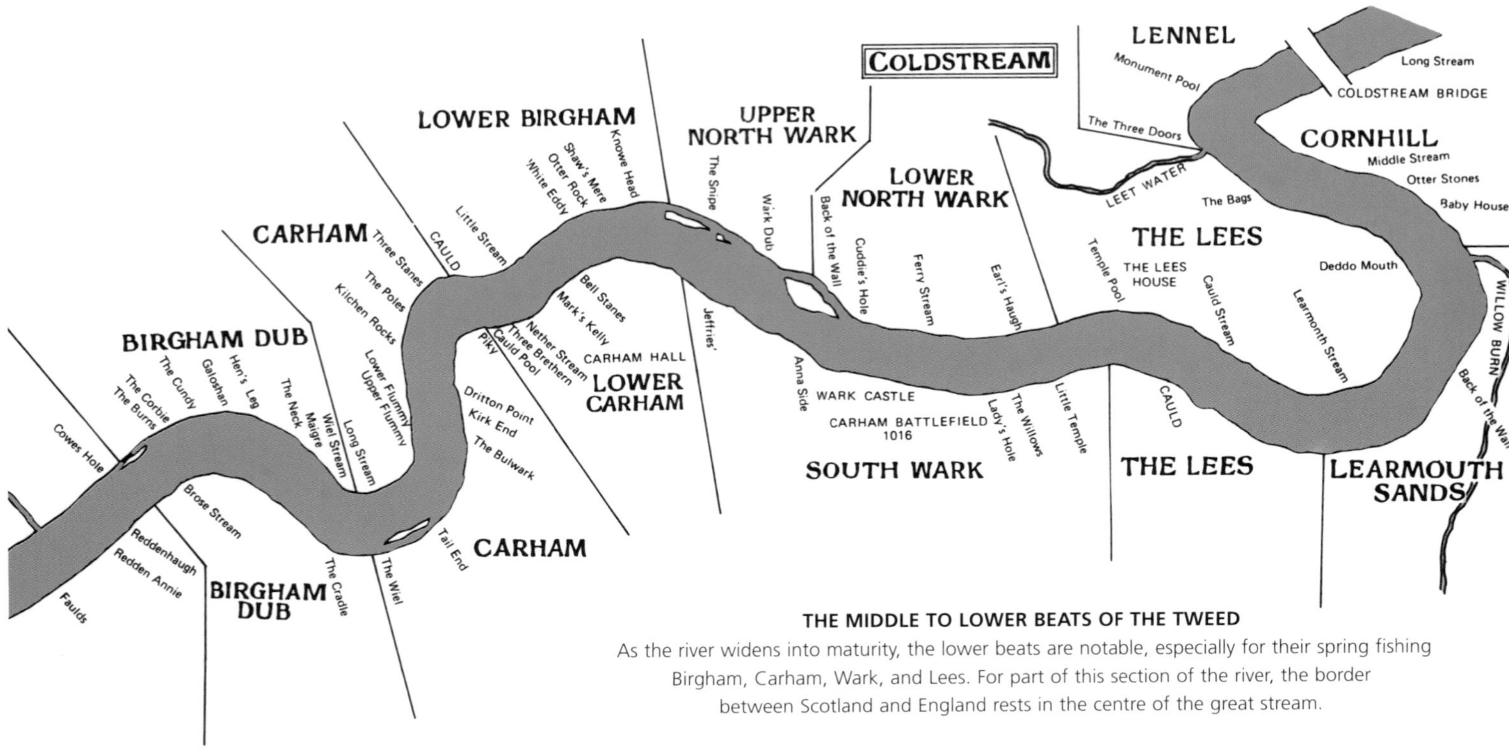

THE MIDDLE TO LOWER BEATS OF THE TWEED

As the river widens into maturity, the lower beats are notable, especially for their spring fishing Birgham, Carham, Wark, and Lees. For part of this section of the river, the border between Scotland and England rests in the centre of the great stream.

Right: The River Tweed. There are many fine ghillies on the Tweed. Their input to your enjoyment cannot be overstated. Who else can know the lies on their beat, where the salmon are and what they may take?

Opposite: The River Tweed near Coldstream. Typical of mid to lower Tweed, this type of pool fishes well in most water heights, but needs a boat if you wish to cover all the lies. This is the place to hook one of these 'back-end' salmon when the season is over in the rest of Scotland.

Upper Floors Beat, River Tweed:
Classic Tweed water. Wide and full of lies for fish to rest. In spring the banks are alive with birdsong and fresh with wild flowers. In summer, the warm breeze wafts insects onto the water for the trout to splash to. In autumn, the colours intensify into reds and burnished golds.

these lower beats unless buoyant water levels draw them higher into the system. The Tweed is blessed with superb water for fly-fishing with streamy glides prevalent throughout its length. It also benefits from efficient management co-ordinated by the Tweed Commissioners and Tweed Foundation whose sterling work contributes significantly to the river's healthy status.

Having suffered from over-fishing, the Tweed is showing significant increments in trout due to proper management of the fishing itself and to improvements in the banks and pools of the river and its tributaries. By maintaining productive water throughout the whole catchment area the stocks of juvenile fish are growing into fine adults and the river has become one of the best trout waters in the country. An increase of grayling and stocks of large sea trout have also been welcomed by anglers.

The Tweed comes a very close second to the Tay for annual salmon catches in Scotland. It is a superb river for fly-fishing with miles of pools and glides, streamy runs and deeper holding pots where the great silvery torpedoes edge in quietly to take up residence, and hopefully, to take your well-presented fly.

The runs of fish in the Tweed are reflected by the seasons. February can be cold and forbidding with the ice grue in the river only relenting during the middle of the day, but the prospect of a hard silver springer warms the very core of all anglers.

The warmth of spring brings a welcome re-emergence of life everywhere you look. Buds and blossom burst out on bushes and riverside trees, birds twitter in courtship display and flies hatch from the river, the trout rising tentatively to take them, not strictly sure that the sun has risen high enough to warm them from their winter torpor. Salmon run in from the sea.

During the summer, flies rise and fall over the pools, swifts and swallows swoop across the water and the air is mellowed by the scent of bankside

TWEED TRIBUTARIES: ETTRICK & TEVIOT

Location Details
Ettrick Water: one of the larger Tweed tributaries.
River Teviot: a principal tributary of the Tweed.

Type of Fishery
Each are fine salmon and sea trout streams, but each are even better-known as excellent brown trout waters.

Description
Small rivers, running through highly picturesque Border countryside.

Species
Brown trout, with runs of salmon and sea trout from the main stem of the Tweed.

Season Details
Trout: March 15th to October 6th.
Salmon: February 1st to November 30th.

Permit Contact(s)
Ettrick Water: Buccleuch Estates, Bowhill, Selkirk. Tel 01750 720753.
Teviot: Hawick Angling Club, 6 Sandbed, Hawick. Tel 01450 373771.

Favourite Flies & Baits
Standard salmon patterns: Willie Gunn, Munro Killer, Ally's Shrimp.
Sea Trout: Dark Mackerel, Stoat's Tail, Teal, Blue and Silver. Trout: Greenwell's Glory dry and wet, olive patterns and Iron Blue Dun, GRHE nymph, March Brown in springtime.

How to Fish
Upstream dry fly for brownies, downstream nymphs when no rises visible.
Salmon: conventional fly-fishing with floating or sink-tip lines.

flowers. Evening fishing for trout simply cannot be bettered, with active grilse splashing in the pools as soon as there is a decent rise in water level.

Autumn brings colour to Tweedside, and the trees are cloaked in rich gold and russet hues. The trout seem intent on taking every morsel of food in preparation for winter's deprivations and the runs of salmon are huge and productive. They ascend the Tweed in prodigious numbers, anxious to be upstream and active in spawning.

The Tweed's salmon fishing season extends until the end of November to accommodate fishing for the late-running blue-backs. As your line tightens there is no way of knowing whether this is a small red fish of ten pounds or a great silver thirty-pounder fresh in from the North Sea. The vigour of these late ascending salmon simply has to be experienced.

The River Ettrick: One of Tweed's main tributaries, the Ettrick offers great salmon and trout fishing. There are good grayling stocks too, especially in the slower pools. This is livelier water than main-stem Tweed, but none the worse for that.

PERTHSHIRE, FIFE, ANGUS & CENTRAL

The River Tay runs through the very heart of Scotland. It is has been seminal in its influence on the development of game fishing and continues to provide a huge contribution to Scottish angling. But Perthshire does not rely solely on her great river and its tributaries, for there is a huge range of lochs to visit and to enjoy. There is coarse fishing in many of these lochs and in the rivers, but in common with most of Scotland, it is game angling that is the most developed and accessible.

The countryside around the Tay is a microcosm of Scotland in landscape. The high mountains give way to wide valleys with forests and moorlands marching over the horizons. This is tourist country, with many visitors enjoying the views, the warm hospitality and of course Tayside's fishing.

The old cliché states that 'variety is the spice of life' and you simply could not hope to have a more spicy angling variety than is available in Perthshire, Fife, Angus and Central, everywhere you look there are streams and stillwaters. It is a land of plenty when fishing is considered.

One of the greatest assets of the central part of Scotland is its ready accesssibility. You may be just a score of miles from a major city yet you are truly in the country when you fish in central Scotland. The Kingdom of Fife has great charm in its land and people, while its fishing has been developed to the highest standard. Angus is a hilly county with five finger-like glens sculpted into the Grampian Mountains, rich in history and interest, and the fishing is simply grand.

There is something here for everyone.

Loch Lee:
This is the land of peregrines, eagles and ospreys. Red deer look down on you as you drift in splendid isolation along the steep shores of Loch Lee in upper Glen Esk. The wild brown trout are as swift as anywhere and rise through the whisky-coloured water to take your bob-fly quicker than your eye will register. Tranquil and remote, and totally relaxing.

Lochs of Perthshire, Fife, Angus & Central

Butterstone Loch, near Dunkeld:
A fine rainbow trout fishery of justified renown, Butterstone offers attractive surroundings, excellent facilities and a good head of responsive rainbows. The wide variety of successful techniques reflect the fun that you may have here. Try lures and sub-surface tactics early in the year, then come closer to the surface with nymphs, buzzers and dries when the trout are 'up'.

BUTTERSTONE LOCH

Location Details
Near Dunkeld (on the road to Blairgowrie).

Type of Fishery
Fly-only, from boats (no bank access).

Description
Attractive fishery in lovely tree-lined setting with hills surrounding. A fine fishery and well worth visiting.

Species
Primarily rainbows with a few natural brownies. Good quality rainbows in decent numbers.

Season Details
March to October.

Permit Contact(s)
Rick Knight, (Manager) Butterstone Loch, by Dunkeld. Tel 01350 724238.

Favourite Flies & Baits
Standard rainbow lures (Cat's Whisker and Black lures). Boobies, dries and emergers. Growing use of buzzers – to good effect. Try Dunkeld, Silver Invicta or Silver March Brown, Kate McLaren, or Bibio, if you wish to fish conventional patterns, sizes 10s - 12's

How to Fish
The loch is relatively shallow with some deeper areas. The best fishing is around the margins and on the drop-offs around these deeper areas. The top bay can provide shelter in gusty conditions. Try alongside reed-beds close-in to the side. Medium sink and intermediate lines unless booby fishing (deep line).. Floating lines when surface activity observed.

Perthshire's lochs have some of the best stillwater fishing in the country due to several factors, the most influential being the climate, which is conducive to fish growth, and the fact that the lochs are, or have at some time been, actively managed as fisheries.

The most famous of Perthshire's lochs are divided by their species. Some hold rainbow trout whilst others are occupied by their natural cousins, the ubiquitous brownie. There are large lochs in wilderness desolation like the great sprawl of Loch Rannoch and the moorland expanse of Loch Laidon, then there are intimate little lochs tucked away in the hills and dusky valleys. Some are wholly natural, while some like Loch Faskally and those of the Tummel system, are impounded for electricity generation. If you fished a different location every day of your life in Perthshire you would never experience the same day twice, such is its diversity and charm.

Butterstone Loch sits on the Dunkeld to Blairgowrie road and is a jewel of a rainbow loch. Sub-surface lure fishing is popular in the early part of the year, and small flies and nymphs become successful in the warmer parts of summer. Some lochs give rise to the use of specific flies like Loch Ordie in the surrounding hillsides above Dunkeld, the birthplace of the effective bushy brown and white fly of its name. Loch Ordie is in good company within these heathery Perthshire hills for nearby are the lochs of Benachally, Dowally and Rotmell each of which offer excellent fishing.

The Pitlochry Angling Club has several small lochs including Loch Bhac in the forested hills above Loch Tummel, and Loch Kinnardochy, under the flanks of the conical mountain Schiehallion, and these are stocked with fine brown trout, rainbows and brook trout.

Loch Tay and Loch Earn are larger and deeper sheets of water, each within the catchment area of their respective rivers and each with salmon, native trout, charr and rainbows from their local fish farms. As with most large waters a little local knowledge is highly desirable, but if unsure, fish the shallower parts for trout, where the feeding is most likely to be. This is true of the other larger Perthshire lochs like Loch Tummel, Loch Garry and Loch Ericht. Most of the larger lochs have populations of charr and ferox trout which can be an interesting diversion from standard trouting. The great Moor of Rannoch is cleaved by Loch Laidon, and at its western end by Loch Rannoch itself. The area has fine wild trouting, but do not expect huge fish – most are small, but they are vigorous. Amongst the wee ones there lurks the grandaddy of them all however – hook him, and watch the sparks fly from your reel! Ferox brown trout are present in a number of Scottish lochs, especially in the Highlands. Ferox are cannibals, taking smaller brown trout and feeding on the shoals of charr that live at depth in the larger lochs. Loch Rannoch and Loch Arkaig are good venues for ferox brown trout, but most of the larger lochs will provide examples if suitable methods are applied. Deep trolling of dead baits or large plugs behind a slow-moving boat are usually best for attracting large Highland ferox.

Loch Earn, at St Fillans: Loch Earn holds fine populations of brown trout, charr and rainbows. Fishing is good and some fine baskets are likely to come off the loch, especially in late spring and early summer. Bank fishing is supplemented by a good provision of boats for hire. Traditional Scottish patterns take the browns and more-modern lures attract the 'bows'. Fishing is best along the shallower contours of the tree-lined shores.

LOCH EARN

Location Details

Shimmering between St Fillans at its lower end and Lochearnhead at the top end, Loch Earn lies under mountains of grandeur in central Perthshire. It is about six miles long. The A85 runs along its shore.

Type of Fishery

A mixed fishery with excellent boats for hire, and many fine bays for shore fishing with fly and bait.

Description

The loch is very deep so it is the margins and shallow bays (especially at each end of the loch) that hold most fish. There are many water skiers and wind surfers.

Species

Brown trout (stocked in good numbers, plus wild trout), ferox trout, Arctic charr (large specimens), perch and pike, and many 'escapee' rainbow trout. Very few salmon and sea trout run into the loch.

Season Details

Brown Trout season 15 March to 6th October.

Permit Contact(s)

St Fillans Post Office, St Fillans, Perthshire.
Tel 01764 685309.
Lochearnhead Post Office, Perthshire.
Tel 01567 830201.
Drummond Estates Boat Station (hire of boats with outboard engines) near Lochearnhead, Perthshire.
Tel 01567 830400.
Four Seasons Hotel, St Fillans, Perthshire.
Tel 01764 685333.

Favourite Flies & Baits

Spinning with small Rapalas, Tobies and Mepps-type lures is popular, as is shore bait-fishing with worms or maggots. Fly fishing is effective along the treed shores, in shallower water, using black flies like Kate McLaren, Connemara Black, Bibio and tinsel-bodied flies like Silver Invicta. When shoals of rainbows are about, try larger lures, otherwise size 10 to 14 or even 16 in quiet conditions.

How to Fish

Charr grow to unusually large size close to fish farm cages (they probably feed on waste/pellets from the cages). Fish for them nearby with flies or baits, using sunk line tactics.

Brownies live in the shallower parts and may be caught using conventional floating line/intermediate line sunk-line tactics.

Rainbows follow available food – they may be found almost anywhere, but most likely close to cages and along shore-sides.

Pike and perch should be caught by spinning in likely spots where reeds or 'snags' give them protection.

Lochan Reoidhte, Trossachs: There are many small lochans tucked away amongst the hills in this area. They are set in wild country amongst silver birches, native oaks and alders, and hold natural brown trout, pike and perch. The hills are rocky, the fishing is traditional Scottish-style, and the area is hugely appealing. Most are lightly fished and offer great days out.

Some lochs seem to hold bigger fish than others, Dunalastair Reservoir being a typical example. A small loch raised by impoundment to provide water for hydro schemes further down the Tummel system, Dunalastair still has the remains of trees growing in its shallower parts. It has a pike population to be reckoned with, and some of the bonniest brownies in Scotland – big, golden and brightly-speckled – just the way they should be. The great low-lying swathe of mid-Scotland bounded by the rocky outcrops along the Highland Boundary Fault at its northern margin and the

THE TROSSACHS LOCHS: LOCH KATRINE, LOCH VENACHER AND LOCH ACHRAY

Location Details
Near Aberfoyle, Stirlingshire.

Type of Fishery
Mixed fishery – bait, spinning and fly.

Description
Lovely lochs set in picturesque surroundings. Productive too. This is 'Rob Roy country' – rich in texture and history. This is also where Sir Walter Scott created the romance of the Trossachs in his novels and poems. Very attractive.

Species
Brown trout, pike (some very large!) and huge numbers of perch.

Season Details
March 15th to October 6th for brown trout.

Permit Contact(s)
Loch Katrine: W M Meikle, 41 Buchany, by Doune, Perthshire. Tel 01786 841692.
Loch Achray: Loch Achray Hotel, by Callander, Perthshire. Tel 01877 376229.
Loch Venacher: J Bayne, Main Street, Callander, Perthshire. Tel 01877 330218.
W M Meikle, 41 Buchany, by Doune, Perthshire. Tel 01786 841692.

Favourite Flies & Baits
Bushy bob-flies like Bumbles and Soldier Palmer; old patterns like Poacher and Greenwell's Glory, Wickham's Fancy and modern midge and buzzers do well.

How to Fish
Traditional-style Scottish drifting-boat fishing at its best. Let the boat drift broadside in front of the breeze and fish through the waves downwind – truly conventional – truly effective – truly fun!

Fishing the Shoreline, Loch Lee:
Where a steep slope on the shore clearly continues under the water, it is best to fish in the shallower margins where sunlight fuels aquatic life. This is where the fish will exploit food items and be more likely to respond to your offerings.

gentler hills of the Southern Uplands to its south, is known as Central Scotland. Here you will find some of the best fishing lochs of southern Scotland – from the Trossachs waters to the west, to the water supply reservoirs in the middle, and countless small first class trout lochs dotted liberally throughout the area.

The Trossachs lochs are simply beautiful. Set in high heather-clad hills with rocky tops, and surrounded by ancient forests, they are home to fine trout, occasional salmon and some of the largest pike in the UK. Put quite simply, they are amongst the best in the world for fishing.

Loch Katrine is the quintessential Trossachs water and is set in stunningly beautiful country, especially at its eastern end. Drive from Callander, through the Pass of Achray, to reveal the Victorian pier where the the Sir Walter Scott paddle streamer is generally moored. The dark rocks and ancient trees provide a deep contrast of bright sunlight and dappled shade. Even in high winds there is shelter here. Beyond this haven, the loch opens out to around a mile in width and runs westwards for about 8 miles to Stronachlachar. Loch Katrine has excellent stocks of brownies which respond to traditional loch-style fishing.

Just west of Loch Katrine is Loch Arklet, deep and narrow under the heights of Ben Lomond to the south and An Caisteal and Beinn a' Choin to the north, with lovely Ben Venue for company. Pike, perch and trout swim in its clear water ready to take an angler's offering. There are numerous lochs in the Trossachs, each with an individual attraction. Try a day on Loch Ard near Aberfoyle or Loch Drunkie and Loch Chon – lovely lochs each offering good brown trout fishing.

Loch Tummel, Perthshire:
Many tourists are familiar with Loch Tummel's 'Queen's View'. Queen Victoria probably could not have known how good the fishing was in the loch beneath her – nor how it might continue to be a productive and popular fishery a century later.

LOCH TAY

Location Details
With the picturesque central Perthshire towns of Killin and Kenmore on its shores, Loch Tay nestles under high hills in fine countryside. The loch is large and popular.

Type of Fishery
Fishing is from boats (mostly trolling for salmon and brown trout) and bait and fly-fishing for trout in the bays and along the undulating shoreline.

Description
The loch is very deep – deeper even than the majority of the North Sea – so it is the margins and shallow bays that hold most fish. At Kenmore, where the River Tay flows out of the loch, the opening ceremony for the salmon season takes place each January 15th.

Species
Salmon (often very early in the season), brown trout (natural stock), ferox brown trout, Arctic charr (large shoals), perch and pike, and the almost ubiquitous 'escapee' rainbow trout.

Season Details
Salmon fishing starts on January 15th and ends with the rest of the Tay system on 15th October.
Brown trout season 15 March to 6th October.

Permit Contact(s)
Loch Tay Lodges, 'Remony', Acharn, Kenmore. Tel 01887 830588.
Ardreonaig Hotel, Killin, Perthshire. Tel 01567 820400.
Kenmore Hotel, Kenmore, Perthshire. Tel 01887 830205.
Mr J Rough, Newsagents, Main Street, Killin, Perthshire. Tel 01567 820362.

Favourite Flies & Baits
Trolling baits for salmon are Rapalas, and big spoons, with Waddington flies also used to good effect. The Arctic charr will take small tinsel-bodied flies at the surface especially around late-May and early June. Trout patterns are standard loch dressings with bushy bob flies and slimmer point flies (try dark-fly/dark day, bright fly/bright day tactics). For ferox trout, big plugs and trolled dead baits take these cannibals.

How to Fish
For ferox, you need to find the best contour – just at the point of the drop-off into much deeper water (around the 20' to 30' mark). This also favours the charr shoals (but as ferox feed on charr this is no surprise). Brown trout favour the areas where food is plentiful – and that's where sunlight can penetrate to fuel the food cycle – in shallower water up to 6-8 feet deep. Fish for trout on shallower points and in bays and also around the many sub-surface 'crannog' prehistoric lake dwellings. Salmon need to be trolled for over recognisable 'marks'. Firbush Point is a real favourite.

Lintrathen Reservoir

LINTRATHEN RESERVOIR

Location Details
In lower Glen Isla – not far north of Alyth, Perthshire. Signposted from the B954 Alyth to Glenisla road.

Type of Fishery
Brown trout (only), fly-fishing (only) from boats, (no shore fishing access).

Description
A lovely, wide, tree-lined loch set in rolling hills of lower Glen Isla. This is a public water supply and the policies are kept in beautiful condition. Good boats and engines. You are obliged to wear a life jacket.

Species
Brown trout – stocked in good numbers and at decent 'pound-plus' size. Perch also present.

Season Details
Early April to October 6th.

Permit Contact(s)
Lintrathen Angling Club. Tel 01575 560327.

Favourite Flies & Baits
Conventional brown trout flies – especially black colour in the earlier parts of the year. Tinsel bodied patterns also excel. In a wave, expect trout to splash at muddlers and bushy bob-flies. At other times, fish slowly just below the surface with size 12s or smaller. Buzzer patterns growing in popularity. Dry fly tactics are a good prospect in calm conditions.

How to Fish
This is a deep loch with good shallow margin areas – so fish in 3-9 feet depth. The top end – furthest from boathouse – is probably the most productive (shallower), but give close attention to the dam walls and rocky promontories.

Above: Lintrathen Reservoir, Glenisla, Angus. Well-managed and well-stocked with fine brown trout, Lintrathen is a grand place to enjoy an early-summer day or mid-summer evening. The rises of trout can be exceptional.

Lintrathen lies at the foot of Glenisla, one of the five main Angus glens that penetrate into the Grampian massif like the fingers of an open hand. The environs are picturesque and carefully kept, and the vista opens out to reveal a wide loch fringed by rhododendrons and stands of larch and pine.

The name Lintrathen derives from the gaelic *Linn–an-t'Abhainn* (the fall of the river) referring to the nearby waterfall on the River Isla, the Reekie Linn. Here the river plunges into a misty spray-filled gorge. Visit here in the depths of a frosty winter and you will see mammoth icicles the likes of which you may not encounter elsewhere.

This is a brown trout loch, it is stocked with takeable sized trout to supplement the small natural brownies which grow in the feeder burns. Most of the year it is a 'wee flee' water, larger patterns not attracting the canny brownies. Most of the time, it is a surface fishing loch, which is a significant bonus as many waters seem to have developed the habit of providing their fish at depth. Rising fish are likely to be seen throughout the year and this is what attracts so many visitors to the loch.

As with most waters which have significant depths, fishing is best around the margins where the shallow water allows sunlight to penetrate, thereby fuelling the life of food item species. Lintrathen has great midge hatches especially in spring when black chironomids fill the air.

Small dark patters are the obvious choice for traditional and modern artificials, but summer-hatching ephemerid up-wing flies should be imitated when they appear, as should the sedge flies even later still.

Boat fishing is the only way onto this loch and the fish are brownies, becoming a rarity in the ever-increasing realm of the rainbow. You will enjoy Lintrathen – it is a bit of a secret which should be carefully explored and relished.

Opposite: Loch Tay, Perthshire. A large sheet of water which requires the help of a boat and ghillie for trawling for salmon. If it is trout that takes your fancy, try the shallow bays and rocky promontories. Free-drifting along the shore offers the best trout fishing. Charr and ferox are found at depth in this lovely loch.

Loch Leven

Loch Leven, Kinross: Always take advice from the fishery office or from the locals before venturing out on 'The Loch' as Leven is affectionately known. The new facilities of the National Angling Centre opened in 2001 and resulted in the loss of the harbour-side tackle cabin pictured above.

The home of traditional Scottish 'loch-style' fly-fishing for trout, Loch Leven holds a special place in most game anglers' hearts. It is a large and attractive sheet of water (over 3000 acres) with an average depth of around 10 feet, and is highly productive. Rather mysteriously, however, trout are often found in its two deeper parts, the eighty-feet - deep 'North Deeps', and the 'South Deeps', bucking the conventional wisdom that fish tend to inhabit food-rich shallow areas in stillwaters.

The fishery has changed substantially over recent years from solely brown trout to mixed rainbows and brownies. Loch Leven's fish populations have changed from plentiful half-to-three-quarter pound brownies taking small, surface-fished, artificial flies, to the present day when most anglers adopt tactics for the larger fish using styles more common on rainbow-stocked reservoirs.

The reasons for this change are varied and complex and include: enrichment of the in-flowing tributaries with agricultural fertilisers and inappropriate discharges from surrounding towns and villages has lead to eutrophication and algal blooms; increased land drainage, has lead to the lowering of the water tables in the watershed around the loch, causing inadequate flows in the spawning burns; lethal levels of predation by cormorants (possibly because they struggle to find food supplies easily in the sea), and the changing aspirations amongst modern game angling devotees.

LOCH LEVEN

Location Details
The closest town is Kinross, adjacent to M90 motorway. The loch is signposted from the town's main street.

Type of Fishery
Large (3000-plus acres) stocked loch, which holds a distinct sub-species of brown trout. Excellent rainbow trout.

Description
Daunting for beginners, the loch is nearly 3 miles across – you need to know where to start – the staff are genuinely helpful.
The loch has many islands and wide bays, and has vast areas of productive shallow water, most of which holds fish.

Species
Brown trout (both wild and stocked) and rainbow trout.

Season Details
Opens in early April and closes at the end of the brown trout season on 6th October.

Permit Contact(s)
Loch Leven Fisheries, the Pier, Loch Leven, Kinross.
Tel 01577 863407.

Favourite Flies & Baits
There is probably more variety in fly choice at Loch Leven than anywhere, due in part to the many competitions held there. Lures attract rainbows, imitative patterns attract brownies, but the reverse is also true. Conditions dictate your tactics and tackle: calm summer evenings favour smaller flies (12-16s) whilst robust windy days favour bushy 10s. Try a mix of lure on the point, nymph in the middle and a palmered fly on the bob.

How to Fish
Fish will be encountered almost everywhere in Loch Leven. The trick is to know where to find the greatest activity, and the best method of finding out is asking. Most Leven anglers would suggest to fish in four to six feet of water and if that didn't draw a response, try a bit deeper around the 'drop-offs'. Use deep sinking lines, unless the fish are higher in the water column.

Not everyone welcomed the introduction of rainbow trout into what they saw as a bastion of survival for wild brown trout. Many anglers hold the view that the Loch Leven strain of brownies is unique, perhaps resulting from the land locking of migratory trout before the building of sluice barriers to raise the loch's level, and preventing passage down the River Leven. But none will argue the extraordinary growth rate and superb condition of Loch Leven rainbows. Love them or loathe them, they are simply wonderful examples of their kind.

Loch Leven has many game angling attributes, not least its capacity to provide long drifts over productive areas. Depending on wind direction, it is possible to drift the boat for a couple of miles without having to make changes. The size and sturdiness of the traditional clinker-built boats makes a day afloat on Leven a great pleasure.

Fishing around the islands is recommended, especially around St Serf's Island while the lee of Castle Island, the Reed Bower, Roy's Folly and Alice's Bower will offer shelter in stout winds. The west shore from the Scart to the Green Isle and Burleigh Sands is often productive along with the west-most point of St Serf's Island, the 'Hole o' the Inch', 'The Horseshoe' and the 'Thrapple Hole'. These names burn brightly in the memory of anyone who has enjoyed Loch Leven's fishing.

Above & Below: Loch Leven.
When quieter conditions favour, try small dry-flies to tempt the big natural brownies or the fast-naturalising rainbows.

Rivers of Perthshire, Fife, Angus & Central

Fishing Hut, South Esk:
At the end of a fishing day, the fishing hut is a convivial place to share the company of like-minded friends.

Mention Perthshire and fishing in the same breath and most anglers make the quantum leap straight into the River Tay, but there are many other rivers in Perthshire which offer superb fishing. Admittedly, these may be tributaries of the mighty Tay, but they are so distinctive in nature that they should be given individual consideration. Whether you fish for salmon, sea trout, trout, or coarse fish, the rivers of Perthshire will have much to attract you. Tayside is called the 'Region of Rivers' and thoroughly deserves this accolade for there is an abundance of wonderful streams.

Flowing through the Braes of Atholl is the charming River Tummel. Famous for its historic association with the Battle of Killiecrankie, the river is equally notable for its salmon and trout.

The Tummel's main tributaries, the River Garry (a shadow of its former glory due to water abstraction) and the River Tilt (collecting the snow-melt from mighty Beinn a'Ghlo and the flanks of the Grampian mountains), keep the main river in good ply by collecting rainfall from different areas. By the time the Tummel slows into the impoundment of Faskally Dam near Pitlochry it is decently proportioned. Faskally Dam is a hydro-electricity facility which alters the downstream flow during times of power generation, so you may find the water level suddenly overflows the top of your waders when there's a great surge of water!

The river holds good stocks of brown trout and large grayling, especially in the grand pools and glides between Faskally Dam and the confluence with the Tay at Logierait, and has runs of salmon early in the year. If you would like to watch salmon as they run the system, the dam has a viewing chamber at the fish ladder and during the height of the run in autumn you can see the excited salmon forging their way upstream to the spawning areas.

Faskally Dam has great shoals of stripy perch, and lurking with deadly intent, many large and voracious pike. The river benefits from sensible stocking by Pitlochry Angling Club and permit prices are very reasonable. The River Tummel runs through lovely country, is wholly accessible, and provides some extremely fine fishing.

The River Earn is a tributary of the Tay, yet in some ways it almost isn't. The Earn does run into the Tay estuary a few miles downstream of Perth but in almost every other respect it is a river in its own right. It flows through its own wide strath, drains a large loch of its own name, has a completely different catchment area, and even has a different season for salmon fishing. The only significant thing that defines it as a Tay tributary is the fact that it flows into the Tay estuary.

If the Tay is primarily a salmon river, with some

Bottom right: The River South Esk, Angus.
One of east-coast Scotland's great sea trout rivers. This is a place for summer night-time fishing with small flies over the inky darkness of the pool, with just a glimmer of light left in the sky.

THE RIVER EARN

Location Details
From Loch Earn, the River Earn flows through the attractive valley of Strathearn to its junction with the River Tay in the Tay estuary.

Type of Fishery
Excellent salmon and sea trout river, with plentiful wild brown trout and grayling.

Description
Progressively slower-flowing as it nears its outflow into the Tay, the river is moderately-swift, rocky and tree-lined in its upper reaches, but winding and sedate in its lower parts.

Species
Salmon, sea trout, brown trout, grayling and 'escapee' rainbows.

Season Details
Salmon and sea trout: 1st February to 31st October.
Trout: March 15th to October 6th.

Permit Contact(s)
Upper beats: Tourist Office, High Street, Crieff. Tel 01764 652578.
CKD Finlayson Hughes Ltd, Barossa Place, Perth. Tel 01738 625134.
Lower beats: Country Pursuits, Bridge of Allan, Stirling. Tel 01786 834495.
Trinity Gask Estate Office, Old Schoolhouse, Trinity Gask, Perthshire. Tel 01764 663237.
James Haggart, Haugh of Aberuthven, Auchterarder Perthshire. Tel 01738 730206.

Favourite Flies & Baits
Salmon: small 'Waddingtons' and tube flies in dark patterns (Stoat's Tail), and also try Ally's Shrimp and Willie Gunn.
Sea trout: tinsel-bodied flies like Teal Blue and Silver, Dark Mackerel, but don't miss out the Silver Stoat's Tail.
Trout: ephemerid (olives) imitations – in dry fly form and in nymph form. Try Iron Blue Duns, Gold-Ribbed Hare's Ear and Wickhams Fancy.

How to Fish
Salmon fishing in conventional manner – down and across. You may need to retrieve the fly or 'back-up' in slower pools.
Trout and grayling fishing with dries when fish are rising and with nymphs when they are not.
Sea trout fishing at dusk and through the night where permitted.

brown and sea trout, then the Earn is primarily a sea trout river with brownies and salmon too. It is curious why some rivers hold brown trout without migrations to the sea, whilst others somehow encourage their trout to seek the salt. Is it all to do with available food supply, or is it based on the genetics of the fish stock? Another mystery is why some rivers favour salmon and others sea trout.

From the tumbling burns that chase and chatter brightly down the rocky slopes of Ben Chonzie and Beinn Odhar, the river rests for a while in the shimmering stillness of Loch Earn before setting off towards the sea. Picking up the contributions of its upper tributaries, the river flows through a long series of fine pools and runs in central Perthshire, past quaint towns like Comrie and Crieff, set amongst hillsides which sport a fresh coat of bright green in springtime, and gleam burnished gold in autumn. There can be few more pleasant landscapes to fish amongst than this, but the Earn is not only visually attractive, it's also highly productive too.

Sea trout start to arrive in late spring although

The River Earn, near Comrie: Pool-follows-glide-follows-pool on this lovely section of the Earn. The overhanging bank-side trees provide shelter for resting migratory fish, and for the local populations of brownies and grayling. The Earn is bonnie, productive, not expensive and highly regarded.

The River Ericht:
A high proportion of the salmon running the main-stem of the River Tay ascend the River Ericht. It also holds fine brown trout.

they seem to be appearing earlier and earlier each year. The runs peak in June and July when the river is excellent for night fishing. What could be better than standing in an Earn pool in the deep dusk of a July evening with the inky dark water rolling into great concentric waves as sea trout after sea trout leap around.

Salmon slide in to the river from opening day until the end of the season, and are always there, sometimes ready to accept a well-placed fly. If you

THE RIVER ERICHT

Location Details
Flowing from Glenshee to its junction with the River Tay, the River Ericht runs through north-central Perthshire.

Type of Fishery
A salmon river of considerable note, with good brown trout too.

Description
Very fast flowing in its rocky, upper reaches, then running through a wonderful series of deep pots and swift glides, partly in gorges.

Species
Salmon, brown trout, and 'escapee' rainbow trout.

Season Details
Salmon: 15th Jan - 15th Oct.
Brown trout: 15th Mar - 6th Oct.

Permit Contact(s)
Kate Fleming (Tackle), Allan Street, Blairgowrie. Tel 01250 873990.
CKD Finlayson Hughes, Barossa Place, Perth. Tel 01738 630926.

Favourite Flies & Baits
Salmon: Ally's Shrimp, Willie Gunn, Hairy Mary, Munro Killer, Yellow and Black, and Orange and Black as Waddingtons. Spinning baits include: Flying C, Devons, Rapalas, Tobies.
Worm fishing is still permitted on some beats.
Trout: Early season – March Browns and Dark Olives, then later in the season – light olives, Greenwell's Glory. Try deep-sunk nymphs (especially weighted and woven variety).

How to Fish
For brown trout try upstream dries or conventional teams of wets and nymphs. The Ericht is a small river so you need not use a huge fly rod for salmon. Fish 'down and across' with long casts so that the fly tracks across the pool as slowly as possible (speed up when grilse are about). Floating line in summer, otherwise, sunk lines of different rate depending on temperature and flow.

enjoy fishing for grayling, then look no further than the Earn. This river is highly accessible through local estates and riparian owners and there are superb angling improvement associations and clubs.

Few visiting anglers may be familiar with one of the Tay's finest tributaries, the River Ericht, but this crucial contributor to the mother stream far excels many similarly-sized rivers in its productivity. Indeed, its stocks of salmon and trout seem to be flourishing at a time when many other rivers are in steep decline. The River Ericht is a typically-highland hardstone stream in its upper parts above Bridge of Cally, where the Blackwater, Ardle and Shee tributaries fast-fall through a series of lovely pots and pools, interspersed with attractive slower glides and more-rapid gravely runs. The terrain is wonderfully mixed too, with the heath and heather of the upper mountains giving way to stands of mature native trees.

Lower downstream, the river enters a deep chasm called Craighall Gorge, a few miles above the town of Blairgowrie. Here, the deep dark pools support a very good stock of wild brown trout. Some very fine brownies have been caught in recent seasons throughout much of the river with richly-spotted trout of 2–3 lbs becoming increasingly common. The best salmon pools on the Craighall Beat are the Upper Boat Pool, The Cauldron and the Piper's Cave.

At the lower end of the ravine is the famous Cargill's Leap, a waterfall chain over which the river flows through a narrow chasm into a series of deep churning pools.

The lower river, below Blairgowrie, is a fine series of runs and pools which provide good early-season sport. The confluence of the River Ericht with the River Isla, itself a major Tay tributary, marks its final outflow. The river has followed a fast-descending journey born of snow-melt amongst the heather, saxifrages and juniper of the rocky 'Munro' tops (over 3000 ft high) of Glas Maol, Carn an Tuirch, and Glas Tulaichean.

The patterns of salmon flies in popular use tend to be fairly conventional with traditional favourites like Silver Stoat's Tail, Munro Killer, Willie Gunn, and small Blue Charms featuring regularly (especially when the grilse have run in). These may be tied on doubles, trebles or small tubes. The ubiquitous Ally's Shrimp takes a significant proportion of fish (especially in its yellow version) reflecting its popularity as much as its undoubtedly attractive features.

As with other rivers, fly size varies according to water clarity and height, with most anglers using 6s and 8s in high water and down to long-tailed 12s and even 14s for grilse in the clear water of high summer. Tackle is best kept lighter with rods of around 12–14 feet, as the river is rarely wider than a decent cast and is often tree-lined. A sinking tip or floating line is recommended in all but the

The Witches Pool, The River Ericht:
This crucial contributor to the mother stream (the River Tay) far exceeds many similarly-sized rivers in its productivity.

The River Tummel, below Faskally Dam at Pitlochry: A great trout-fishing river, with excellent stocks of grayling, the Tummel is perhaps best known for the salmon that ascend from the Tay. The salmon ladder at Faskally Dam is a great attraction when fish are running.

heaviest water. Standard spinning gear may be used with confidence, toby and Devon spinners justifying their popularity and Flying C's proving an effective alternative.

For trout, early season hatches of March Browns and Dark Olives dictate dry flies and nymph imitations of these species, whilst later, there are the large Summer and Autumn Duns and the ubiquitous Blue-winged Olive to add variety. The river has huge numbers of stoneflies, particularly the Large Stonefly *(Perla microcephala)* and the Yellow Sally *(Isoperla grammatica)* and it is unusual to catch a brownie which does not have stonefly nymphs of some species in its stomach. Not surprisingly, nymph fishing with stonefly imitations is a highly effective way of catching trout.

For those with something of a fixation about

RIVER TUMMEL

Location Details
Flows through the lovely Vale of Atholl to its junction with the River Tay in Perthshire.

Type of Fishery
Moderately swift-flowing river of medium size. Good pools and glides for game angling – especially fly-fishing.

Description
Flows from the west to the east, running through Loch Rannoch, Dunalastair Reservoir and Loch Tummel to fill Faskally Dam at Pitlochry, then downstream into the River Tay. The River Tilt and Garry are its main tributaries.

Species
Salmon, brown trout (natural and stocked) and grayling (some big grayling).

Season Details
Salmon: January 15th to October 15th.
Trout: March 15th to 6th October.

Permit Contact(s)
Pitlochry Angling Club, (Ross Gardiner, weekends and evenings only) 3b Robertson Crescent, Pitlochry. Tel 01796 472157.
Mitchell's of Pitlochry (Nick Mitchell, proprietor), 23 Atholl Road, Pitlochry. Tel 01796 472613.
Ballinluig Post Office (trout permits).

Favourite Flies & Baits
Salmon: Tummel Shrimp, Willie Gunn (Gold-bodied version particularly), Ally's Shrimp, Munro Killer, Garry Dog.
Trout and Grayling: ephemerid imitations like Greenwell's, Light and Dark Olives, nymphs and dries, Iron Blues, March Browns early in season. Use weighted woven nymphs for fast runs.

How to Fish
Conventional fly-fishing and spinning for salmon but be careful of water level which may rise rapidly when Faskally Hydro-electric Power Station generates. Spinning lures include Devons, Rapalas and spoons. Trout and grayling can be caught on dries and deep-sunk nymphs.

the great River Tay itself, why not give the River Ericht a try – you won't be disappointed. And for those who have yet to develop their Tay fixation, you won't be disappointed by a visit to the exquisite Ericht either.

One of the most charming glens in Perthshire, and perhaps in the whole of Scotland, is lovely Glen Lyon. The intense autumn colours and the freshness of the glen in springtime simply have to be experienced. The lower River Lyon has salmon running from the earliest months of the year, although they generally do not ascend above the gorge section, some 6 miles or so upstream of the confluence with the Tay, until water temperatures rise.

The river runs nearly 30 miles from Loch Lyon to the river Tay and has numerous fine pools, waterfalls and gravely runs. Loch Lyon was heightened by 70 feet when a dam was built to form a hydro-electric generation facility, and freshets of water are released at intervals. Runs of salmon correspond with these increments in flow – the trick is to know when they will be allowed to happen! When you fish the Lyon, you are in an enchanted natural realm – you will be watched by deer, sung to by all manner of birds, and have a very good chance of a fine salmon and a basket of fit river brownies.

Above: The River Lyon: near the Bridge of Balgie, Perthshire.

Below: The River North Esk. at The Loups, near Edzell in Angus.

The Tay System

'Harling' on the River Tay: This traditional approach to fishing from the boat is operated on the middle and lower beats of the river. Baits are trawled behind the boat over the best lies. When a salmon takes, the boat and angler are taken to the bank to play the fish.

THE RIVER TAY

Location Details

Running from Loch Tay in west Perthshire to its outflow in the North Sea near Carnoustie.

Type of Fishery

A large river with countless pools and glides – highly suitable for game angling. Rocky and rough in its upper course, more sedate but deceptively swift-flowing in its lower reaches.

Description

The largest river in Scotland with the highest number of salmon caught each year.

Species

Salmon, brown trout, sea trout, grayling, 'escapee' rainbow trout, roach, pike, eels, flounders, sea fish in the estuary.

Season Details

Salmon: 15th Jan – 15th Oct.
Brown trout: 15th Mar – 6th Oct

Permit Contact(s)

There are far too many sources of permits to include all, the following are amongst the best:

Michael Smith, 'Cuilaluinn', Aberfeldy. Tel 01877 820302.
Mansfield Estates, Scone Palace. By Perth. Tel 01738 552308.
Strutt & Parker 13 Hill Street, Berkeley Sq, London. Tel 0171 6297282.
Tay Salmon Fishery Company Ltd, St. Leonards Bank, Perth. Tel 01738 636407.
Country Pursuits, 46 Henderson Street, Bridge of Allan. Tel 01786 834495.
CKD Finlayson Hughes, Barossa Place Perth. Tel 01738 625134.
Mr P King, Estate Office, Murthly and Strathbraan Estates, Murthly, Perthshire. Tel 01738 710303.
Taymount Estate Office, Taymount, Perth PH1 4QH. Tel 01738 828203.
Ballathie House Hotel, Kinclaven, Perthshire. Tel 01250 883268.
Ballinluig Post Office (trout permits)
Robert Cairns, Easter Cluny, Edradynate, Aberfeldy. Tel 01887 840228.

Favourite Flies & Baits

Salmon: Ally's Shrimp, Willie Gunn, Hairy Mary, Munro Killer, Yellow and Black, and Orange and Black as

Waddingtons. Spinning baits include: Blair Spoon, Flying C, Devons, Rapalas. Kynoch Killers and Tomic lures (plug baits primarily for 'harling'). Worm fishing is still permitted on some beats.
Trout and Grayling: Early season – March Browns and Dark Olives, then later in the season – Light Olives, Greenwell's, Iron Blues, Badger dries. Deep-sunk nymphs (especially weighted and woven variety) work well too.

How to Fish

The Tay is a big river, you will need to wade to reach the salmon lies and where trout may most be expected to take. Take great care of shelving slopes of shingle as these may slide into deep water carrying you with them, especially if the flow is swift.
Fish 'down and across' with long casts for salmon so that the fly tracks across the pool as slowly as possible (this may be speeded up later when grilse are about). Floating line in summer, otherwise, sunk lines of different rate depending on temperature and flow. Try upstream dries for trout or conventional teams of wets and nymphs.

Of all the Scottish salmon rivers the River Tay is undoubtedly the greatest. It's the longest river in Scotland, possesses the greatest flow, drains the largest catchment at around 2000 square miles, and enjoys the greatest number of running salmon. In a humble spring in a corrie on the eastern flank of Ben Lui, a tiny trickle sustains bright green mosses which also distil droplets from the misty clouds before coalescing and draining away. From such a tiny capillary the great arterial flow of the River Tay develops.

The clear water splashes noisily down the mountainside joining other burns along its way to form the River Cononish. Below the village of Tyndrum the stream adopts the new name of the River Fillan. Passing through Strath Fillan and the village of Crianlarich, the river flows through Loch Dochart and Loch Iubhair then assumes the name of the River Dochart as it empties out of Loch Iubhair. Down through Glen Dochart to Killin, the

The River Tay at Islamouth:
There are many fine and famous beats on the Tay and Islamouth is numbered amongst the best of them. Fish that wait to ascend the River Isla, then the River Ericht, lie at Islamouth, offering a great prospect of sport.

SALMON POOLS OF THE RIVER TAY

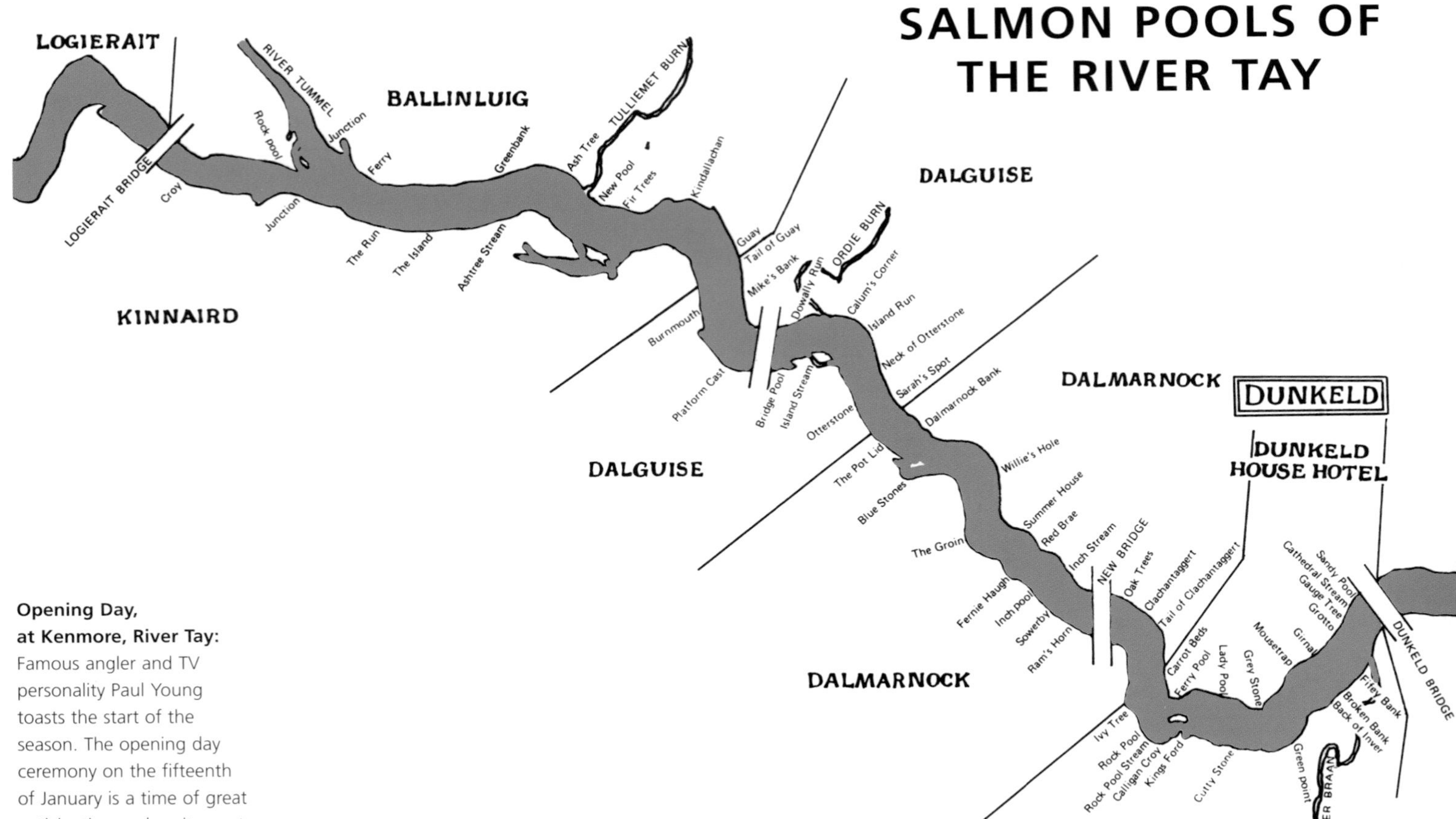

Opening Day, at Kenmore, River Tay: Famous angler and TV personality Paul Young toasts the start of the season. The opening day ceremony on the fifteenth of January is a time of great anticipation and excitement.

river roars over the rocky Falls of Dochart and enters Loch Tay. Loch Tay, at nearly fifteen miles long and over 500 feet deep in places, offers excellent prospects for catching salmon from boats, especially in the early months of the season.

The river slips out of Loch Tay at Kenmore where, on the fifteenth of January each year, the opening of the Tay salmon season is celebrated. On this day, a large crowd gathers by the riverside and pays tribute to the salmon and to the mighty river herself. A toast is made by sluicing whisky from a silver quaich, over the bows of a fishing coble, and the season is proclaimed open to a cheer from the anglers and watchers. It's a time of excitement and anticipation – rich in character and tradition.

The river now grows in stature, flowing through tree-lined Strath Tay. The first main tributary, the River Lyon, joins a little upstream of Aberfeldy and the river sets off in fine style to its meeting with its next tributary, the River Tummel, some fifteen miles downstream. Each of the tributaries of the Tay are fine fisheries in their own right carrying populations of ascending salmon

MIDDLE RIVER TAY

From the meeting of the waters as the Tummel joins the main stem of the river, the Tay is wide, productive and thoroughly absorbing. Great pools follow each other in a procession of fame: Dalguise, Dalmarnock, Dunkeld, Newtyle, Murthly, Stenton, Glendelvine (where Miss Ballantine caught her huge fish), Burnbane, Baldarroch, Kercock and Meikleour.

The River Tay, at Kenmore.
In spring, ascending salmon push well upstream into Loch Tay, where they may be caught from the start of the season.

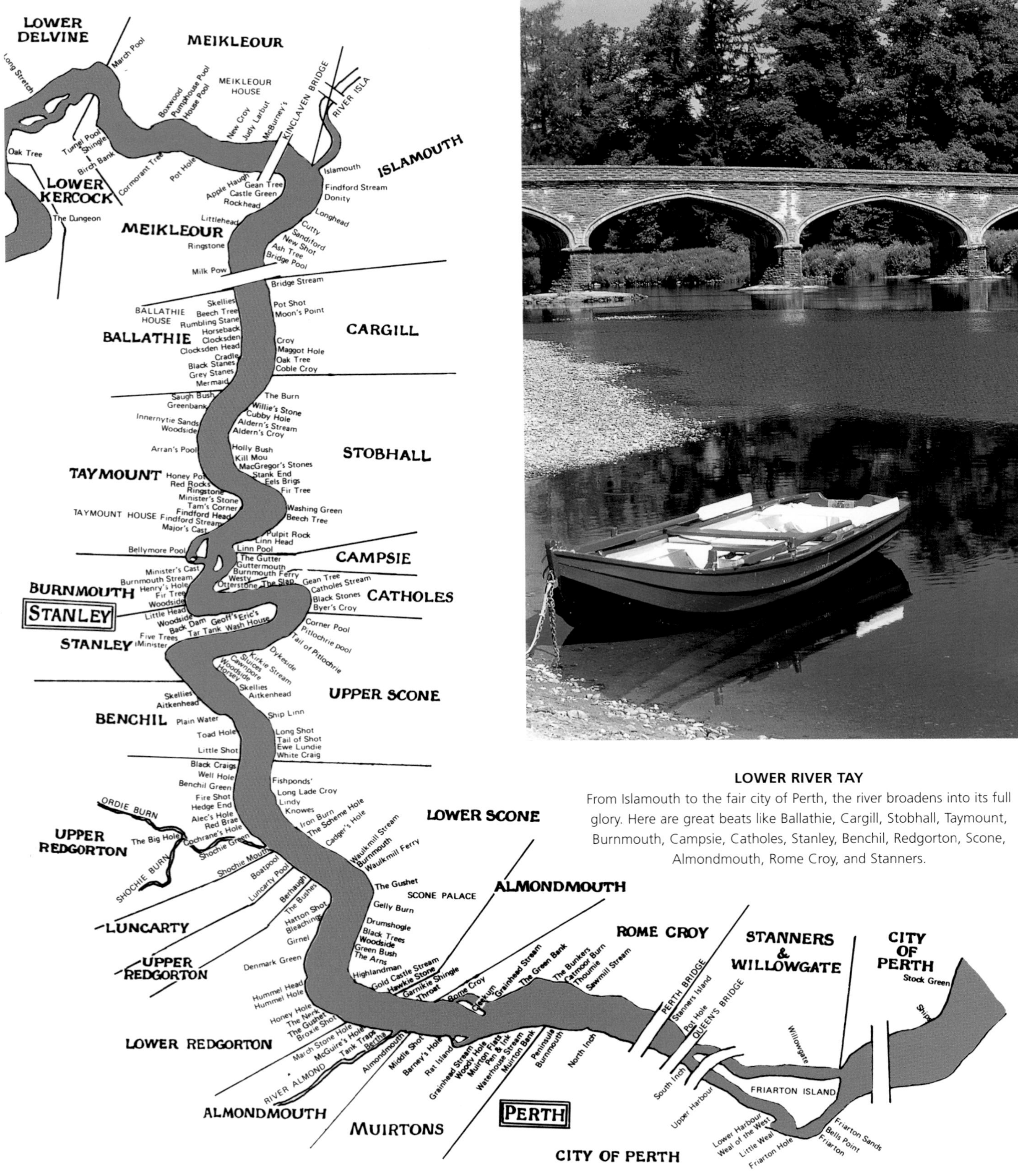

LOWER RIVER TAY

From Islamouth to the fair city of Perth, the river broadens into its full glory. Here are great beats like Ballathie, Cargill, Stobhall, Taymount, Burnmouth, Campsie, Catholes, Stanley, Benchil, Redgorton, Scone, Almondmouth, Rome Croy, and Stanners.

The River Tay, North Inch, Perth: In these lower reaches of the river, the water level rises and falls with the influence of the tide. Here, salmon prepare for their long journey into the headstreams to spawn.

plus a commendable head of brown trout and grayling. This 'Region of Rivers' is a land of plenty as far as game fishing is concerned and the splendour of the surrounding countryside is unmatched.

With the addition of the River Tummel, the Tay nearly doubles in flow. Not far downstream of Dunkeld the River Braan augments the flow, then, a few miles further, the River Isla adds its contribution at the Islamouth salmon fishing beat. Most of the Tay's tributaries have tributaries of their own, for example the River Isla and the River Ericht – both first class salmon rivers.

The Tay has now become a formidably large river – its flow may seem smooth but it is deceptively fast and strong. The last two tributaries to join the mother stream are the River Almond and the River Earn. The river is influenced by the swell of the ocean's tide although it still has nearly thirty estuarial miles to flow before it passes Dundee to meet its destiny in the North Sea near Carnoustie's famous golf courses.

The Tay flows nearly 120 miles over rocks as ancient as time; through forests, valleys and fertile fields; through villages, towns and two major cities; and throughout its journey it is home to a wealth of freshwater life. It's contribution to the development of modern game fishing, especially for Atlantic salmon, is simply unsurpassed anywhere. Little wonder that it has a special place in the hearts of anglers from all over the world.

Trolling is the recognised method of salmon fishing on Loch Tay. Most of the larger hotels at Ardreonaig, Aberfeldy, Killin and Kenmore will make the necessary arrangements for boats with gillies. There is no substitute for local knowledge on such a large loch so a gillie is invariably essential. Favourite spinning lures include Rapala,

Opposite: The River Tay, Kinclaven Bridge. In lower water conditions, the boat may be left on shore, most anglers prefer to cover the salmon lies from the bank. The trout fishing in middle Tay is superb.

Opening Day on the Tay: There may be deep frost and your line may freeze in your rod rings but the prospect of a 'springer' after the dark days of the close-season warms the heart.

shops and is best in late May/early June although late evening sessions in high summer can be very productive. Standard bushy patterns work well on the surface in sizes 10-14 while bright attractor patterns like Silver Invicta and Dunkeld, and nymphs imitators provide extra stimulus when fished deeper.

Recommended fishing spots include the shallower areas at each end of the loch and also around promontories and bays. The large number of prehistoric man-made island dwellings, 'crannogs', are also worth fishing around as they provide reef-like conditions where fish congregate to feed in the shallows.

The River Tay has the largest catches of salmon of all Scotland's rivers; trout catches are also good and are improving due to regulation under the Protection Order. Salmon fishing on the Tay consists of bank fishing, mostly fly and

Toby and Kynoch, while larger tube flies and Waddingtons are often trolled to good effect.

It is surprising how early in the year that large spring salmon are caught in the loch, sometimes still bearing sea lice, a great distance from the tide and especially in the cold water of late winter when their metabolism is a bit slower. Trout fishing may also be arranged through local hotels and tackle

spinning, with some beats permitting worm fishing, and boat fishing, which is called harling.

Harling allows greater cover of the wider pools than casting from the bank, although sitting in a boat waiting for a salmon to take the trolled lure or fly is not to everyone's taste. Nevertheless, many salmon are caught by harling and many anglers hook their first salmon this way. Harling is most

Above: The River Tay. There is nothing quite so satisfying as casting a line over a pool where fish lie, except maybe hooking one.

practised in the middle and lower beats as the smaller pools of the upper river can be cast over more easily from the banks.

The Tay's trout are not necessarily easy to catch, but are amongst the fittest in the world and a worthy quarry. In the spring, big hatches of March Browns occur, and great speckled backs appear in the glides, rising slowly to take the fluttering flies.

The lovely thing about Tay trout is that they seem to occupy lies just like salmon. You will see the same fish in the same place if you regularly visit a particular pool. Dry fly is very effective when hatches start. While small nymphs are good when the fish are feeding sub-surface. Keep in mind that some of the Tay pools are powerful and many feet deep, so weighted nymphs really have to be generously weighted. This is also true when you try for a Tay grayling.

There is ample association trout fishing water on the Tay and permit prices are realistic, many of the main estates and hotels offer day and weekly tickets. For salmon fishing, hotels and estate offices are a good first step to finding details on salmon fishing, and the tourist offices are ever-willing to help.

If you wish to fish a large river in wonderful country, then the Tay is the natural river of choice.

Left: The River Tay. On a morning when penetrating frost ices your deepest bones, maybe there is a hint of an excuse for a medicinal dram.

THE NORTH EAST

Opposite: The Upper River Dee at Linn o' Dee, near Braemar.
Mountains and conifers, rocks and splashing rivers – the real stuff of Scotland. The famous Royal Dee flows many lovely miles to the sea at Aberdeen, from high in the Cairngorm Mountains.

The right shoulder of Scotland is rich country. The farms are productive and the commercial fishing communities have been accustomed to the wealth gleaned from the North Sea.The area has few lochs but it does have superb rivers. These are trout streams of considerable excellence but it is the mighty salmon that holds most sway.

This is also a royal area of Scotland. The River Dee runs through a charming strath, so charming in fact that Queen Victoria decided to make her Scottish home at Balmoral Castle, Deeside. The present royals spend time here too and enjoy fishing the Royal Dee. The rivers of the region descend through rich pasture land sometimes in rocky turmoil and at other times in quieter mood with smooth swirling trout-filled glides. This is a land of abundant and varied fishing.

The trout fishing is unequivocally first-class in these royal glens, but it is the salmon that remains king. Most of the rivers of the north east carry stocks of salmon throughout the year, and most also have fine runs of sea trout as soon as summer rain breaks the late-spring drought. From the cool of the North Sea the burnished-silver fish slip into the lower pools trying to avoid the ever-present danger of predatory seals. Then they steel themselves for the arduous journey upstream through the rocky shallows, over rushing cascades, through the countless pools, until at last they find that elusive place amongst the gravel to ensure the survival of their kind in this landscape of magical charm.

Lochs and Rivers of the North East

Opposite: The River Don.
In its tranquil sections the Don has some of the finest trout fishing in North East Scotland. The dry-fly fishing is amongst the best in Britain.

THE RIVER YTHAN

Location Details
Near Newburgh, Aberdeenshire, on the Newburgh to Peterhead road.

Type of Fishery
Recognised as a sea trout fishery, the Ythan also provides catches of salmon and grilse.

Description
The best part is probably the estuary and lower reaches, as the middle and upper river flows through wooded farm land, is now quite heavily weeded in summer, and requires spate to bring it into good fishing ply.

Species
Sea trout, salmon and some brownies.

Season Details
11th February to end October, statutory brown trout season.

Permit Contact(s)
Mrs A Forbes, Newburgh Fishings, 3 Lea Cottages, Newburgh, Aberdeenshire.
Tel 01358 789297.
The Buchan Hotel, Ellon, Aberdeenshire.
Tel 01358 720208.

Favourite Flies & Baits
Ythan Terrors and Blue Elver patterns (long streamer lures) work well, as do Teal, Blue and Silver, Dark Mackerel, Delphi, and Silver Stoat's Tail.

How to Fish
Boat fishing (with fly) in the estuary is an unusual and effective Ythan pursuit. Otherwise, conventional river fly-fishing tactics from the bank, in the glides of the lower river, pull some very fine sea trout, the occasional salmon, and bright silver grilse when runs of these lively young salmon are about.

North of Aberdeen there is a shoulder of land jutting out into the North Sea pointing towards Norway and the far north. Through this scapula of Scotland run some fine rivers, each attracting discerning anglers 'frae a' the airts'. In the hinterland to this coastal plain lie the foothills of the Cairngorms, while down the straths run clear rivers which are small but highly productive.

The lower reaches of the rivers are often rich and slower, while the beats of the headstreams offer fishing that is characteristically 'Highland'. The migrations of silver salmonids penetrate into the

Left: The River Ythan, near Newburgh.
The Ythan is a sea trout river par excellence. Especially in its lower and tidal reaches, the return of the enigmatic sea trout is eagerly awaited each summer.

The River Deveron, Bridge of Alvie.
The Deveron has some fine salmon and sea trout runs each year – and superb brown trout too.

highest parts of the upland burns. It is not unusual to be out hill-walking in the late autumn, and jump across a burn, and see the great surge of a startled fish which had been lying in the tiny shallow pool, thousands of miles from, and thousands of feet above, its previous home in the deep ocean. This is surprising country.

Running eastwards is the River Ythan, perhaps the most famous sea trout river of the far north east. Rising high above Huntly, the River Ythan comes to life in the bubbling springs called the Wells of Ythan, and the river turns and twists through partially wooded banks from Auchterless to Methlick before passing through Ellon and running towards its sandy estuary to Newburgh and the North Sea. Sea trout are the mainstay of the Ythan although salmon also ascend when the water is high. Fishing takes place in the estuary and within the river and is readily accessed through local hotels and angling associations. Contact Aberdeen and District AA, Fyvie AA and the Newburgh AA (through local tourist offices).

The River Deveron flows from the hills of west Aberdeenshire towards the North Sea. Some very large salmon run the Deveron, much larger than such a modestly sized river might be expected to have, so be prepared for a specimen-sized tussle when you visit this attractive river. Like the Ythan, the Deveron can be accessed through local associations and nearby hotels. There are good runs of sea trout and night fishing can be exceptional.

The River Ugie is a small river which enters the sea at the fishing port of Peterhead. Strictly speaking it would be more accurate to describe the

THE RIVER DEVERON

Location Details
Flowing into the Moray Firth near Banff the Deveron rises in the hinterland behind the great coastal plain of Aberdeenshire and Moray, flows through fine countryside and provides excellent salmon and sea trout fishing.

Type of Fishery
A premier salmon and sea trout river.

Description
Faster and rockier in its upper reaches, the river slackens pace a little and runs through superb glides, forming really fine salmon and sea trout fishing in its middle and lower beats.
There are many estate and riparian owners and good association water with easy accessibility.

Species
Fine runs of salmon and good runs of (sometimes large) sea trout.

Season Details
11th February to end October, statutory brown trout season.

Permit Contact(s)
Banff & Macduff Angling Assocn., 20 Shore St., Macduff. Tel 01261 832891.
Huntly Angling Assocn., Murdoch, McMath and Mitchell, 27 Duke Street, Huntly.
Tel 01466 792291.
Huntly Castle Hotel, Huntly.
Tel 01466 792696.
Savills, 12 Clerk Street, Brechin, Angus (Laithers Beat).
Tel 01356 622187.

Favourite Flies & Baits
For salmon, shrimp patterns (Ally's and GP), Willie Gunn, Comet, Munro Killer, Hairy Mary.
Sea Trout: Stoat's Tail, Teal Blue and Silver, Dark Mackerel.
Trout: Greenwell, Grouse and Claret, Dark Olives wet flies, Wickham's Fancy and Light Olive, and Hare's Ear dry flies.

How to Fish
Standard approaches to daytime salmon and for sea trout fishing (especially dusk and night-time).

Top right:
The River Deveron.
The hut at Montcoffer is perched over the river to enable you to see the fish as they run into the pool below.

Ugie as the fusion of two rivers coming together near Peterhead – the North Ugie Water and the River South Ugie. Like its near neighbours, the Ugie(s) also carry sea trout and some salmon and provide visiting anglers with inexpensive and accessible fishing.

There can be no doubt that Scotland has its share of the world's famous salmon rivers. Few serious salmon anglers can be unaware of the famous River Dee in Aberdeenshire, most will have

Bottom right:
The River Don.
The Don holds very fine brownies in its lovely pools as it slips under broad trees and past rich farm land. This is 'downstream nymph' and 'upstream dry-fly' country at its best.

The River Don:
as it passes under the Bridge of Don not far from the granite city of Aberdeen.

used flies which were developed especially for the river, and some of the luckier anglers will have cast a line over her enigmatic pools. In common with the other main rivers of Scotland, the Dee has contributed much to what we know about Atlantic Salmon and how we fish for them. But this is not an academic river – it is one which offers practical sport in wonderful surroundings.

The raindrops and snowflakes that fall on the high tops of the Cairngorm mountains unite to build the river. These humble drops percolate through heather roots and over hard rocks to form tiny streams which eventually come together amongst the wildest and highest mountains in Scotland. The water travels down through the rocks of the hillpass called the Lairig Ghru, over the well-known cataract the Linn o' Dee to head downstream to Braemar and Royal Deeside, where Balmoral Castle overlooks the pools. The middle and lower sections of this river are simply wonderful and have some of the finest fishing anywhere. Finally, the river meets the sea at Aberdeen harbour amongst the supply ships for the North Sea oil fields and the trawlers landing their hard-won catches.

Despite yielding some trout, the heartbeat of the river is salmon, although catches have declined significantly and anglers have been returning the salmon that they catch to try and increase numbers.

THE RIVER DON (IN ABERDEENSHIRE)

Location Details
Running from the hills around Tomintoul to the sea near Aberdeen, the Don is Highland in its upper reaches and typically east-coast river (glides and pools) in its lower parts.

Type of Fishery
A salmon river, with runs of sea trout, and excellent brown trout river fishing.

Description
Tumbling through rocky gorges, and heavily-treed in its upper parts, the Don makes its way down Strathdon then opens out a bit to form a wider more-accessible (larger) river which has fine glides and pools

Species
Salmon, sea trout and brown trout.

Season Details
11 February to end of October, statutory brown trout season.

Permit Contact(s)
Colquhonnie Hotel in Strathdon, Aberdeenshire.
Tel 01975 651210.
Mr F. Milton, Kemnay House, Aberdeenshire.
Tel 01467 642220.
Grant Arms Hotel, Monymusk, Aberdeenshire.
Tel 01467 651226.
The Estate Office, Castle Forbes, Whitehouse, Alford.
Tel 01975 562524.

Favourite Flies & Baits
Blue Charm, Stoat's Tail, Munro Killer, Willie Gunn, Ally's Shrimp.
Dry Flies for brown trout – Badger Quill, Wickhams Fancy, Light olives. Wet Flies, Greenwell's (when olives are hatching) March Brown (early season)
Teal Blue & Silver and Silver Stoat for sea trout.

How to Fish
Salmon fishing is conventional, using short rods where it is awkward to cast and full size rods in the more open reaches.
Dry Fly fishing for the fine brown trout is amongst the best anywhere – under-rated and under-exploited.

PARK BEAT, RIVER DEE

Location Details
Park House, Drumoak, Banchory, Kincardineshire.

Type of Fishery
Prestigious salmon fishing and sea trout fishing. The type of truly classy fishing that stands head and shoulders above the more mundane.

Description
Sumptuous facilities for salmon fly-fishing on the middle Dee.

Species
Salmon and sea trout.

Season Details
1st February to 30th September (subject to variation by the District Fishery Board – intention to increase numbers of spawning fish).

Permit Contact(s)
The Estates Office, Craigie Farm, Leuchars, Fife. Tel 01334 839218.

Favourite Flies & Baits
Standard salmon patterns are used: Blue Charm (traditionally), Ally's Shrimp, Munro's Killer and Willie Gunn, Tubes and Waddingtons in higher water, smaller doubles and trebles in lower conditions. As fish are returned, the use of single and barbless hooks is also encouraged. For sea trout, there is little to beat a Silver Stoat's Tail.

How to Fish
The Long Pool is a slower glide which may need a little retrieve or backing up in lower conditions, otherwise, conventionally 45 degrees cast and mend, then allow the fly to track over the lies. Sea trout in the 'gloaming' can be an utter joy and well worth postponing the after-dinner drinks for.

The Upper River Dee pours over hard-stone boulders which sparkle with mica and garnets, its clean water comes from snow melt in the high Cairngorms. This is a typical Highland river with wide course when the water is low, but full to brimming in the power of a real spate.

The River Dee:
Flowing swiftly under the soaring stonework arch of the Old Brig 'o' Dee. Many great salmon swim under this bridge on their way to the gravel of their spawning redds in the upper reaches.

In what is a comparatively short season, running from the first of February to the end of September, fishing is at its best in the middle and lower beats until higher water levels draw the fish further upstream. Some very large salmon are caught in the Dee and there is a real chance of some first-class sea trout fishing in late summer.

Special beats are Invercauld near Balmoral, where resinous Scots pine trees and aromatic heather give a lovely ambience to the river bank; sumptuous Park Beat near Crathes, where there is a special classic elegance and productivity, and the Cairnton Fishings where Wood developed his thinking about fly size and presentation.

The River Don, on the northerly outskirts of Aberdeen has salmon and sea trout runs too, but it

The River Dee at Braemar:
A small Blue Charm or Stoat's Tail may be the downfall of a silver salmon amongst these meandering bends.

River Dee: Help from the ghillie will keep the enthusiasm levels at an appropriate level and will make all the difference to your chances.

is more noted for its wild brownies – great, fat, butter-yellow, crimson-speckled trout which rise keenly to a well-presented dry fly. Hardly a winter's day goes by without the Cockbridge to Tomintoul Road being mentioned on British radio as being blocked by snow. This is the high country which drains to form the upper Don.

The river runs under tree-clad hills and by the rich fields of bonnie Strathdon, then widens by the time it reaches Alford and Monymusk and it is here that the best trout fishing is to be had. Modestly priced and readily available through the local estates and hotels, there is enough to keep an enthusiastic dry fly exponent fulfilled for many delightful days. If you are seeking quiet days of fine fishing for trout in pleasant tranquil country, then the Don will be very hard to beat.

River Dee: The river slows into deep still pools when the level is low, but becomes a raging torrent in spate conditions. Salmon parr grow in these lovely pools until the time they head off downstream for the sea.

THE HIGHLANDS

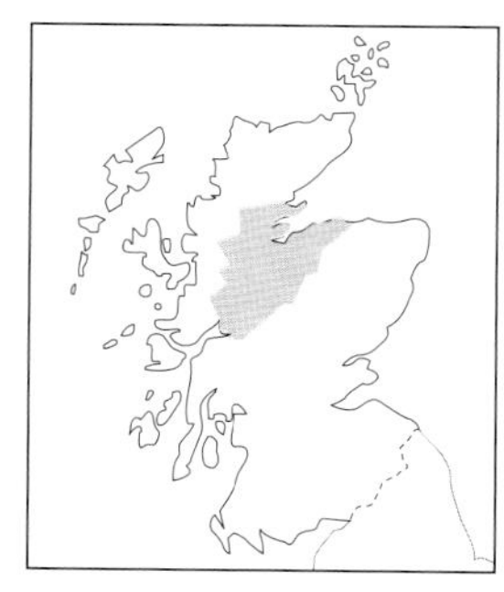

The River Findhorn, Cawdor Estate:
The Findhorn runs through wide valleys in its upper reaches, then into deep-cut gorges nearer the sea before emerging into a fine estuary at the village of the same name. Salmon, sea trout and brown trout live here amongst the boulders, pours and runs, and may be caught with small flies strategically placed in front of their noses.

There can be fewer areas of Britain more synonymous with 'getting away from it all' than the wild Highlands of Scotland. With high mountains, deep glens, mature forests and wild moors, this is an area of unsurpassable natural beauty. It is here that solitary anglers enjoy some of the best natural fishing in Europe – maybe the world. The definition of exactly where the Highlands start and finish is a bit superfluous. Once you leave the central area of the country, you enter a different landscape with fewer farms, smaller villages and greater expanses of wild country. The hills are higher, the place more deserted – the Highlands are an unspoilt wilderness full of opportunity for dedicated anglers.

Highland trout are not the great slab-sided, stew-pond monsters of the south, but are as wild as they come, especially if you put a hook in their lip. They are lean, magnificently speckled with dark markings and brilliant red spots along their silver lemon flanks. They eat well too, but an increasing number of anglers are adopting the habit of returning them to live out their lives in their natural environment. The rivers and lochs hold trout, while many of the lochs also hold charr, pike, and perch.

Traditional methods of fishing are favoured and evocative artificial flies catch as many fish as their modern brethern. There is something special about using ancient patterns and tactics when fly-fishing in the Highlands – a kind of timelessness that is so attractive and enjoyable. Fishing is all about enjoyment, and you certainly will enjoy fishing in the Highlands.

Highland Lochs

Loch Morlich:
Situated near Aviemore and Coylumbridge, this loch is a popular water sports venue set close to the snow-filled corries of the Cairngorms and Ben Macdui. The loch is surrounded by conifer forests and is highly attractive. The fishing is mixed with some very good trout putting in an appearance from time to time.

Typically, a Highland loch is a rocky stillwater bounded by heather clad braes, often peat-stained, and almost invariably filled with teeming populations of brown trout. This section deals with those Highland lochs which have not been considered in other sections. This does not suggest that the others are not 'Highland' in nature, rather that they have been fully dealt with under different geographical areas.

What makes a Scottish Highland loch different? Probably, it is the wildness of its location, combined with its roughness of terrain, that characterise its essential 'highland-ness'. Most of these lochs are not afflicted by agricultural fertiliser run-off and consequent eutrophication. Indeed they are more likely to suffer over-acidity through afforestation, acid rain and peaty catchments. Some have islands which still retain

LOCH RUTHVEN
Location Details
Set in the rolling hills to the south of Loch Ness not far from Inverness.
Type of Fishery
Loch Ruthven is a boat-fishing, fly-fishing-only loch.
Description
This loch is a grand place to spend a tranquil day. It is big enough to offer that sense of exploration (around two miles long) yet intimate enough to allow you to try out most of its area in a day.
Species
Brown trout (some quite large for a high loch of this type).
Season Details
March 15th to October 6th.
Permit Contact(s)
J Graham & Co (Tackle shop), 37 Castle Street, Inverness. Tel 01463 233178.
Favourite Flies & Baits
Bushy bob flies – Loch Ordie, muddlers and bumbles (especially Claret Bumble), with Silver Invicta, Dunkeld, Silver March Brown down the cast. Emerger and hopper patterns work extremely well when the fish rise – sometimes a stupendous evening rise, if it does not get too cold.
How to Fish
Outboard motors are not permitted so be prepared to row. Fish the margins (keeping clear of the reed beds where nesting wildfowl may be in the spring/early summer). The standard approach of 'keep around the 6 foot contour' is a good basic principle.

Opposite: Loch Laggan.
Close to the A86 to Spean Bridge, Loch Laggan rests under the bulk of Creag Meagaidh (1130m). The road has many lay-bys along the loch's northern shore and the opportunity for a quick cast is rarely missed by visiting anglers.

stands of ancient Caledonian Scots Pines, left there because they were too difficult to remove, remnants of a time when much of northern Scotland was blessed by these quintessential Highland trees.

The lochs of the Highlands are mostly located in poorer quality valleys and moorlands more suited to upland sheep farming and forestry than classical agriculture. They are comparatively poorer aquatic environments than their southern counterparts where warmer conditions and richer sub-strata are more likely to exist. The rocks are harder, the climate more bracing, with higher winds, shorter summers and longer winter nights, and the height above sea level of many Highland lochs makes them more prone to the effects of cooler climatic conditions. Nevertheless, they possess some excellent wild brown trout fishing.

Highland trout are wild and natural – not the huge slab-sided rainbows stocked at an unnatural density and dimension common in southern waters – for these are real fish. They come to your surface fly with speed and alacrity, but they may not be easy to hook for those of slow response! If you wish to enjoy the best of traditional Highland trout fishing a visit to Glen Affric is thoroughly recommended. Loch Mullardoch and Loch Affric are simply superb – good fishing in splendid scenery. Access is readily available through the Glen Affric Hotel at Cannich.

Slightly less remote is Loch Ruthven near Inverness, a great loch to fish for larger brownies. The boats are good, access is easy and the dancing waters of Ruthven should not be missed. Moving south, you will encounter several long narrow lochs which provide trout fishing, some much

Loch Cluanie, Inverness-shire: The rocky shores of this loch, close to the roadside on the A87, offers some good fishing, especially from a drifting boat hugging the natural contours of the shore. The fish are typically 'three-to-the-pound', but they fight as though they believe they are much bigger.

better than others, but all worth investigating.

Further north still is the attractive Millbuies Loch near Elgin where fishing is for brown trout from boats. Not far away, on the Forres to Carrbridge road lies Lochindorb where small brown trout will rise two at a time to a bushy fly fished on the surface. Lochindorb has a great stock of brownies and is always a pleasure to fish.

LOCHINDORB

Location Details
On the Forres to Carrbridge road, Lochindorb is easy to find and access.

Type of Fishery
Primarily a boat fishery, it has a huge population of brown trout of natural but relatively-small size.

Description
Not a large loch – about two miles long by half a mile wide – the island with its sinister castle is a major landmark. This was the keep of the notorious Wolf of Badenoch.

Species
Brownies – mostly under a pound in weight, but fast and furious.

Season Details
Standard brown trout season.

Permit Contact(s)
The Caretaker's Cottage at Lochindorb Estate, Glenferness. Tel 01309 651270.

Favourite Flies & Baits
Work a team of small bushy flies through the surface – Soldier Palmer, Claret Bumble, Bibio, Zulu. Kate McLaren. Otherwise almost anything else will draw attention – try bright flies on bright days, and dark flies when the weather is dull.

How to Fish
Long drifts are best – try to arrange to drift parallel to the shore. If the wind is westerly, try the shallow south end. The loch is not deep so fish should be encountered over much of its area – but shorelines where food items live and gather are most productive.

Lochindorb:
The A939 road from Grantown-on-Spey to Nairn runs close to historic Lochindorb. The Wolf of Badenoch's island castle seems to dominate the loch, especially in the fading light of dusk - it is curiously eerie under these conditions, but the hard-fighting brownies care nothing for such flights of fancy - they grab your fly and fight furiously.

Loch Affric:
There are fewer more beautiful fishing lochs in Scotland than those of the Affric area – and Loch Affric itself, nestling under Carn Eighe (1183m), is a shining example. Typically, there is a good population of trout – some very small, but some fit for the glass case on the mantle-shelf. Stunning fishing in stunning landscapes.

GLEN AFFRIC

Location Details
Glen Affric lies west of Cannich (which is on the A831 between Drumnadrochit and Struy).

Type of Fishery
Bank and boat fishing in a splendid Highland loch setting. The upper part of the River Affric, where it flows into the main loch, is well worth fishing too.

Description
Dramatic Highland loch with remnants of the ancient Caledonian Pine Forest on the shore.

Species
Wild brown trout. Most are mature at around half a pound but there are some considerably larger fish.

Season Details
Standard brown trout season March 15th to Oct 6th.

Permit Contacts
CKD Finlayson Hughes will provide details of Affric Lodge accommodation (contact at Barossa Place, Perth. Tel 01738 639017). Alternatively, contact the Glen Affric Hotel, Cannich, Inverness-shire. Tel 01456 415214.

Favourite Flies & Baits
Palmered-pattern flies do well – Soldier Palmer, Zulu, Bumbles, Loch Ordie – anything that creates a bit of surface wake. Similarly, you may expect activity to a medium sized Muddler in breezier conditions.

How to Fish
The loch is typical of Highland Scottish waters and requires typical Highland Scottish tactics. Use bushy bob flies to rise a decent trout at or near the shore and where jumbles of rock offer a good hiding place for fish. Hug the contours of the loch-side where the water is around 4 – 6 feet deep. The 'foot o' the wind' (lee shore) is also a very good bet.

Left: Loch Beinn a' Mheadhoin.

Right: Loch Oich.

Loch Lochy:
Part of the Caledonian Canal, Loch Lochy is popular with cabin cruisers passing through the canal. Some very fine trout are caught in this loch each year, and shoals of perch are chased by mighty pike.

Highland Rivers

River Ness near Inverness: The River Ness is a short river but has fine trout, sea trout and salmon stocks. It benefits from being clear much of the time, even in high spates. The great loch takes out the suspended matter which comes down the tributaries in floods. Salmon run throughout the year and the trout fishing in late-spring to mid-summer can be spectacular.

For many, the Highlands of Scotland start wherever you meet high ground. Dunkeld is sometimes referred to as the 'gateway to the Highlands', especially when you pass into higher terrain travelling northwards through the narrowing of the Tay valley.

Others maintain that the Highlands lie on the north side of the Highland Boundary Fault. Exactly where the Highlands commence or cease is not really relevant, for much of the northern part of our country is typically 'highland' in its terrain and climate.

The great north-east to south-west incision of the Great Glen divides the north from the rest of the mainland. This deep glacial strath has major lochs within it – mighty Loch Ness, Loch Oich and Loch Lochy – each joined by a system of locks to form the Caledonian Canal, allowing boats to make passage from the North Sea to the Atlantic Ocean. Loch Ness is a large loch by any standard at over 24 miles long and over 800 feet deep but the River Ness is quite short at only six miles from Loch Ness to the sea and falling only 50 feet or so over its course. It is a prolific salmon river and is very accessible through hotels and tackle shops in the Inverness area.

LOCH NESS AND THE RIVER NESS

Location Details
Nestling in the hills of the Great Glen, Loch Ness is a deep (800 feet) and narrow loch. The River Ness is short, running from the Loch, through the centre of Inverness, then into the Moray Firth just five and a half miles away.

Type of Fishery
The loch is a mixed fishery for bank and boat angling, spinning, bait and fly fishing for many species. The river provides many salmon and sea trout, with some fine brown trout too.

Description
The loch is large without the benefit of deeply indented bays – it is therefore the shallow shoreline that produces most of the action. The river is a typical Highland stream of significant size except that it remains very clear at almost all times due to the water clarity of the loch.

Species
Loch Ness has salmon, brown trout and ferox trout, Arctic charr, pike and the odd monster.
The river has runs of salmon and sea trout with a population of fine river brown trout.

Season Details
Salmon: 15th January to 15th October.
Trout statutory season.

Permit Contact(s)
The Estate Office, Glenmoriston Estate, Invermoriston. Tel 01320 351300.
J Graham & Co (tackle shop), Castle Street, Inverness. Tel 01463 233178.

Favourite Flies & Baits
Trolling in the loch with Rapala plugs and Toby lures is popular, while fly-fishing around the shores with conventional trout flies is successful in some places. The river salmon take the standard offerings – Willie Gunn, Hairy Mary, Green Highlander, Tosh, Ally's Shrimp – but use a size smaller than comparative rivers due to the normal clarity of the water (even after high rainfall).

How to Fish
Hug the banks of Loch Ness – not necessarily to avoid all the monsters which lurk out in the depths – but to stay close to where the trout tend to be.
The river is large enough to require long casts and conventional fly-fishing.

The side arms of the Great Glen also have lochs and rivers of note. The River Moriston, a fine salmon river, empties into Loch Ness having drained Loch Cluanie and Loch Loyne. The river passes through spectacular wooded banks and is mostly swift of pace. Fishing opens early, on the 15th of January, and early salmon are regularly caught. A lovely rocky river of great character and decent productivity, with a slower mid section, it is generally the lower beats that offer the best prospects, and these can be quite extraordinary under optimum conditions.

The River Garry flows into Loch Oich at Invergarry having tumbled through mountainous terrain in its course from Loch Quoich, through Loch Garry. The waters of the Garry are used for hydro-electricity generation and low compensation flows tend to impede the passage of migrating fish until later in the spring when more buoyant summer flows are established. Nevertheless the River Garry provides fine fishing in superb surroundings, particularly in its lower beats.

River Ness:
Locals have access to this fine river and visitors can make arrangements easily for a day or two's fishing. A large river when compared to its short length, the Ness is swift-flowing and attractively tree-lined in most parts.

River Farrar, Strathfarrar:
The Rivers Farrar and Glass are tributaries of the River Beauly and each run through wonderful wild country. Typically Highland in nature they have superb pours, glides and deep pots interspaced with boulder-strewn runs and 'rattles'.

River Affric in Glen Affric: If you imagine a real Highland river, with deep peaty water and cascading rushes between ancient water-worn boulders, lined with native trees and flanked by banks scented by wild flowers, then the River Affric is what is in your mind's eye. It is a lovely river full of small darting brownies and salmon parr, and the occasional large fish to catch you unawares.

Lovely Loch Arkaig fills the short river of the same name to pour into Loch Lochy. This is a river of salmon during summer months, brown trout all through their season, and pike whenever you care to give the lower reaches at try. The loch has a good head of ferox trout and many anglers have had tussles with these cannibalistic brownies.

On the opposite side of the loch, the River Spean combines the outflowing waters of Loch Treig and Loch Laggan to join the River Roy before reaching Loch Lochy. Curiously, the River Spey rises within a mile or two of the source of the River Roy and yet flows east to the North Sea while the Roy flows westwards to the Atlantic.

The tree-lined River Lochy is a brilliant diamond set in a rich seam of rivers, with some of the bonniest salmon pools in the locality and the most prolific catches. Access is readily obtained through tackle shops in Fort William and through local hotels and tourist offices.

Entering Loch Linnhe, near Fort William, is the Nevis, probably one of the most spectacular streams in the area. Glen Nevis runs through wild unspoilt country, impressive with the great buttresses of the Ben Nevis massif hanging majestically overhead and is home to runs of salmon during summer spates and vermilion-speckled trout.

Salmon run into the lochs of the Great Glen and ascend the connecting rivers. It seems that the lochs buffer the temperature during periods of winter cold, attracting more salmon than the rivers which often flow several

River Findhorn: A small river with a big reputation for fine and large salmon.

degrees colder. This means that salmon fishing in the lochs may hold significant prospects. There is also a teeming population of brown trout, summer incursions of sea trout, pike, perch and abundant shoals of charr in the deeper lochs.

River Beauly:
The River Beauly is as prolific as it is magnificent. The salmon fishing is relatively inexpensive for its quality and the sea trout fishing from mid June is excellent. Some very nice brown trout lurk in the deep pools and will come shyly to a well-presented dry-fly.

Further along the top flank of the north-east corner of Scotland, and running in a more northerly direction, are the River Findhorn, the River Nairn and the River Lossie. The Findhorn, at around fifteen miles long, is the result of the joining together of two quite different waters, the River Cro and the Eskin Water. It carries salmon and sea trout throughout much of its wild and rocky gorge sections before flattening out into a fine sandy estuary near the RAF Base at Kinloss.

The River Nairn also has runs of sea trout and salmon and is well worth fishing when in the area. It is a small river which drains the land to the south of the infamous battlefield of Culloden. A spate river, the Nairn does best when incursions of fresh fish come after rises in water level.

River Avon, Ballindalloch:
The River Avon starts its rapid descent as soon as it flows out of Loch Avon on the high flanks of Cairngorm itself. Free falling in countless rapids and cascades it finally joins the Spey and carries some of the migratory fish that enter that river. In the Avon's lower reaches particularly, there are decent brownies.

The River Lossie passes through the elegant town of Elgin before reaching the sea on the sands near the harbour at Lossiemouth. The River Lossie has seen extraordinary improvement in salmon and sea trout catches over recent years due to hard work on the part of the local angling association. The river is not long, but now carries excellent runs of migratory fish.

The River Spey

The River Spey, Boat of Garten: Where rainbows of the climatic variety rather than the trout type, span the heavens, and where ospreys nest in full public view.

Running clear and cool from the heights of the Cairngorms, the River Spey is a fast flowing river of great fame. It has no major barriers against ascending migratory fish so salmon and sea trout tend to distribute themselves throughout the whole system. This results in good fishing over most of the Spey's wonderful miles. There are also fine brown trout, plus pike in the slower sections at Spey Dam and Loch Insch, so a rich feast awaits visiting anglers. Add to this the fact that the river runs through some of Scotland's finest scenery and it is clear why the Spey has such pride of place in our angling heritage.

The Spey rises in the Monadhliath Mountains which lie between the Great Glen and Strathspey. Flowing roughly north east, the upper river collects the contributions of its major tributaries the River Truim, the River Calder and the River Tromie. This part of the country is definitely Highland in nature. Rocky-topped hills jostle against the grander mountains beyond and the deeply-cut river valleys are swathed in stands of alder, birch and rowan all adding to the natural wild beauty of the area.

SALMON POOLS OF THE RIVER SPEY

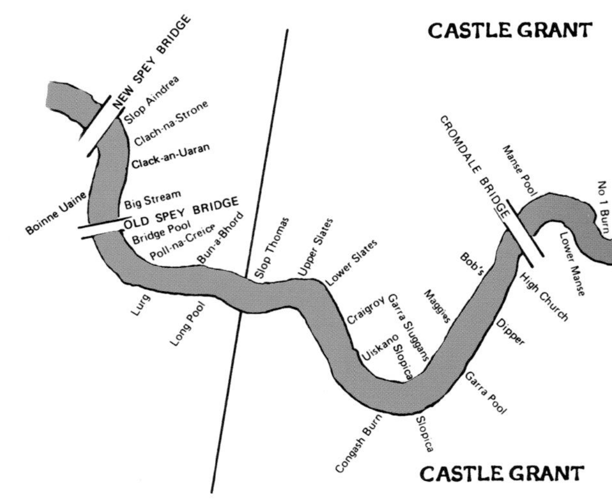

THE RIVER SPEY

Location Details
Meeting the sea at Spey Bay and running from the heights of the Cairngorms, the Spey runs fast through Moray.

Type of Fishery
A premier salmon river with good runs of sea trout and buoyant stocks of brown trout.

Description
Fast flowing and productive – this is one of best salmon rivers in Scotland. Sea trout fishing is a huge attraction too. Good access through excellent angling associations.

Species
Salmon, sea trout, brown trout and pike in slower sections (and Loch Insch).

Season Details
11th February to end of October, statutory brown trout season.

Permit Contact(s)
Mortimers, High Street, Grantown-on-Spey, Moray, will advise on the wide availability of permits.
Tel 01479 872684.

Favourite Flies & Baits
Spey patterns for salmon include Munro's Killer, Arndilly Fancy, Green Highlander, Willie Gunn, Ally's Shrimp (or General Practitioner), Tosh and Hairy Mary. Sea trout will come to Stoat's Tail and the Teal, Blue and Silver.

How to Fish
Wading is required to gain the best advantage from the Spey (but wade very carefully for the flow is fast and the bottom rocky).
Spey casting was developed to allow the fly to be cast without catching in high banks or trees behind the angler.
Sea trouting at dusk and into the dark is a must when they are fresh in from the sea.
Dry fly for brown trout can be exceptional in places.

Downstream of Loch Insch where the river's flow becomes sluggish as it passes through the impoundment, the Spey accelerates to a much faster pace, running over glides and long pools. The River Nethy and the River Dulnain both rattle down the Cairngorms into the Spey before the major tributary, the River Avon, joins the main stem of the river. From Grantown-on-Spey to Spey Bay on the North Sea coast, the river runs through a wonderful succession of famous fishing pools and beats which are etched in the minds of all salmon anglers, regardless of whether they regularly enjoy fishing the Spey or simply read or hear about it.

Many of the Spey pools have high banks and many are thickly wooded, this is the origin of the world-famous style of casting known as the Spey Cast, when the line is rolled from in front of the angler rather than conventionally back-cast, risking hooking in the trees or bank. Who has not heard of famous beats like Castle Grant, Knockando, Arndilly, Tulchan, or Ballindalloch? Who has not aspired to landing a Spey salmon or sea trout in wonderful scenery in the heart of Highland Scotland? One of the best features of the Spey is open access to superb association beats. This is not the preserve of the rich – you may fish Spey in excellent water for a fraction of the cost of more exclusive beats.

The snows of the Cairngorms, northerly

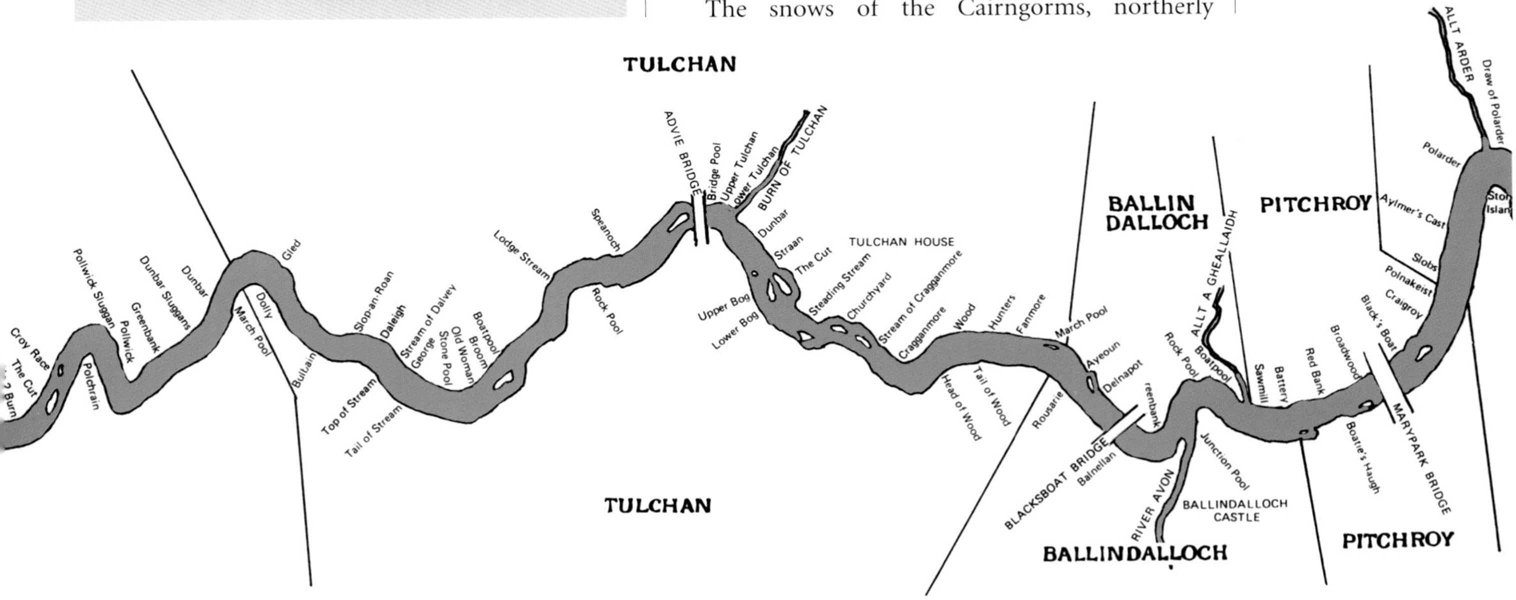

THE UPPER BEATS OF THE MIDDLE SPEY

Crystal clear water runs through pine-clad valleys in a succession of famous salmon beats.
Names that are synonymous with Spey heritage and angling sport familiar the world over: Castle Grant, Tulchan, Ballindalloch.

Right: Lower River Spey: On the Brae Water not far from Fochabers. These lower reaches tend to benefit from low water – holding the fish rather than encouraging them further upstream.

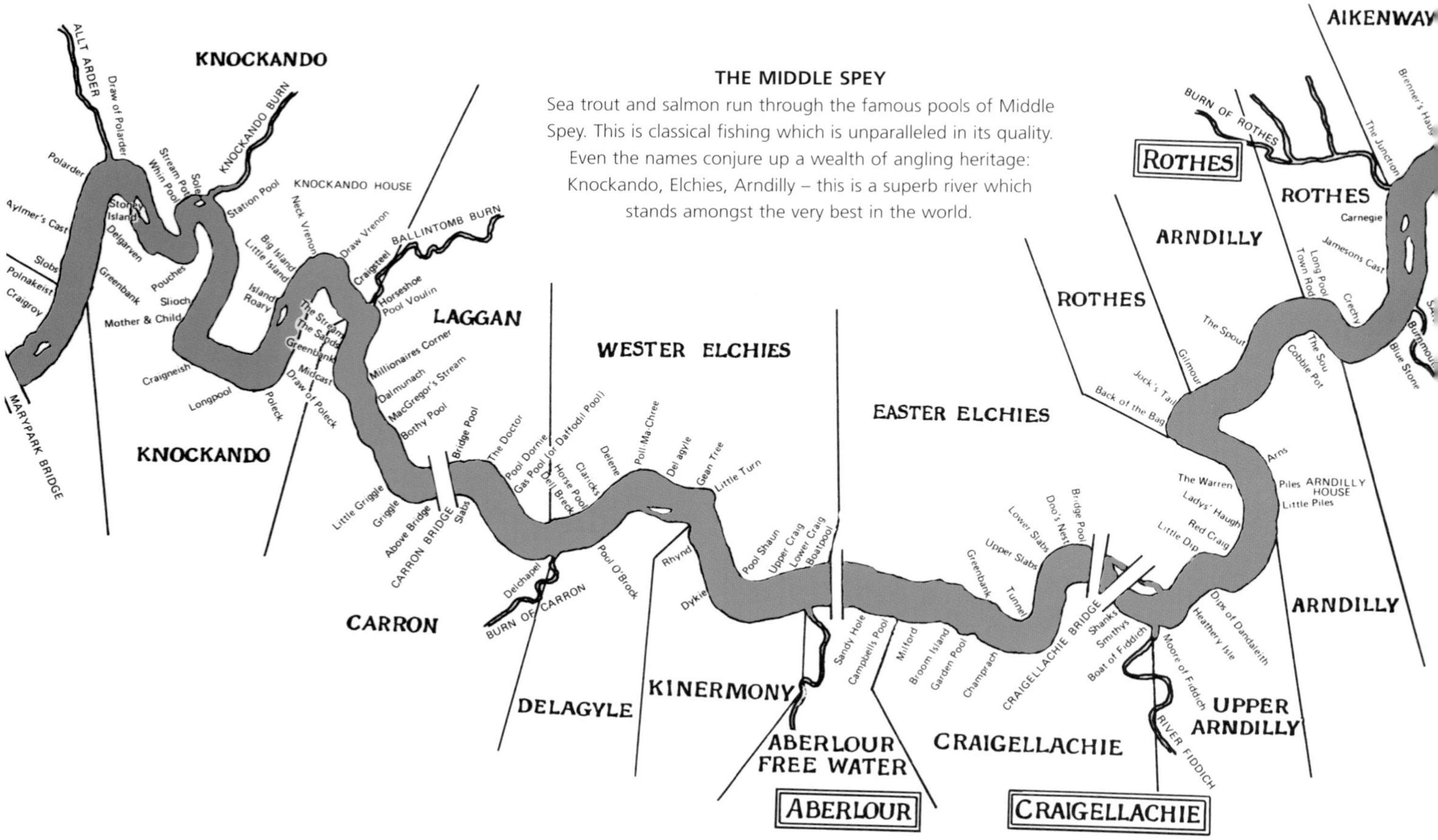

THE MIDDLE SPEY

Sea trout and salmon run through the famous pools of Middle Spey. This is classical fishing which is unparalleled in its quality. Even the names conjure up a wealth of angling heritage: Knockando, Elchies, Arndilly – this is a superb river which stands amongst the very best in the world.

Grampians and Monadhliaths melt slowly throughout spring and early summer providing a sustained flow of cool water to keep the river level buoyant and fresh. The tumbling River Avon carries a large proportion of the juvenile stock throughout its long course probably because there are no obstructions preventing fish from ascending to spawn. The whole river provides excellent nursery areas for young fry and parr. The Spey system is highly productive and utterly charming, attracting dedicated anglers from all over the world to its fast runs and holding pools. Spey salmon are not the largest in the world – averaging around 12 lbs, but they are wild and fresh. The sea trout fishing in the lower and middle river can be spectacular and is a huge attraction in its own right.

THE LOWER SPEY

The early-running salmon and summer-time sea trout pass through these lower beats at speeds depending on temperature and water height. If the weather is cool and dry – the lower beats provide fast and furious sport. If however there is plenty rain and it is mild, the fish tend to run faster and further.

SPEY BAY
Sea Pool
Market Pool
The Groyne
Bridgepool
NET WATER
CASTLE WATER
Braehead
The Pot
Cumberlands Ford
Essil
Horne's
The Willows
The Spout
Birks
The Quarry
NET WATER
Bulwark
Bridgepool
Dipple
Grilse
Intake
FOCHABERS BRIDGE
BURN OF FOCHABERS
CASTLE WATER
GORDON CASTLE
BRAE WATER
Lennox
Upper Auldearg
Otter's Cave
Lord March
Lower Auldearg
Cruive Dyke
FOCHABERS
Ewe
Rock Pool
Turn Pool
Twenty Pound
Island Stream
Island Point
ORTON HOUSE
ORTON
Lower Cairnty
Upper Cairnty
Couperee
New Pool
Wood Pool
BRAE WATER
DELFUR
Spurden
…addies
Island Stream
Willows
House Pool
The Collie
Broom
Otter Hole
DELFUR LODGE
BURN OF MULBEN
BOAT O' BRIG
Bridge Pool
Holly Bush
Burn Mouth
Two Stones
Beaufort
ORTON
DELFUR

Right:
The Middle River Spey close to Craigellachie. Broad runs and wonderful glides run into what seems to be a never-ending series of tremendous pools.

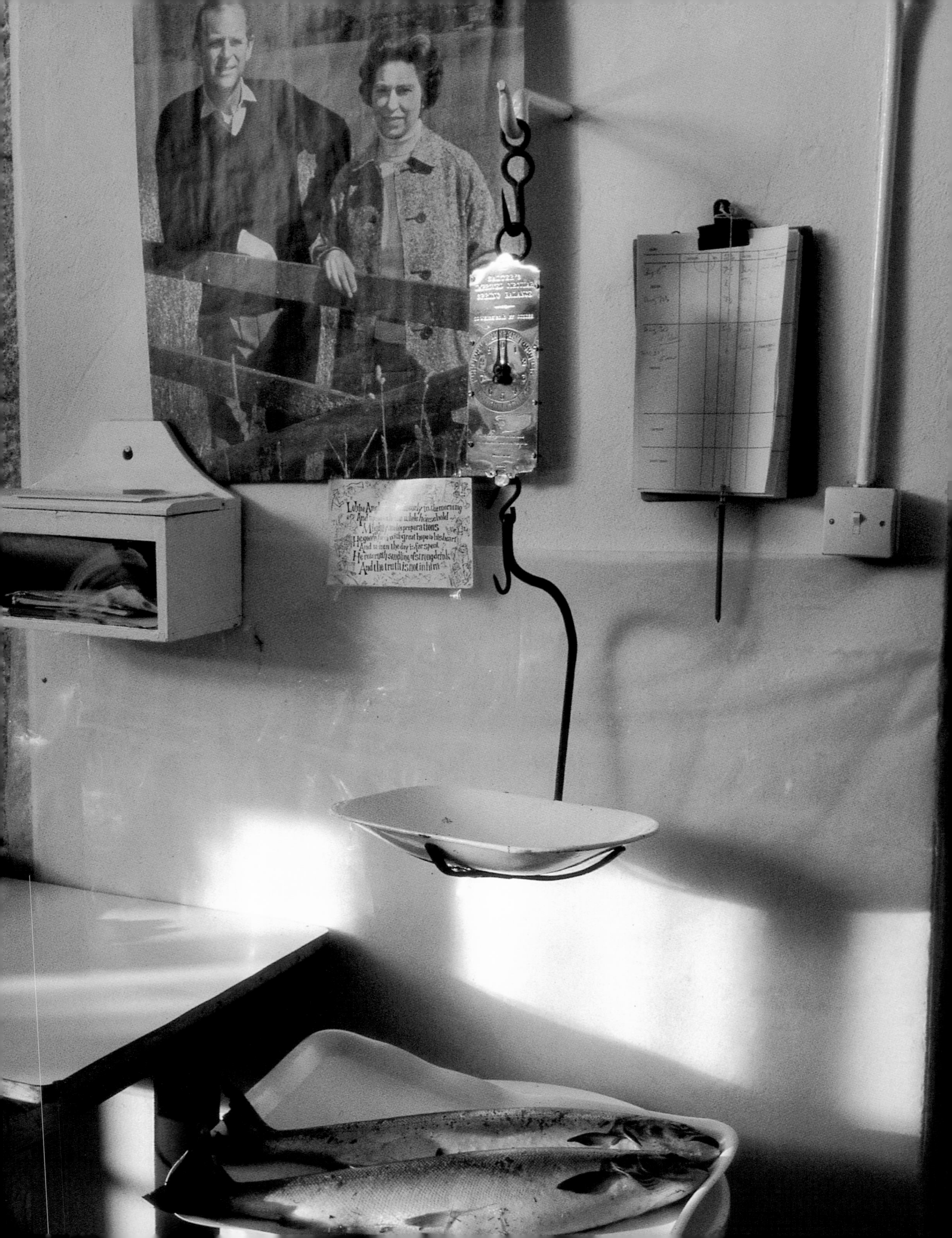
in the morning
preparations
with great hope in his heart
And when the day is far spent
He returneth smelling of strong drink
And the truth is not in him

THE NORTH AND THE NORTHERN ISLES

Opposite:
Fishing Lodge Interior, Loch More.

The 'black gold' drilled and drawn from deep within the earth's crust changed the far north a few decades ago. The region was once remote, neglected and ill-served with roads but now it is an easy, if long, drive from the south. Easier accessibility and wider appreciation of the area's natural beauty have benefited tourism but have brought pressure on wild fishing.

There are hundreds of fine trout lochs in the far north, salmon rivers of remote but productive glory and sea fishing of genuine excellence. Further north are the wonderful islands of Orkney and Shetland which are quite different in character from the mainland. You raise your eyes in Orkney and you cannot avoid seeing the influence of prehistory on the landscape.

Shetland is actually quite near to Norway and shows the effects of incursions by Vikings past and Scandinavians present. The islands bustle with voices from all over the world and their fishing is marvellous.

If you relish wild country and warm people when you go fishing, then the far North of Scotland is definitely the destination for you. You will find fishing far away from it all, under clear skies, with the soaring crescendo call of the curlew for company. At the waterside, the sandpiper warns you to stay clear of her nest, the grasses sway to the gentle pull of the breeze and there is a taint of the sea amidst the land perfumes which surround you. In the height of summer, the skies do not darken, they hold on to the 'simmer dim' of light and day without end. This surely is a magical place.

Lochs of the North and the Northern Isles

Loch Caladail, Cape Wrath, Durness: One of the best limestone-based lochs in Scotland. The water is clear, so fine tackle and great care are required to tempt the fish, but be careful, there are really heavy trout in this rich environment.

The lochs of the far north vary widely: some lie in the catchment of major salmon and sea trout rivers, these include Loch Loyal, Loch Naver, Loch More and Loch Stack, while some sit on top of limestone strata which increases their pH and productivity, including the Durness lochs Croispol, Borralie and Caladail. Others like the Caithness lochs of Watten, Calder and St Johns are famous and attract visitors from all over the country. The remainder may not have such a wide reputation or special geological attributes, but for those who know their whereabouts, they quietly

LOCHS BORRALIE, CROISPOL AND CALADAIL (DURNESS LIMESTONE LOCHS)

Location Details
Durness, Cape Wrath, Sutherland.

Type of Fishery
Brown trout lochs of high pH (due to limestone sub-strata), boat and bank fishing strictly fly-only.

Description
Lovely lochs in natural settings. Ultra-clear water and simply superb brownies – full and fit, and coloured the way brownies should be – silver under-flanks, butter yellow sides, burnished golden-backed with jet-black, and huge vermillion-red speckles – fin perfect and tremendous sporting quarry.

Species
Perfect brown trout and a few fine charr.

Season Details
March 15th to 6th October.

Permit Contact(s)
Cape Wrath Hotel, Durness Sutherland.
Tel 01971 511212.

Favourite Flies & Baits
Dry flies work but you must fish fine and far-off in such gin-clear water. De-grease your leader and use small flies. Emerger patterns and nymphs also work well, as do conventional wet-fly patterns. Try 'Daddies' in high summer, Greenwell's and Hare's Lug dries, Silver Invicta and Wickhams's Fancy. Don't be reticent to try new ideas – for instance, Cul-de Canard dry flies work a treat.

How to Fish
You must keep in mind that the water is exceptionally clear so your smallest tactical indiscretion will be noticed by the fish. They are catchable, but you have to be good, or lucky or both.

Loch Borralie, Cape Wrath, Durness: A loch where fish may appear anywhere at any time from its gin-clear depths. The average weight of fish is far higher than other Highland lochs, due to the enriching limestone that forms most of the bed of the loch.

LOCH WATTEN

Location Details
Watten village near Thurso, Caithness.

Type of Fishery
Fly-only mostly from boats. Brown trout fishery.

Description
A three-mile by half mile shallow loch set in low hills. Often windy. Trout are surface active, and in good density and size (due to alkalinity of water).

Species
Brown trout.

Season Details
March 15th to 6th October.

Permit Contact(s)
The Loch Watten Hotel Watten, Caithness.
Tel 01955 621232.
John Swanson, Aspen Banks, Bank Road, Watten.
Tel 01955 621326.

Favourite Flies & Baits
Bushy bob-flies of 10-14 depending on wind strength/brightness. Try Olive Bumble, Claret Bumble, Loch Ordie, Zulu, Ke-he and Clan Chief. Otherwise, Greenwells and Light Olives when hatching ephemerids are about – Silver Invicta and Wickham's Fancy are also productive.

How to Fish
Try to keep to the right depth contour on just where you can make out the stones on the bottom (around 4-6 feet). Alternatively, in a brisk wind try along the foamy wind-lanes. These often hold fish much further out in the middle of the Loch.

and simply provide the finest wild trout fishing in the region.

The Cape Wrath peninsula in the far north west is a microcosm of differently proportioned lochs, some dark, peaty and a bit daunting, others so crystal clear that you can see twenty to thirty feet down into their depths and would swear that no fish lived there – but of course they do, it is just that they see you long before you see them. The limestone lochs near Durness produce some stunning fish, richly speckled and large, but they are not easy to fool in such clear conditions. They best time is when a decent mild breeze scuds the racing clouds onto the nearby mountains and the water looks correspondingly dark. A bushy fly bounced around in the waves may bring a shining torpedo from the depths, but be warned, these fish do not take kindly to being hooked and they will struggle to stay in that wonderful clear water. You can arrange days on Caladail, Croispol and Borralie via the Cape Wrath Hotel. The hotel has several other non-limestone lochs which are well worth enquiring about.

At the eastern shoulder of Caithness lie Loch Watten, Loch St Johns and Loch Calder plus a bunch of less well-known stillwaters which are all worth a visit. Watten is perhaps the most famous

Loch Hope, Sutherland: A grand sea trout loch whose outflow is northerly through the lovely sea loch, Loch Eriboll. Fish with confidence along the shores especially around the promontories and shallower drop-offs.

Above: Loch Stack, Sutherland.
You can't help feeling excited when you push the boat out on one of these wonderful remote lochs.

and provides some fine top-of-the-water sport. It may suffer from over-fishing, although the stock density is still high. Loch Calder nearby is a big deep loch and has a huge head of small brownies, while Loch St John's is a productive trout loch. The remote lochs around Forsinard and the top end of Strath Halladale are a particular pleasure to visit and attract many visitors each year. Typical of the type of waters in the area, Lochs Badanloch and nan Clar are joined to Loch Rimsdale – a delightful

Right:
Loch Stack, Sutherland.
For remoteness and that elusive feeling of getting away from it all, Loch Stack takes some beating. The air is perfumed by bog myrtle, juniper and heather, the waves slap on the clinker planks of the boat, and your reel protests loudly as yet another fish shows you the backing line.

tangle of wild fishing using traditional tactics and tackle.

All the lochs in the region are unspoilt and lovely, sharing a mystical combination of wild terrain, wide horizons and attractive water. The whole area offers fishing which is unsurpassed and although too few anglers may be aware of the delights of these lochs, this is not neccessarily a bad thing, for if too many made the journey into their remoteness, the lochs would undoubtedly suffer.

Above:
Loch Naver, near Altnaharra, Sutherland. Home of visiting salmon, sea trout and native brown trout, Loch Naver is a lovely place to fish. The wind can make boat fishing difficult and the bank is a good fall-back when conditions get too rough.

Left: Loch Loyal. Sandwiched between Ben Loyal (764m) to the west and Beinn Stumanadh (527m) to the east, Loch Loyal sits in splendid isolation. Fish as close as you can cast to the shore and draw your flies outwards into the deeper water and look forward to a day of wild brown trout fishing the likes of which you can only dream of.

Orkney and Shetland

Loch of Harray, Ring of Brodgar, Mainland, Orkney.
A better fishing loch can scarcely be designed – rocky skerries abound, weeded bays provide shelter and rich feeding for butter-yellow brownies which fight with every ounce that they possess.

Hoy, Mainland, South Ronaldsay, Shapinsay, North Ronaldsay, Rousay, Stronsay, Eday, Sanday and Westray – a necklace of green isles set within a blue sea. These are the Islands of Orkney, an archipelago separated from the main part of Scotland by the Pentland Firth and site of some of the finest fishing in the country. Here are super lochs with fine brown trout plus sea fishing which would be hard to beat anywhere. Further north still is Shetland, Unst, Bressay, Yell, Fetlar, Whalsay and Mainland Shetland – another group of angling gems set in the shimmering Atlantic.

Orkney and Shetland do not have rivers, as there is insufficient catchment area to produce streams of any size, but they do have freshwater lochs and these have small burns which feed them, some draining into the sea allowing the passage of sea trout into the lochs. The finest feature of these lochs, however, is the brown trout fishing notable for its remarkable and consistent quality.

Shetland has a fair number of small lochs spread over its individual islands, the most notable on Mainland being the Loch of Tingwall. Many of Shetland's waters have limestone strata running beneath them and are consequently rich. Tingwall is no exception. The other 'must-fish' loch is the the Loch of Spiggie situated near Sumburgh to the south of Mainland. This is a relatively large, shallow pan of a loch which is best fished from the bank, although you will have to wade out many yards from the side until you reach deeper water.

Orkney has some of the best stillwater brown trout fishing in Scotland with famous lochs like Harray, Boardhouse, Stenness and Swannay. The Orkney Trout Fishing Association (OTFA) manages the fishings in most lochs and access is straightforward and inexpensive. Take advantage of a local boatman if at all possible for the location of the many rocky skerries is better established before you run the outboard onto them.

Fishing is top-of-the-water sport and is likely to be a splashy affair in the stiff breeze and rolling waves. The trout cream out of the sides of the waves to attack your bushy Ke-he, a highly-effective Orcadian bob-fly pattern. Orcadian fly dressers have developed a superb range of patterns which prove to be useful wherever they are wetted.

Fishing in the sea around the scatter of islands is a joy. This may be done from the shore where locals catch sea trout on fly amongst the tangle of seaweed in the voes, or from boats under towering rocky cliffs where superb skate, halibut and cod willingly take the bait.

LOCH OF HARRAY

Location Details
Mainland, Orkney not far from Stromness.

Type of Fishery
Brown trout fishery of considerable renown.

Description
A shallow loch with many skerries on which trout love to gather and feed.

Species
Brown trout – often silvery-lemon coloured.

Season Details
March 15th to October 6th.

Permit Contact(s)
Merkister Hotel, Harray, Orkney. Tel 01856 771366.
Orkney Trout Fishing Association (OTFA) per W Sinclair, 27 John Street, Stromness. Tel 01856 850469.

Favourite Flies & Baits
There is a culture of fly-design in Orkney by very-able trout anglers. Their patterns have become standards for the rest of the UK: White-Hackled Invicta, Sedgehog, Blue Loch Ordie, and the Ke-he (the black and the brown versions). Muddlers will rattle them too. Silver flies also attract.

How to Fish
Fish on, and around, the skerries, hug the contours of the shores at the correct depth (the trick is to find what depth the fish are lying at). There will be action, especially if the wind is warm, there's always wind in Orkney.

Rivers of the North and the Northern Isles

River Laxford, Sutherland: One of the loveliest rivers in the north, the River Laxford has seen better times as far as its sea trout stocks are concerned, although summer salmon still present great sport. Access is not too readily available for the River Laxford, so if you receive an invitation from someone with fishing there, don't turn it down.

The quality of its fishing make Caithness and Sutherland a charming part of the world for anglers regardless of any prevailing weather. The region has excellent salmon rivers, trout lochs and sea fishing from boat and shore.

Venturing southwards from the very north west tip of the mainland at Cape Wrath there are several spate streams, each with small insertions of summer sea trout and salmon, but the jewel in the crown in the area is the lovely River Laxford. A spate river, the Laxford benefits from the flow from the two lochs in its catchment, Loch More and Loch Stack. Famed as one of the most productive sea trout rivers before the reduction of their numbers, the Laxford still fishes well for summer salmon and sea trout. It runs in spectacular country below the towering Ben Stack and nearby Arkle, with Foinaven beyond. Loch Stack was once a Mecca for sea trout anglers, although its eminence has faded somewhat in recent years. It is hoped that the fortunes of sea trout will recover to their former glories. You may not catch as many sea trout as you once might have but this river system is still truly exceptional.

Rhiconnich sits in a grand area for game angling and for shore and boat fishing in the sea lochs, and beyond. For an area so far to the north of the British Isles the average temperature and weather is surprisingly good. Often, when the rest of the country is cold and wet, this little corner basks in fine weather, although the reverse is sometimes the case, so pack your sun oil and your wellies.

If you travel along the north coast from the furthest west headland at Cape Wrath to the furthest east point at John o' Groats, you will pass rivers as scenic and productive as any in Scotland. The River Dionard runs northwards through wild mountainous country to meet the sea in Balnakeil Bay at the seaward end of the Kyle of Durness. This

Above: River Halladale. A wild river at Forsinard, Sutherland, which needs the freshness of extra water to gain the best fishing. Small flies worked through the runs and into the deeper glides will produce responses from salmon and sea trout when they are fresh.

river has good runs of salmon throughout the year, and sea trout venture in from mid summer onwards, although recently they seem to have spread their ascent, running both earlier and later into the season. Loch Dionard holds fish, especially when the river level drops, and is an excellent fishery in its own right.

The River Hope system comprises of the main stem of the river and Loch Hope, plus their mountainside tributaries, and runs into the lower part of Loch Eriboll. Salmon run this system mostly in summer with a few fish making an earlier start. In common with most north and north west

THE RIVER DIONARD

Location Details
Near Durness on the road to Laxford Bridge in Sutherland.

Type of Fishery
Migratory fish river.

Description
Set in superb wilderness scenery under the dramatic peak of Foinaven, this productive small river is a true gem. Loch Dionard, within the river's course, fishes well from bank and boat for salmon and sea trout too.

Species
Salmon and sea trout.

Season Details
February 11th to the end of October.

Permit Contact(s)
Estate Office, Gualin, by Durness, Sutherland.
Tel 01971 521282.

Favourite Flies & Baits
Salmon accept small flies of shrimp pattern – (Ally's Shrimp, Oykel General Practitioner etc) and small tube versions of Willie Gunn, Garry Dog, and Munro Killer. Sea trout readily attack Stoat's Tail (particularly the 'jungle silver' tying) and Teal, Blue & Silver and a Peter Ross is worth a wetting.

How to Fish
The Dionard is not a large river so you should be able to 'read' where the lies are likely to be. Work over these making your fly dance in enticement over the silver beauties. Shore fish the loch, especially at the 'narrows'. There is almost always a fish or two waiting there.

Right: River Dionard, North West Sutherland: Remote and attractive, the River Dionard sits below the magnificent peak of Foinaven (915m). Salmon and grilse run in as soon as water levels allow; summer sea trout provide great sport too.

LOCH NAVER AND THE RIVER NAVER

Location Details
By the Bettyhill to Altnaharra road in North Sutherland.

Type of Fishery
The Loch and River hold salmon and sea trout plus good brown trout stocks.

Description
Unspoilt country surrounds these waters, and in them are wild, strong fish. This is land of strong character – rocky and steep – so the river cascades and foams through a tough and torturous course with deep dark pools interspersed with many small falls.

Species
Salmon, sea trout and brown trout.

Season Details
Salmon season: 12th January to 30th September, statutory brown trout season.

Permit Contact(s)
The river is not all open fishing but the odd day may be arranged through The Store at Bettyhill, Strathnaver. Tel 01641 521207.
CKD Finlayson Hughes, Barossa Place, Perth.
Tel 01738 639017.
Altnaharra Hotel, Lairg, Sutherland.
Tel 01549 411222 for loch and river.

Favourite Flies & Baits
Garry Dog, Munro Killer and Willie Gunn (gold version) on small tubes take salmon as does Ally's Shrimp and the Oykel GP.
Sea trout accept Dark Mackerel, Teal, Blue & Silver and Stoat's Tail on tubes or double hooks.

How to Fish
On the loch you will need the services of a ghillie to find the fish. Take your time, up here there is plenty of time to enjoy the take and run of the fish.

Above:
River Shin, Sutherland.
The Shin rises on the west side of Scotland and runs eastwards to flow into the Kyle of Sutherland and thereby into the North Sea. The river falls through wild and wonderful country.

rivers, modern runs of sea trout have reduced but are starting to show positive signs of returning. Loch Hope is a superb loch to fish for salmon and sea trout. A decent breeze to lift the waves, plus a trusty boatman and a selection of favourite bushy flies, and a day afloat on Loch Hope promises great fun.

The River Borgie is a pretty little salmon stream running between Beinn Stumanadh and Ben Loyal. This is another of the several northern rivers which run in and out of a loch within its system, and Loch Loyal is a particularly attractive loch which offers fine fishing. The River Naver also has the advantage of draining a loch in its catchment – and a large loch too – for Loch Naver is six miles long. The Naver is amongst the very best of the northerly

Left:
River Naver,
Bettyhill, Sutherland.
Bonnie and blithe, the Naver runs from Loch Naver to the sands of the bay at Bettyhill. The estuarial pools are amongst the best and most accessible, but salmon and sea trout ascend the river in numbers, when good water conditions prevail.

River Hope at Loch Eriboll, North Sutherland: Some large sea trout, an excellent chance of a summer salmon, and wild brown trout. How can you fish when there is so much to charm your eyes?

salmon and sea trout rivers and has a succession of superb pools below the Loch to the sea pools near Bettyhill. Access is best achieved through local hotels, the angling club water is an excellent prospect.

Further east, the Halladale River suffers only a little from not having a loch in its track to sustain its level but benefits from attracting early spring fish if the water level is right. It really is a spate river requiring increased flow to bring in the runs. The Halladale may not convey a great impression on you when you first see it, running through bleak boggy ground at its top end near Forsinard and rather slowly in some of its lower reaches, but it does have some good pools and glides.

Possibly the most actively managed river system in the far north is the River Thurso, which river is kept at reasonable fishing levels by releasing water from Loch More. The river drains many small lochs, and natural flows are generally good with fish

LOCH HOPE AND THE RIVER HOPE

Location Details
Altnaharra, Sutherland.

Type of Fishery
The Hope system favours migratory fish, and whilst salmon are present in numbers from early each year, and grilse turn up in early summer, it is the sea trout that constitute the prime element of this superb fishery.

Description
A large sheet of water, over six miles long by around one mile across, Loch Hope sits in its mountain setting like a glistening jewel. The River Hope runs its one mile-plus course to the sea through a series of productive pools, but is mainly reserved for private use.

Species
Salmon and wild brown trout, with runs of sea trout.

Season Details
An early start to the salmon season on 12th January to the end of September, statutory brown trout season.

Permit Contact(s)
Altnaharra Hotel, Lairg, Sutherland. Tel 01847 601272.

Favourite Flies & Baits
Conventional salmon patterns in small sizes may be fished with success from the boat. For example: Willie Gunn, Green Highlander and Hairy Mary, but bushy flies more-often targeted at trout work well: Loch Ordie, Bumbles Ke-he and Zulus.

How to Fish
Ghillies will keep you to favoured drifts, mostly along shore-sides. There is no fishing from the shore anyway, so close-in tactics from the boat are generally successful. Give the fish time to turn with your fly after you see the rise on the surface.

RIVER HELMSDALE

Location Details

Flowing eastwards into the North Sea this Sutherland river is one of the best known and sought-after in Scotland. It enters the sea at Helmsdale village. The road to Kinbrace follows the river's strath.

Type of Fishery

Quite exclusive fishery for much of its water although the Association beat is accessible to visitors.

Description

A salmon and sea trout river descending through a typical east coast strath with falls and pools, runs and pots – a gem of a river.

Species

Salmon and sea trout. There are small river brownies, of course, but it is the Helmsdale's migratory fish that hold attention.

Season Details

Early opening on 11th January – salmon season closes on 30th September.

Permit Contact(s)

Strathullie Craft Shop, Dunrobin Street, Helmsdale. Tel 01431 821343.
Brian Lyall, Badanloch Fishings, Kinbrace. Tel 01431 831232.

Favourite Flies & Baits

Oykel General Practitioner (it also works on the Helmsdale), Tube and 'Brora' flies dressed as Willie Gunn and Green Highlander also take fish, as does Ally's Shrimp and Silver Stoat's Tail. Keep in mind that treble hooks are disallowed from May 1st.

How to Fish

Helmsdale is a fairly small river so wading is not often needed (it is rough anyway so it is best to keep out of the water unless absolutely necessary to cover a lie). Being of intimate size it is possible to 'read' where the lies are likely to be, and to cover them effectively. Fish your fly as slowly as possible, even dangling it enticingly, until the big silver takes it. Floating lines only, during summer (local restriction).

Above: River Helmsdale, near Kinbrace.
The epitome of Highland river salmon fishing – open in places and running through landscapes as wide as the sky.

entering the system progressively throughout the season. The netting does not commence until June so the chances of an early fish are as high as they could be. Good annual runs are maintained by restocking the river with juvenile salmon grown on in the hatcheries – a tribute to hard work and sound management practice.

The northern rivers which flow east into the North Sea include some of the finest in Scotland. Entering the sea at the town of Wick, the Wick River drains out of Loch Watten, a fine brown trout loch, before running eastwards to meet the salt water of the estuary. Not considered one of the classic northern rivers it still provides good salmon fishing and sea trout runs when conditions favour. Perhaps more favoured for spring fish, the nearby Berriedale River carries a good stock of relatively small salmon. The lower river runs in a strath incised into the eastern Caithness hills and is joined near its mouth by the smaller Langwell Water. The best times to visit the Berriedale/Langwell are during the summer months when freshets raise the levels and encourage fish to ascend.

Perhaps the epitome of Highland river salmon fishing, especially in the spring when the river has bucked the trend of decreasing spring runs, is the River Helmsdale. Bolstered in flow by several lochs, the river

Left: River Helmsdale, Strath of Kildonan.
Quintessential small-river fishing for salmon. Run your flies through the dark pools, and the foaming cascades with real expectation – and wonder at the vigour of the fish when the line tightens.

River Thurso, Caithness: One of the most prolific salmon rivers for its size in Europe. Well managed and cared for, the Thurso drains a wild tract of Caithness moors and small lochs. It runs over characteristically flat rock formations in a delightful series of fine pools and glides.

runs through Kinbrace and the Strath of Kildonan. The River Helmsdale passes through rocky gorges, deep pots, streamy pools and lovely runs, over cascades and turbulent sections interspaced with foam-flecked glides. A highly attractive river, the Helmsdale and is also highly productive when good conditions prevail.

The River Brora is another example of a stunning northern river, excellent stocks of salmon and grilse with a fair head of sea trout. Not only does the Brora offer first class spring fishing, but the autumn runs seem to come later and the season reflects this by staying open until mid October. Most anglers fish the Brora with larger-than-usual tube flies, Waddingtons or the specially designed 'Brora' flies, because the water is often heavy with

RIVER THURSO

Location Details

Entering the sea at the county town of Thurso, the River Thurso flows north from its source amongst the peat in central Caithness.

Type of Fishery

A small river but one of the most productive for salmon in the north.

Description

The upper river runs through peaty heathland then descends through a series of gliding pools inter-spaced by rockier sections. This is a typically northern river, interesting to fish with deep pots and fine streams where you imagine fish to be lying.

Species

Salmon mainly, with a few sea trout and brownies.

Season Details

January 11th to 5th October.

Permit Contact(s)

Estate Office, (River Thurso Fisheries), Thurso, Caithness. Tel 01847 893134.

Favourite Flies & Baits

Small tube flies – General Practitioner, Hairy Mary, Golden Willie Gunn and Ally's Shrimp. A Stoat's Tail is a good fall-back.

How to Fish

The river has wide open banks for most of its course and wading is not often needed as the river is not wide, so keep back from the edge and work your fly over the likely lies. Making the fly skate over streamier water sometimes draws a fast response.

RIVER BRORA

Location Details
East Sutherland river flowing to the North Sea through a fine strath.

Type of Fishery
One of the finest smaller Scottish salmon and sea trout rivers.

Description
Rocky river in most parts, descending through superb pools and runs. Classic salmon fly-fishing, and very productive.

Species
Salmon (in prodigious numbers) and good sea trout.

Season Details
1st Feb to end of September.

Permit Contact(s)
CKD Finlayson Hughes, Barossa Place, Perth. Tel 01738 625134.
The Estate Office, Sutherland Estates, Duke Street, Golspie, Sutherland. Tel 01408 633268.

Favourite Flies & Baits
Willie Gunn – it was originally dressed for use on the Brora. Brora style Waddington flies dressed as Black & Orange, and Black & Yellow, Ally's Shrimp or a GP.

How to Fish
The Brora is not a big river but it is fast-flowing and rocky. You need wade only a little to improve the angle of attack but it is best to keep clear of the water. Floating lines or slow-sinkers are all that is required. Being a small enough river to work out where the fish should be definitely helps, but look out for those fish that do not conform to our perceived wisdom. There's plenty of salmon which have not read the right books.

snow-melt or summer rain; this does not hinder the fishing as the river fishes best in high water. Small tubes are best in low conditions, sometimes even skating them across the 'white water' on streamy runs to elicit a bite.

Another group of rivers which have justifiably good reputations for salmon and sea trout all come together in the long inlet called the Kyle of Sutherland which in turn runs into the Dornoch Firth. Many people drive up the A9 road over the bridge just north of Tain and miss the shore-hugging trip around the Kyle through Bonar Bridge – but this denies you the feeling of close proximity to some of the best small rivers in the area. Anglers should take time to absorb the atmosphere and gauge the prospects of the Rivers Cassley, Carron, Oykel, Einig, Evelix and Shin, six of the best.

The Oykel and the Cassley come cross-country to their eastern outflow, for they rise on the west side of the country and gather precipitation from this wetter catchment. For this reason, it may be totally rainless when you are fishing the Oykel or Cassley, but the rivers may still show rising levels. This is true of several rivers in Scotland – even the mighty Tay – which also rises in the west but flows far across the land to its eastern outflow. The Oykel carries wonderful runs of salmon and sea trout and has lovely clear pools interspersed with turbulent headstreams and small falls. The geology of the river's course is fascinating with gorges slicing through metamorphic rock strata which are tilted at bizarre inclines, jagged and wild.

The rivers Carron and Einig are characterised by many waterfalls as they crash down from the high

Above: River Thurso, Caithness.
Curlews call out in their wonderful watery crescendo overhead, and waterside sandpipers join with the dippers to let you know you have entered their domain.

Below: River Brora, Sutherland.
Wild banks, untamed country, deep pools, frothy cascades, and leaping salmon and sea trout all feature on the Brora.

Above: River Cassley, East Sutherland: There is always a fish lying beneath foam in Scottish rivers.

Below: River Oykel, Bonar Bridge, East Sutherland: Running into the Kyle of Sutherland, the River Oykel has a prodigious reputation.

Opposite: River Carron, Bonar Bridge, East Sutherland.

ground into the Kyle of Sutherland. Fortunately, none of these are lasting obstacles to the passage of salmon at normal levels, and fish may be taken throughout much of the rivers' length in wild Highland surroundings. The nearby River Shin is another attractive river which is affected by a major hydro-electric generation scheme on Loch Shin. Some hold the view that control of water flow creates better management and improved runs, while others believe that the river would be better off without any man-made dams and interference. Regardless, the Shin does attract excellent runs of salmon, although sea trout are less plentiful.

RIVER OYKEL

Location Details
East Sutherland – flowing into the North Sea through the broad expanse of the Kyle of Sutherland.

Type of Fishery
Salmon and sea trout river. One of the best in the country (exclusive).

Description
Classic Scottish salmon river, rattling through sections of rocky gorge, tumbling and splashing over ancient rocks, stunningly gorgeous in bright conditions, only magnificent when the weather is at its worst.

Species
Salmon (grilse in summer) and sea trout (in excellent numbers).

Season Details
An early start on the 11th January, closes at end of September.

Permit Contact(s)
The Inver Lodge Hotel in Lochinver.
Tel 01571 844496.
Oykel Bridge Hotel, Lairg, Sutherland.
Tel 01549 441218.
But don't hold your breath – the Oykel is not easy to book, it is a case of 'dead man's shoes'.

Favourite Flies & Baits
The variant of the General Practitioner – the Oykel GP – is renowned. Green Highlander, Yellow Torrish, Hairy Mary, Willie Gunn (golden version particularly). Stoat's Tail and Teal, Blue & Silver for the sea trout.

How to Fish
Small river tactics: stay out of the water if possible, and cast over the likely lies. Night fishing for sea trout can be very rewarding.

THE NORTH WEST, SKYE & THE WESTERN ISLES

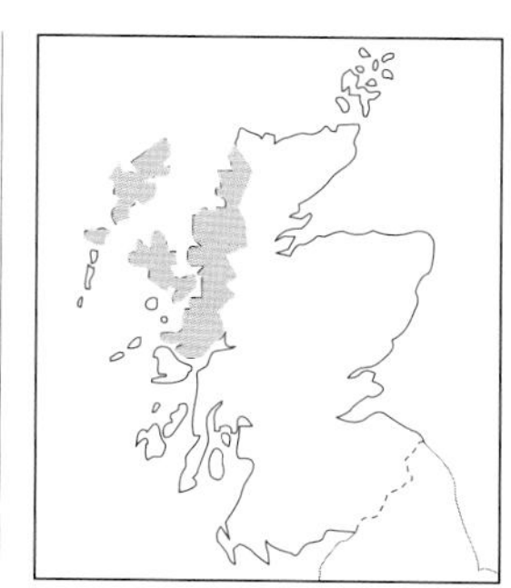

If it is remoteness and a sense of grand scale that you crave, look no further than the north west of Scotland. This is open country with wide vistas. Countless lochs sweeten the colourful views, deep sea lochs incise ancient rocks and high mountains rise from landscapes.

Offshore are countless islands, some large enough to have lochs and small river systems, others not much more than a jumble of rocks. Those islands that do have freshwater resources have some of the finest game fishing anywhere in the world.

The fishing is varied – deep lochs vie with tiny pools for the reputation of offering the best fishing. The machair lochs with their sea shell lime richness are vastly different from the dark peaty pools just a few hundred metres inland, and so are their trout. The large freshwater lochs draw salmon and sea trout into them and offer an excellent chance of catching these fish on fly. This is country closely knit with the ever-changing patterns of weather, and in this respect, the fishing holds no exception. Rivers fill with rain and in come the runs of silver salmon and sea trout, but only when spate augments their flow.

The names of the main areas are magical and wonderfully mysterious - the peninsulas of Kintail and Knoydart, the Outer Hebrides, Wester Ross and Assynt. Whether it is a small silver salmon, only minutes off the salty tide, or a yellow, vermilion-speckled brownie that you aspire to catch, then this is where to look for them.

River Kirkaig, Wester Ross:
A jumble of ancient rocks, wild vegetation and water cascading noisily in sparkling sunlight make the Kirkaig one of the most attractive rivers in west Scotland. Add in the magnificent backdrop of Suilven (731m) and decent runs of summer salmon – and the Kirkaig takes on a further glorious dimension.

Loch Scourst, Isle of Harris: If you long for deserted lochs and wilderness fishing, then the outer Hebrides have a charm entirely of their own. Escape is the order of the day – breathe in the cool, clean air and catch fine fish.

Lochs & Rivers of the North West

The north west of Scotland is a wild tract of land consisting of igneous rocks, intruded into by lavas and basalts, and bounded by metamorphic rocks of ancient and more-modern deposition. This complex milieu of geological substrate has been ground down by huge ice sheets, etched deeply by the ocean's breakers and eroded through aeons of above-average precipitation. Little wonder that there are hills and mountains crust-folded into groups, or standing like monuments to their prehistoric volcanic nativity. And little wonder that there are peat bogs standing full of water, alongside pools and lochs of all sizes, the larger of which have burns running into them, and rivers flowing from them. This is a region of rock, peat, water and most of all fish.

There are countless lochs in the area. Most have wild brown trout of all sizes and those connected to the sea have runs of sea trout and a few salmon. Some of these lochs sit on seams of limestone and are clear and rich, the trout growing prodigiously in the alkaline waters. Others are acidic and much poorer – the trick is knowing which is which – not easy without local guidance!

The stupendous number of lochs southwards from Scourie, through Kylestrome, towards Lochinver and Assynt are renowned for their accessibility and utter charm. If you climb Quinag you are in the epicentre of an aquatic landscape peppered by lochs of every size and shape. Many a fine summer fishing holiday has been enjoyed by families in this area, tramping over the heather to loch after loch – some providing few big fish, and some yielding dozens of tiddlers. This has always been a fishing area with local hotels and guest houses catering for visiting anglers. You'll find information about access readily available from hotels and tourist offices.

River Inver, at Lochinver: The River Inver flows around five miles from mighty Loch Assynt to the sea pools at Lochinver. The sea pools hold salmon and sea trout amongst the sea weed, as the fish wait for fresh water to run upstream into the wild country of Assynt.

Assynt

Loch Assynt, Wester Ross: Remnants of the ancient Caledonian Pine Forest still cling to the islands. This is wild country and wild fishing. A place to enjoy tranquil isolation and fine fish.

There can be few parts of Scotland as wild or beautiful as Assynt where boundless moors are punctuated by literally thousands of crystal-clear lochs. For the angler there is something new at every turn – from the large lochs like Loch Assynt itself to the countless small un-named lochans, some no bigger than puddles. Every cleft in the ancient hills has a stream of some kind. There are sparkling burns and fascinating spate rivers, with brown trout, sea trout and summer salmon. Some of the lochs also gain from the penetration of migratory salmonids where rain-swollen rivers and burns offer passage from the sea.

There are exquisite gems of lochs – like the

LOCH ASSYNT

Location Details
The road to Lochinver in Sutherland runs along the shore of wild Loch Assynt under mighty Ben More Assynt and sultry Quinaig.

Type of Fishery
A natural loch of raw beauty – sometimes ravaged by wind, sometimes sizzling in sun-baked calm. Deep in places, the loch is around six miles long with bays and promontories to fish around.

Description
A bank and boat fishery for wild game species – boat fishing is probably the best option as you can gain access more easily.

Species
Salmon, wild brown trout and ferox trout.

Season Details
Salmon: 11th February to 15th October, statutory brown trout season.

Permit Contact(s)
The Inchnadamph Hotel, Assynt, Sutherland.
Tel 01571 822202.

Favourite Flies & Baits
Bushy flies in more robust overcast conditions (size 10, or even 8). Palmered patterns work well – Bumbles, Soldier Palmer, Clan Chief. Bright flies work too: Dunkeld, Wickham's Fancy, and Butchers.
For salmon: Blue Charm, Ally's Shrimp and Hairy Mary.

How to Fish
As for most West Highland lochs, the best fishing is in the shallow bays and around the promontories. Cast right into the side 'at the foot of the wind' as this is where food gathers. Fish exploit this fact.
Fishing is mainly with a floating or an intermediate line.

THE RIVER KIRKAIG AND THE FIONN LOCH

Location Details
A few miles around the headland from Lochinver, Sutherland the river flows into the sea at Inverkirkaig. The Fionn Loch sits at the head of the short river – about three miles of uphill panting from Inverkirkaig.

Type of Fishery
Salmon river with a few sea trout, and a very fine brown trout loch.

Description
The River tumbles down a very rocky and precipitous series of cascades, deep pots and fast runs. The Fionn Loch shines in stunning splendour under Cul Mor and Suilven. Tremendously picturesque and very productive.

Species
River – summer salmon (they are unable to surmount the falls in the upper river and do not enter the Loch).
Loch: fine wild brown trout and Arctic charr.

Season Details
Salmon: 11th February to 15th October.
Trout: 15 March to 6th October.

Permit Contact(s)
Inver Lodge Hotel, Lochinver, Sutherland.
Tel 01571 844496.

Favourite Flies & Baits
Salmon: Willie Gunn (especially the golden version), Blue Charm, Hairy Mary and shrimp patterns.
Trout: Bushy palmered flies on the bob, with nymphs in the middle, and tinsel-bodied flies on the point (size 10's and 12's).

How to Fish
The River needs some care for the slopes are steep and treacherous – it is best to have someone with you. Place your fly just below the boil at the head of each pool and let it track across – and hold tight.
The Fionn Loch is exposed in windy conditions – but it can suffer from flat calms too. Fish from the boat or land and work along the headlands casting to where the water is just deep enough not to see the bottom. There are plenty trout – and charr too.

lovely Loch Sionascaig shimmering under the rocky scarps of Cul Mhor on its east side, and the fractured ridge of Stac Pollaidh a couple of miles to its south. The buttresses of the heights of Caisteal Liath and the rest of the Suilven ridge prominent to the north, with Canisp lurking beyond, make the vista around Sionascaig truly unparalleled in natural beauty. The fishing is superb with many vermilion-speckled brownies around the attractive bays, most of which are willing to accept a bushy fly placed lightly on the water's surface.

Another absolute 'must to visit' is the stunning Fionn Loch (The White Loch) also nestling under Suilven's sandstone peaks. The route into this diamond of a loch is a walk up the valley track of the foaming River Kirkaig, where salmon fin

River Kirkaig, Inverkirkaig, Wester Ross:
Thrashing down one cascade into the next, the Kirkaig is turbulent and fast. It also draws runs of grilse and salmon as soon as spates break the summer droughts. Not for the un-energetic – but stunning for those with the will to climb in and out of this superb valley.

Above:
Near Lochinver in Assynt.
A typical West Highland river. Open vistas with mountain backdrops, low-growing native trees hugging the rocky banks, and fishing which is tremendous when summer spates fill the river with fresh water and freshly-run fish.

Opposite:
Fionn Loch, Inverkirkaig, Wester Ross.
The steep slopes of the Caisteal Liath buttress on Suilven slide into one of Scotland's most beautiful lochs – the Fionn Loch (From Gaelic – White Loch). Here are charr, and red-speckled brownies in number and quality. Fish the shores with bushy flies and enjoy West Highland fishing at its best.

strongly against the rushing white water and hide in the deep darkness of its pools. Fishing on the Kirkaig is often successful, particularly when grilse rush in from the tide, but be warned you must be able to climb up and down very steep rocky slopes. The straight fifty foot drop at the falls 2.5 miles from the sea, means that salmon cannot ascend further into the Kirkaig. At the top of the track you open out onto the broad shimmer of the Fionn Loch where the sandy bays offer abundant butter-yellow trout.

In the same glen, a little to the east, lies Loch Veyatie, a deep loch, best fished around its margins. In this respect it is very similar to its attractive and conjoined near neighbour, the Cam Loch. You start to get a feel for the place when you realise that one loch inevitably leads to the next in a superb chain of discovery.

The wildness of the north west is its basic attraction – this is a landscape of depth, texture and lavish colour. It also has scents which are peculiar to it, with the subtle fragrance of bog myrtle and thyme entwining to enhance the soft heathery perfume.

The fishing is remarkably varied. Some of these lochs have populations of tiny trout – fish which are fully adult and of significant age but which will never grow to appreciable size through lack of feeding. Others however, have under-strata of limestone which, leaching away, provide a richness of feeding that nurtures wild trout to sizes that surprise and delight. Some of these lochs are peaty and dark – some are gin-clear. You may walk from one to the next and find that no two are the same. Even the lochs which are close enough to be able to cast into two from the same point can be utterly different. They are irregular in shape with sweeping bays and rocky promontories, absolutely ideal for stravaiging gently along the shore with a fly rod.

If you are into wild fishing and wild fish, this area simply cannot fail to enchant. Stay at Inchnadamph or Lochinver and you will be staying in hotels and guest houses wholly focussed on visiting anglers. They understand fishing in this area – it is a genuine way of life and one which is wholly engrossing and entertaining.

Wester Ross

Loch Maree, near Poolewe, Wester Ross: Loch Maree was once unquestionably the best sea trout loch in the world. Regrettably it has now lost this ranking, but it is recovering once more and is a lovely loch to fish. The bulk of Slioch (980m) in the background gives the loch a dramatic and magical air.

Wester Ross is stunningly beautiful, especially if you take time to penetrate into the country away from the main roads. The River Kanaird is a typical west coast stream, the hydro schemes in the nearby hill lochs giving it extra water when flows might otherwise be low. Salmon and sea trout ascend the Kanaird while other attractive salmon streams include the River Broom which runs into the sea loch Loch Broom, and the smaller Ullapool River.

Draining the slopes and backland around the serrated crest of one of Scotland's finest mountains, An Teallach, the River Dundonnell ends up in Little Loch Broom some miles south of its greater sister. On the other side of the An Teallach massif, the River Gruinard and the Little Gruinard flow into the Bay and you have a very good chance of catching a fine sea trout or salmon in early to mid-summer in the Gruinard rivers when the rains break a drought.

Further south still is the wide expanse of Loch Ewe, a typical West Highland sea loch, and running into it one of the finest rivers of the west, the River Ewe. Tremendous runs of sea trout used to ascend the river into lovely Loch Maree, under the high flanks of the glorious peak of Slioch, and although numbers have declined in recent years, it is to be hoped that the population of sea trout will build up once again, restoring Loch Maree to its prominent position amongst the finest anywhere.

Torridon and the Applecross peninsula are famous for their mountains – Liathach, Beinn Eighe, and Beinn Alligin – but there are several small spate rivers well worth a try for a salmon, provided that conditions are right. The River Torridon itself and the Applecross River are typical examples, as are the Rivers Balgie and Shieldaig. The difficulty arises when you lift your eyes to look at the surrounding grandeur of the brooding mountains and miss the take of a fish – little consolation perhaps, but there's nowhere lovelier to do it.

LOCH MAREE AND THE RIVER EWE

Location Details
The Gairloch Road in Wester Ross hugs the shoreline for a few of Loch Maree's 12 miles. The River Ewe drains the Loch and flows to the sea loch – Loch Ewe.

Type of Fishery
Once the most famous (justifiably) sea trout loch in Europe, now trying to regain that lost reputation.

Description
A superb example of a West Highland stillwater. Many bays and islands (some blessed with ancient conifers). There are many favourite long 'drifts' well-known to the local ghillies.

Species
Sea trout – regrettably not in the prodigious number of years past but returning as the negative effects of fish farming are addressed. Salmon in the river. Brown trout in both (the loch has the largest ones)

Season Details
Salmon and sea trout: 11th February to end October. Statutory brown trout season.

Permit Contact(s)
The Loch Maree Hotel, Wester Ross.
Tel 01445 760288.
Sheildaig Lodge Hotel, Gairloch, Wester Ross.
Tel 01445 741250.
The Keeper's Cottage, Poolewe, Wester Ross.
Tel 01445 781274.

Favourite Flies & Baits
Kate McLaren (created for Loch Maree sea trout), Clan Chief, Zulus and Soldier Palmers, Loch Ordie is used for dapping.
In the River, standard salmon patterns work when fish are fresh in – also small shrimp patterns, General Practitioner, Stoat's Tail.

How to Fish
Loch fishing is almost invariably 'floating line stuff'. Sometimes an intermediate line will pull the fish up too. Dapping used to be the 'de rigeur' method but this thoroughly enjoyable skill seems to have declined a bit.
The River is fairly rapid and quite wide in places so fish from the croys – allow your fly to investigate any likely holding spots. Work right down to the productive Sea Pool – especially at the top of the tide, and especially if the river is high.

River Ewe, Inverewe, Wester Ross:
The river drains mighty Loch Maree and used to have stupendous runs of sea trout and many fine salmon. Now, the salmon outnumber the sea trout.

The South West Highlands

Loch Shiel, Glenfinnan, Moidart: High hills, shimmering light in ever-changing patterns, deep water and lightning-fast trout rising to bushy bob-flies.

There are six main peninsulas jutting out from the mid-west coast of Scotland, sheltered from the great Atlantic gales by the isles of Skye, Rum, Eigg and Mull. This is a remote part of Scotland incised deeply by sea lochs which are more akin to Scandinavian fjords than lower-lying lochs. The high hills and mountains slope steeply into them, creating first-class fishing opportunities. The sea fishing and game fishing of the area are simply exceptional and are relatively under-utilised. It is true to say that fish farming has impacted heavily on migratory fish numbers but this is being addressed and stocks are set to regain their healthy level and recover the great natural attraction that they rightly hold.

In the north of the region are the Five Sisters of Kintail, mountains of considerable grandeur. Beneath them runs pretty salmon rivers: River Croe and the River Sheil of Duich. These are typical west coast spate rivers which are barely trickles until there has been significant rainfall, and then the silvers come in.

In the Knoydart peninsula, on the south side of Loch Hourn, is the Inverie River, which contains salmon and sea trout when the rain brings them in from the tidal reaches of its sea loch, Loch Nevis. Knoydart has many fine trout lochs, too numerous to do full justice to – just go and explore as many as you can.

The next peninsula to the south is lovely Morar, bisected by Loch Morar, the deepest loch in the UK which plunges to an astonishing 1017 feet. The deepest loch in the country gives birth to the shortest river, for the River Morar runs out of Loch Morar, tumbles over the Falls of Morar and threads its way across silver sands into the sea – a modest journey of around six hundred yards. Sea trout and salmon run the Morar leaving behind the shimmering ocean with the isles of Eigg and Rum just a few miles offshore.

On the south side of the Sound of Arisaig lies the picturesque peninsula of Moidart where the River Ailort and River Shiel drain the lochs of their own name, and the River Moidart meets its destiny in the sea at Kinlochmoidart. These beautiful rivers have runs of salmon and sea trout in reduced numbers since fish farming impacted upon their stocks but are still well worth a visit. The River Shiel runs into Loch Shiel at one of the most famous monuments in Scotland commemorating the raising of the standard by Bonnie Prince Charlie before the 1745 campaign. The river forms part of the boundary between Inverness-shire and Argyll – a wonderful tract of land, rich in tradition and history, and rich in its wealth of fishing too.

Ardnamurchan pushes index-finger-like against the surge and swell of the restless Atlantic, pointing towards the isles of Coll and Tiree. There are no major rivers in Ardnamurchan but there are plenty of lochs with vermillion-speckled brown trout.

Morvern is the mainland peninsula which lies alongside Mull. The rivers Rannoch and Aline are the main streams and support good runs of summer salmon and fine sea trout. This is typically remote, West Highland territory where the trout are as wild as the country, bronze-backed and yellow flanked, with red spots as bright as rowanberries.

The Isle of Skye

Land of the mighty Cuillin Mountains, ancestral home of the Clan Macleod – and the aquatic home of many fine brown trout, sea trout and salmon – the Isle of Skye has a justified reputation for its grandeur, history and fishing. The bonniest lochs in Skye must be the Storr lochs, a few miles north of Portree, shimmering at the feet of the huge basaltic pinnacle, the Old Man of Storr. These three interlinked lochs have beautiful pink-fleshed brown trout ever-ready to accept a well-placed fly. There are few finer settings for an evening's fishing.

The rivers of Skye are neither large nor long, but they do carry migratory fish and are very picturesque. Tumbling down the steep slopes of the Red Cuillins, the River Sligachan has runs of salmon and sea trout when rain waters swell the flow. The River Camasunary is well-known for its blue-tailed fly pattern the Camasunary Killer, and the River Snizort is one of the loveliest salmon and trout rivers in west Scotland.

It is not just game fishing that attracts anglers to Skye, Mull and the other Hebridean isles, for the sea fishing is excellent, yet mostly undiscovered. There are many harbours where skippers will take sea anglers to their favourite reefs and wrecks to fish for great conger, skate, halibut, turbot, cod, pollack, saithe, rays, dogfish, sharks and all the other species which live in these sheltered sounds and sea lochs. If there is one under-exploited asset in Scotland's portfolio of fishing it has to be the shore fishing of the western isles. There are many anglers already enjoying the beautiful bays and headlands, but the shoreline is long and often inaccessible and there are vast stretches which have never heard a reel's ratchet.

Above: River Sligachan, Isle of Skye.
Running from the flanks of the famous Cuillin Mountains, the Sligachan is not a large river, but it does hold summer salmon and sea trout. There can be few more magnificent views when fishing than to raise your eyes to Sgurr Alasdair and the rest of the Cuillin Ridge.

Left: River Snizort, Isle of Skye.
This is a typical West Highland burn. It falls over countless small waterfalls into deep pots, then accelerates into faster glides until it free-falls once more. Small trout dart about as you pass by while the larger ones lurk awaiting a well-presented fly.

The Storr Lochs, Isle of Skye.
Fine brown trout lie in these lochs – bronze-flanked with great red spots and black speckles – they charge with a real vengeance to your bushy bob-fly or shiny tinsel pattern.

STORR LOCHS, ISLE OF SKYE

Location Details
A few miles north of Portree on the Staffin road. Under the watchful dominion of the Old Man of Storr – a rocky pinnacle towering over the lochs.

Type of Fishery
Brown trout – mixed population from small darting parr-sized fish to red-speckled beauties of a few pounds.

Description
Two lochs joined together – Loch Leathan and Loch Fada – shallow bays and productive margins – about two miles in overall length. Boat fishing primarily, with good bank fishing too.

Species
Brown Trout.

Season Details
March 15th to 6th October.

Permit Contact(s)
Portree Angling Association, 2 Teraslane, Portree, Skye. Tel 01470 582304.
Jansports, Wentworth Street, Portree, Skye. Tel 01478 612559.

Favourite Flies & Baits
Bushy flies in robust conditions: Golden Olive Bumble, Clan Chief, Loch Ordie, Soldier Palmer, Black Zulu. Tinsel-bodied patterns when fishing under the surface: Silver Invicta, Dunkeld, Butcher, etc Use size 8's in a gale, 10's in a wind and 12's or even 14's in calm weather. Dry-fly and buzzer patterns work well. The lochs are 'fly-fishing only'.

How to Fish
Hug the shorelines, and focus on where the inlet burns run into the lochs. Use floating lines and moderate retrieve, and resort to intermediate or mid-sink lines when the fish will not come to the surface. Evening rises can be spectacular.

Western Isles

North Uist Sea Pools, Near Claddich.

The largest island is Lewis *(Eilean Leodhais)* in the north, with smaller Harris *(Eilean Hearadh)*, slightly southwards. Further south still, are North Uist *(Uibhist a Tuath)*, Benbecula *(Beinn na Faoghla)*, and South Uist *(Uibhist a Deas)*, each linked to each other by causeway roads. A look at the map of Benbecula and the Uists shows how much water lies amongst the narrow tracts of land – it is impossible to travel around without seeing water somewhere in these islands. There are many machair lochs, lying amongst the waving wild flowers on the fertile strip of pasture land just above the sea shore. For the most part, you will fish alone, with only the call of the birds, the soft lilting song of the breeze, and the splash of waves and rising trout for company. The fishing here is just as wild and natural as you could wish it to be.

Lewis has some decent sized lochs, like Loch

South Uist, near Benbecula: Transfixing tranquillity – the Uists provide some of the best fishing in Scotland.

Loch Dibadale, West Lewis.
Typical of the innumerable machair lochs of the Outer Hebrides each has fine trout. The trout can be dour at times – but when the elusive 'purple patch' comes, sport simply cannot be better.

Langavat, to the south west of the island's capital Stornoway, but this loch is surrounded by dozens of smaller lochs with hard-fighting brown trout in every one of them. Langavat has salmon, sea trout and native browns and is central to the fishings of the Grimersta Estate. But the jewel in the crown here is the River Grimersta with its superb runs of salmon. The river is short, under two miles long, but fishing extends through a chain of lochs making it a varied and wonderful place to enjoy game fishing, but it carries a price tag that reflects its superlative quality.

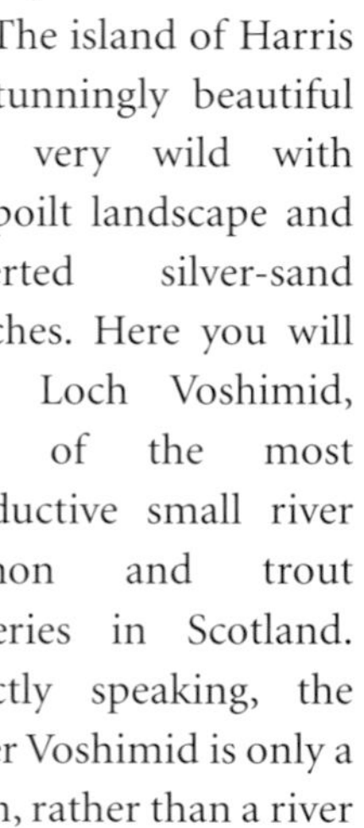

The island of Harris is stunningly beautiful and very wild with unspoilt landscape and deserted silver-sand beaches. Here you will find Loch Voshimid, one of the most productive small river salmon and trout fisheries in Scotland. Strictly speaking, the River Voshimid is only a burn, rather than a river of any consequence or size, but it does carry superb runs of salmon into a system where they may be caught on fly tackle. Like the Grimersta system in Lewis, this is not a budget-priced water, but if you receive an invitation, or find you have chosen this week's lottery numbers, head for Harris and gorgeous Loch Voshimid!

Another expensive but worthwhile fishing area is the River Eaval – known to anglers as the Castle Burn – which runs into the sea at Amhuinnsuidhe. This small river has featured in countless films and videos as the site where sea trout and salmon gather in the bay waiting for rain to draw them into freshwater.

However not all the waters on the outer islands carry an expensive swing tag – a significant number are free. To use them simply contact the estate on whose land the lochs lie, and permission will be granted in a very kind and gracious way – provided

Right: South Uist Landscape.
Everywhere you look in the Uists there are lochs – some large, some little more than pools – and they all contain wild fish.

LOCH VOSHIMID, ISLE OF HARRIS

Location Details
Amhuinnsuidhe, North Harris.

Type of Fishery
A small (only 900 yards in length) but incredibly productive salmon and sea trout fishery.

Description
A short and small river connects Loch Voshimid to the sea, where runs of migratory fish ascend when there is sufficient water height. The loch is shallow and fish accept the fly with abandon – well, at most times. This is an extraordinary loch, in a class all of its own, in stunningly-dramatic surroundings.

Species
Salmon and sea trout, (with brown trout too, but it is the 'silvers' that attract.)

Season Details
11th Feb to end of October.

Permit Contact(s)
CKD Finlayson Hughes, Barossa Place, Perth. Tel 01738 541600.

Favourite Flies & Baits
Bushy patterns prevail – Loch Ordie, Bumbles, Clan Chief, Zulus, Bibio, Goat's Toe, with tinsel-bodied flies also effective – Silver Invicta, Butchers, Dunkeld etc. Loch Voshimid is 'fly-fishing only'.

How to Fish
Boat fishing when wind conditions permit, and bank fishing at other times. Fish with floating lines and short leaders allowing the fish time to really 'inhale' your fly. Dapping is often practised, just don't snatch your flies away from salmon, they take a little time to turn away, and get a real hold.

of course that you agree to abide by all local rules. There is a small charge to fish for migratory fish, but it can be highly productive if you time your visit to perfection.

These are not large streams – they are spate rivers requiring water at the optimum height to bring in fresh fish, but they are a very bright prospect for enjoyment if you like wilderness and seclusion. The wonderful fishings of the Outer Hebrides deserve a book dedicated solely to them – in the meantime, go and see for yourself how marvellous they are.

Above & Below: Loch Voshimid, Isle of Harris:
This is salmon and sea trout paradise. At the end of the day the ghillies gather the gear – and the catch – before the downhill Land Rover ride to a sumptuous dinner.

ARGYLL AND THE ISLES

Isle of Coll, Inner Hebrides, Argyll: Each of the Western Isles has splendid shore fishing, and Coll is no exception. Pollack, cod, saithe and shoals of shimmering mackerel make fishing here a pleasure.

With mild weather, natural splendour, and the abundance and quality of the wild fishing, the Atlantic seaboard of Scotland is blessed in many ways. Argyll is central to west coast Scotland, with rugged mountains looking down over clear lochs and tumbling rivers, to the island dotted western horizon.

The plentiful precipitation retains a light freshness in the land, which may be less marked in the drier parts of Scotland. Each glen nurtures a river system, which all support stocks of indigenous fish. Some of these rivers are wholly dependent on spates, while others are supplied with water from nearby lochs, which keeps their flow fresh and buoyant. Argyll has so much to offer; it is a land of wild magnificence and elegance, with fishing that many would give their eye teeth to enjoy more fully.

The Isles of Argyll have a charm and character quite unlike any other part of the country and their isolation protects the superb quality of their wild fishing. The natural beauty of the islands is simply unsurpassed. These islands do not have big rivers, but they do have varied lochs and numerous small burns. The migrating salmon and sea trout swim in from the ultramarine sea and into the whisky-coloured streams; populations of wild trout swim in the sparkling lochs and will often rise to a well presented fly.

The allure of the tranquil landscape is a magnetic draw for many, but a visit to the Isles is enhanced in huge measure for anglers by the great fishing that is enjoyed there.

Lochs & Rivers of Argyll & The Isles

Above: River Awe, Argyll. The River Awe leaves the great sheet of Loch Awe through the deep-cut Pass of Brander.

Right: River Orchy, Dalmally, Argyll. The Orchy runs into Loch Awe at its north east end and provides most of the spawning for those salmon that come through the Loch.

The contrast within the greater Strathclyde area could hardly be more marked. The urban sprawl of Glasgow transforms suddenly into attractive rural scenery as you head northwards along the banks of Loch Lomond. Similarly, the Clyde estuary brings charming islands like Bute and Arran into immediate accessibility through their regular ferry services and these islands have very fine fisheries. On the westwards side of Mull of Kintyre are the islands of Islay and Jura, famous the world over for their peaty uisghe beatha, but also owning some good wild brown trout and sea trout fishing. Further north still, the land transforms again with classical tumbling rivers, deep-cut lochs and engaging remoteness.

The area's lochs have great diversity – there are large island-strewn sheets of Loch Awe and Loch Lomond alongside smaller more intimate lochs.

Loch Awe is nearly 26 miles long from its northern end under Ben Cruachan and the deep Pass of Brander, to its seaward end where the River Awe runs into the sea loch Loch Etive. Loch Awe is a mixed fishery containing charr, perch, large pike, salmon, natural brown trout and variable numbers of rainbows which have escaped from the fish farm cages. It is a fascinating place to fish especially around the islands and wooded bays.

Fishing on Loch Awe is as you might expect – lures for rainbows, 'top of the water' small bushy flies for the brownies in the shallower parts, trawling for salmon with Rapala plugs or spoons, and plugs or dead-bait tactics around the drop-offs for pike. You can lose yourself in Loch Awe and you will find corners which are free from other anglers, yet the loch is popular and productive. Nearby lies Loch Avich, another super loch, particularly for top of the water fishing for brownies.

Nearly five miles wide at its broadest and over twenty miles in length, Loch Lomond is justifiably famous for its natural beauty. It is a lovely tree-lined loch with sweeping bays and rocky headlands, towered over by shimmering

hills. The fishing is excellent with good runs of salmon and sea trout which ascend the River Leven as they leave the Clyde estuary and swim upstream to spawn in a tributary like the River Endrick. Brown trout, perch, powan, pike and even ruffe enhance the appeal of the loch's fishing.

Top: Allt Brander:
This is the rattling white-water experience which Argyll and the Isles so often offers for angling.

Lying quietly in a north-south direction in its lovely sheltered valley is Loch Eck and flowing from it, the River Eachaig. This small river system runs into the Holy Loch and holds some of the best sea trout fishing on the west coast. It is an oasis of utter calm with excellent prospects for sea trout and summer salmon.

The biggest loch on Mull is Loch Frisa, a long narrow, deep, loch which can be wild and threatening on a dark day, yet tranquil and utterly enchanting when the weather is warm and bright. The Mishnish Lochs on the lovely winding road from Dervaig to Tobermory are a great place to spend a day. They are relatively shallow and productive, and hold a fine population of well-fed brownies.

Left: River Leven at Alexandria.
The River Leven drains out of Loch Lomond into the River Clyde estuary. Many fine salmon and sea trout ascend this short watercourse as it passes through the housing and industrial units of greater Glasgow.

The rivers of Mull fast-fall down steep mountainsides, rattle between water-worn boulders, tumble through rocky gorges and green glens swathed in rhododendrons, then slide across silver sands, to finally merge into the blue depths of the sea. Mull is wild and beautiful, as are its rivers. One of the best is the River Forsa near Salen, which enjoys runs of sea trout in summer and salmon. The River Aros which drains Loch Frisa via its tributary the River

Loch Awe, at Kilchurn Castle: Loch Awe has excellent brown trout stocks, a fair number of 'escaped' rainbows, some very large pike and runs of salmon.

Ledmore has spectacular sections of falls and deep foam-flecked pools and is a lovely place to enjoy typically west coast scenery.

Jura and Islay lie further to the south and enjoy the mildness of the Gulf Steam. They are small islands with superb sea and game fishing. The largest loch on the Isle of Islay, Loch Gorm, is just a stone's throw from the wide Atlantic Ocean across the machair to the west. Other much smaller lochs worth visiting include Loch Lossit, Loch Finlaggan and Loch Ballygrant, which lie between Bridgend and Port Askaig.

LOCH AWE

Location Details
Lying under the bulk of Ben Cruachan alongside the road from Oban to Tyndrum.

Type of Fishery
Mixed large loch with shore and boat fishing.

Description
Large sheet of water: 27 miles long by at least 1 mile wide. It is deep in places with many sheltered (and shallower) bays.

Species
A few salmon, a few sea trout, good stocks of wild and stocked brown trout, ferox trout, escaped rainbows from fish cages, perch, pike (some huge) and Arctic charr. The British record brownie was caught in Loch Awe

Season Details
Statutory season for brown trout, salmon season from February 11th to October 15th.

Permit Contact(s)
Portsonachan Hotel (boats for hire), Dalmally, Argyll. Tel 01866 833224.
Donald Wilson, Ardbrecknish House, (boats for hire) Dalmally. Tel 01866 833223.

Favourite Flies & Baits
Trolling for pike and other species is usually done with rapalas and other plugs.
Fly-fishing for trout is best when May flies are 'up'. Otherwise, small dark and bushy bob-flies and standard wet-flies are the order of the day. Try Wickham's and Greenwell's, Poacher and Clan Chief.

How to Fish
The bays provide the best attractions. They are where the food items are most likely to be obtained by fish, so close in over the skerries and rocky outcrops are 'hot spots'. If you cannot see the bottom you are in too deep water holds true for fly-fishing.
Try around Claddich, Kilchurn Castle and the islands near the entry to the Pass of Brander, or down the loch at Susan's Bay.

Loch Lomond: Soft and gentle, and popular with anglers from all over the world.

Arrangements can be made through the tourist office in Bowmore. The streams around Jura tend to be small, but do attract some sea trout, and you may fly-fish with excellent prospects along the seashore for these silver beauties, using long flashy lures designed to imitate sandeels.

In a micro-environment protected from the oceanic extremes by the Mull of Kintyre lie the lovely islands of Arran and Bute. Arran has several small rivers of note, while Bute has two notable trout lochs – Loch Quien, a small water of around three quarters of a mile in length, and Loch Fad, where there are huge rainbows and a highly-renowned fishery.

LOCH LOMOND

Location Details
The Glasgow to Crianlarich road runs along the south side of Loch Lomond and on the opposite shore there is a road which only goes as far as Rowardennan.

Type of Fishery
A mixed fishery with several species and tactics. Boat and shore fishing.

Description
Loch Lomond is big – over twenty miles long and over 4 miles wide at its wider south end. It has many islands and fine bays bordered by rocky headlands and promontories – good fish-holding spots. The River Leven joins Loch Lomond to the River Clyde and therefore to the sea, while the River Endrick is a major inflowing river (a fine salmon river in its own right).

Species
Salmon, sea trout, brown trout, ferox trout, Arctic charr, rainbow trout (escapees), powan, perch and pike – with exotic introductions like ruffe (escaped as livebait for pike).

Season Details
Salmon: Feb 11th to end of October. Brown trout: statutory season.

Permit Contact(s)
Loch Lomond Angling Association PO Box 3559 Glasgow. Boats may be hired at most of the shore-side hotels and boatyards.

Favourite Flies & Baits
Trolling with plugs and big spoons accounts for salmon, pike and sea trout. Fly fishing is practised along the shores as is bait fishing.

How to Fish
Reconnoitre the area of your choice – find a quiet reach and do your own thing – enjoy the 'Bonnie Bonnie Banks of Loch Lomond'.

THE SOUTH WEST

River Nith, near Drumlanrig: One of the best sea trout rivers of the South West, the River Nith provides excellent sport for night-time fishing in high summer. At other times, salmon make the most impact, but the river's brown trout population is buoyant and of good quality.

Benefiting from the mild influence of the Gulf Stream, the oceanic current which swirls warm water across the Atlantic onto the western seaboard of Europe, the south west is the warmest part of Scotland. While native hardwoods and conifers are the trees of the colder east, the south west is mild enough for palms and subtropical plants, although, in the depth of winter you might wonder how they survive.

There are many small lochs and a few larger ones but the region is not mountainous, and does not have the terrain for large stillwaters. The rolling hills drain to the Irish Sea and lower River Clyde estuary in a succession of small rivers. Only in the most southerly part of the region are there salmon rivers of considerable renown.

In a way, the region misses out on tourism as most visitors drive headlong northwards and don't take sufficient time to explore the south west. They are missing much as the fishing is excellent. Sea fishing along the coastal bays is amongst the most productive in Scotland, coarse fishing is developing apace and game fishing is well supplied from the rivers and lochs. As with elsewhere, there are many small stillwaters providing rainbow trout fishing at modest cost and high quality. Local demand is supplemented by anglers coming southwards from the greater Glasgow area and their discerning competition of demand keeps fishery managers on their toes, all to the benefit of the angler.

The South West of Scotland is a warm corner both in its mild climate and hospitality. After a day's first class fishing, there can be few sights as lovely as watching the sun setting over the calm shimmer of the western sea.

Lochs and Rivers of the South West

Clatteringshaws Loch near Newton Stewart: Wide horizons, open moorland, the call of the wild birds for company and the splash of big trout makes this is a loch worth visiting.

It is extraordinary how some of Scotland's finest fisheries are overlooked. Maybe the locals prefer to keep their attractive fishings to themselves. Whatever the cause of this lack of renown, there is plenty of fine fishing to choose from in the tract of rolling countryside which is bordered by the River Clyde estuary to the north, the rocky Ayrshire coast in the middle, and the low lands of the Solway in the south.

Almost every valley in the undulating green hills of Ayrshire has a reservoir. These were impounded to supply drinking water for the coastal towns or to provide constant water to power the many mills and factories, now obsolete and long gone. This heritage of small, mostly narrow lochs provides local clubs with the opportunity to lease their own water and manage their own fishings. It is encouraging to see so many angling clubs looking after lochs for there are few better methods of managing fisheries than 'for anglers by anglers'.

There are a few wholly natural lochs too, most of which have developed into fine trout fisheries. In addition, there are many more-recent purposely-designed waters dedicated to the cult of the rainbow. With the great population of Glasgow nearby, the area is surprisingly wild with relatively few people enjoying its natural charms. The lochs are not huge, but they are well cared for and provide genuinely good sport.

For club-run, brown-trout-only waters in the northern part of the area, a good day out may be had at Camphill Reservoir or Crosbie Reservoir near Kilbirnie. Rainbows are stocked widely and fine sport should be expected at Busbie Muir near Ardrossan, Knockenden Reservoir and Munnoch Reservoirs (controlled by the Munnoch Angling Club) and the bank-only Caaf Reservoir near Dalry.

Commercial fisheries in the area include the Cowan's Law Country Sports Centre near Moscow; the wooded Craufurdland Fishery near Fenwick; Fairlie Moor Fishery which has huge rainbows released into it regularly, and Skelmorlie Fishery which boasts superb views across the sparkling

CLATTERINGSHAWS LOCH

Location Details
Beside the New Galloway to Newton Stewart road.

Type of Fishery
Bank-only fishing.

Description
A small natural loch, which was raised to provide extra water for power generation in the Doon Valley Hydro Scheme. It can be a wild and woolly place in a grey gale of a day. On the other hand, it is a gem of a place on a fine summer day when white clouds glide across a tranquil blue sky, and the curlews plaintively call in their liquid crescendo, and trout splash at your fly.

Species
Stocked and natural brown trout, pike and perch.

Season Details
Statutory brown trout season (March 15th to 6th Oct).

Permit Contact(s)
Galloway Gun and Tackle Shop, Arthur Street, Newton Stewart. Tel 01671 403404.
Merrick Camp Site, Glentrool, Kircudbrightshire. Tel 01671 840280.

Favourite Flies & Baits
Bushy bob flies attract the trout on the surface. Daddy-long-legs do well later in the season. At other times, Soldier Palmer, Zulus, Bumbles and Clan Chief are a good bet. For sub-surface flies try Silver March Brown and Invicta. Nymph imitations also work well.

How to Fish
Get the wind at your back or on one side and work your way along the shore casting out and retrieving at a moderate rate. Sometimes, fish will come much closer in, so keep out of the water unless you are sure of your footing and feel you need the extra distance from the shore.

The Upper River Clyde: Ask most non-anglers what they know about the River Clyde and they will speak of shipbuilding – but that's not what is found here in its upper reaches, where fine brownies come to natural and well-presented artificial flies.

lower Clyde estuary towards the Arran hills.

To the south are Collenan Reservoir near Troon, the engaging Loch Doon just south of Dalmellington, and the attractive Loch Bradan a few miles to its west, each hydro-electricity impoundments, and each set amongst monoculture stands of Sitka spruce. Loch Doon is a larger loch of nearly eight miles in length by more than a mile wide, and holds fine brown trout and some charr along with decent-sized perch and pike. Nearby Loch Bradan benefits from progressive stock management and some sizeable trout are caught each year.

The Dumfries and Galloway area is not copiously strewn with stillwaters although there are several good fishing lochs. Pernwhirn Reservoir and Loch Ree, both moorland lochs with wild brownies which can be tempted with bushy flies on the surface. Closer to Stranraer are the picturesque Lochnaw Castle Loch and Knockquhassen Reservoir, each well worthy of a visit if you are in the area.

Further east is the slightly larger Clatteringshaws Loch, a hydro scheme loch which is also set in forestry land, and the home of some wild browns. Loch Ken, a long narrow loch north of Kirkcudbright, has many coarse fish as well as a population of browns and the odd salmon.

JERRICHO LOCH

Location Details
Near Lochanbriggs on the Dumfries to Beattock road.

Type of Fishery
One of several small commercial fisheries in the south west, Jerricho provides typically good sport. Stocked rainbow water – small size. A bank-only fishery. Not large enough for boats (around 12 acres).

Description
Well-stocked with rainbows of good weight and condition, also some brook trout and brownies. Really good access for disabled anglers.

Species
Primarily rainbows with some 'brookies' and 'brownies'.

Season Details
April 1st to end of October, statutory brown trout season.

Permit Contact(s)
Glenclova Caravan Park,
Amisfield, Dumfries.
Tel 01387 710447.
The Fishing Tackle Shop,
6 Friar's Vennel, Dumfries.
Tel 01387 252075.

Favourite Flies & Baits
Lures are effective in the early season, then dries and buzzers come into their own. Epoxy buzzers fished very, very slowly – or even static will account for many rainbows and so will hoppers and emergers when the fish have eyes for surface food items.

How to Fish
This is not a large stillwater, so investigate where concentrations of trout are holding. The next trick is to establish what they will accept.

Above: River Doon:
Burns wrote a lovely song about 'Ye banks and braes o' bonnie Doon'. It was bonnie in the eighteenth century and it is still bonnie today. What's more, there are fine fish in the Doon too.

From the Clyde to the Solway along the bonnie Ayrshire coast, the rivers are small but no less attractive. The brown trout fishing in these fine streams is fairly average and not especially notable, but the runs of salmon make them fine sporting prospects.

The River Garnock and its main tributary the River Lugton have quite good trout fishing, especially downstream of Dalry and Kilbirnie, and salmon have been ascending the river in increasing numbers. There is active management here from the clubs and proprietors, so the future of this small river system is assured. Further south, the River Ayr runs nearly forty miles through the moors, woods and fields of central Ayrshire holding mixed stocks of brownies, sea trout, grayling and salmon, although the migratory species only run in high water conditions. The Ayr is another river which also benefits from the excellent efforts of the local organisations' and owners' efforts to sustain the fishery.

Running clear and cool out of Loch Doon, the River Doon is tree-lined and highly attractive with lovely pools and glides throughout much of its length. Not cheap fishing, but very elegant and charming, it's a good prospect for a salmon in the autumn. Just as the River Doon runs out of Loch Doon, the River Girvan slides out of Loch Bradan to run to the sea at the town of its name. Between

Right: River Kelvin, Glasgow:
In the heart of the busy modern city of Glasgow, the River Kelvin has had salmon runs re-established where once pollution reigned. This is a testimony to hard work, and to the capacity of native fish to return once conditions are maintained properly.

THE RIVER DOON

Location Details
Running from the Galloway hills and under the Brig o' Doon where Rabbie Burns' Tam o' Shanter only just escaped the Earl o' Hell and his demonic legions, the river today enjoys a much more tranquil reputation as a very fine fishery.

Type of Fishery
A small attractive river flowing through fine agricultural land.

Description
Small stream – sometimes even smaller due to abstraction – this river is a 'spate river' when it is described as a migratory fish venue, although the wild brown trout seem to relish the gentle flows and rich feeding.

Species
Salmon, occasional sea trout and fine river brown trout.

Season Details
25th February to end October for migratory fish and statutory season for natural brown trout.

Permit Contact(s)
Patna Angling Club, Parson's Lodge, Patna, Ayrshire. Tel 01292 531306.
Skeldon Estate Office, Dalrymple, Ayrshire. Tel 01292 560656.
Craigengillan Estate, Dalmellington, Ayrshire. Tel 01292 550237.

Favourite Flies & Baits
Small Stoat's Tail, Ally's Shrimp and Munro Killer for salmon.
Sea trout will grab a Teal, Blue and Silver or Peter Ross or Stoat's Tail.
Brown trout relish imitative dries, GRHE, Greenwell's, Iron Blue Dun.

How to Fish
Keep out of the water unless you have to wade – to avoid disturbance. Cast down and across for daytime salmon and for sea trout in the dusk and into dark.
Upstream dry fly-fishing (or sunk nymph when the water is high) for the brownies.

River Stinchar, Knockdolian Beat: A spate river for the most part, the Stinchar has fine trout stocks throughout the year, and runs of salmon and a few sea trout when rain fills the river.

THE RIVER STINCHAR

Location Details
The river flows into the sea just south of Ballantrae in Ayrshire.

Type of Fishery
A small west-flowing river. One of several in Ayrshire.

Description
A small river benefiting from rainfall to bring fish into the pools - has suffered like many rivers in farming areas from water abstraction. Now almost a spate river.

Species
Salmon and sea trout. Population of wild brown too.

Season Details
25th February to 31st October for salmon and sea trout, statutory brown trout season.

Permit Contact(s)
The Estate Factor, Knockdolian Estate, Colmonell, Ayrshire. Tel 01465 881237.
Dalreoch Lodge Colmonell, Ayrshire.
Tel 01465 881214.
Donald Love, Almont, Pinwherry, Ayrshire.
Tel 01465 841637.

Favourite Flies & Baits
Salmon: Knockdolian Shrimp and Stinchar Shrimp patterns, Willie Gunn, Garry Dog, Stoat's Tail, Hairy Mary.
Sea trout: Silver Invicta, Silver Stoat, Teal Blue & Silver, Small Devons, Rapalas and Flying C's are also used when water is high and coloured.

How to Fish
Standard approach to migratory fish. The Stinchar is a small river so a small rod (11 - 13 feet) will allow you to cover the water well. Slow pools benefit from backing-up or retrieve otherwise swing the fly over the likely lies.
Upstream dry-fly is a fine way to catch the wily Stinchar 'broonies'.

these two points there is fine fishing, although once again, most salmon wait for high water before entering the system.

Running through lovely stands of trees, and sluicing through sweeping pools of great character, the River Stinchar is perhaps the most picturesque of Ayrshire's rivers. It's not only its visual attraction which places the Stinchar high on the list of have-to-be–fished waters, for the river has much higher than anticipated runs of salmon in high water conditions. From May to September, salmon ascend the river whenever spates chivvy them into action. It is a fair indication of the standing of the river that there are patterns of salmon flies specifically designed for the water, the 'Black Stinchar' being a typical example. Some of the beats, Almont, Bandrochat and Dalreoch, are fairly accessible to visiting rods while others like Knockdolian Estate, tend to be retained by regular tenancies. If you're lucky enough to be invited to fish the Stinchar – don't hesitate.

River Annan at Kirkwood: It is not just salmon, sea trout and native brown trout that may be caught in the Annan, for this river is one of the few in Scotland with a healthy population of chub.

Solway Area Rivers

River Bladnoch: Beat Four at the Spittal Bridge, near Newton Stewart, in Wigtownshire. From the higher moorlands of the South West hill country, to the sea in Wigtown Bay, the Bladnoch carries very nice brown trout, augmented by seasonal runs of salmon and a few sea trout. It also has some sizeable pike in its slower runs.

In a book about Scottish fishing, is there a place for a river which flows for a significant part of its course through England? The answer must be a positive 'yes', especially if the river in question is the River Border Esk. Scotland can claim a justifiable proportion of ownership, as this excellent river flows from the Ettrick hills some forty meandering miles to its merger with the Solway, and most of this course is between Scottish banks.

The Border Esk is primarily a sea trout water, and some of these sea trout are absolutely superb. The river also enjoys runs of salmon and has a good head of fine brown trout, but then you might expect this when large sea trout are plentiful. The Border Esk tends to be clear running unless there has been really heavy rainfall so 'fine and far-off' tactics are the order of the day. The visiting angler can arrange accessible fishing in the towns of Canonbie and Langholm.

If the Border Esk is the main sea trout river of the region, then the main salmon rivers must be the River Annan and the River Nith. The Annan rises in the hills beside the Devil's Beef Tub, where it runs fast and clear over a swift course, before slowing its pace and running through pastoral land to discharge into the Solway Firth near the town of Annan, some thirty odd miles from its source. The River Annan is both attractive and productive, especially for salmon at the 'back end' of the year.

As is common in many parts of Scotland, local anglers were granted fishing rights to parts of the Annan, and it was the famous King Robert the Bruce who granted this right to the four Royal Burghs of Greenhill, Smallholm, Heck and Hightae near Lockerbie in the 1300s. Brown trout, grayling, salmon and sea trout can all be found in the Annan along with decent-sized chub and this lively quarry is a bit of a novelty to most Scottish fishers. Fishings are reasonably accessible through the main tourism offices in Annan and Lockerbie.

The River Nith, at around fifty miles in length, is the largest of the area's rivers. It runs from its several contributing sources amongst the moors and farmlands around Sanquhar, through lovely Nithsdale, past Thornhill, downstream to Dumfries, where there is a large cauld (weir), then slips out over the sands into the Solway Firth. A high proportion of the river's fishings are available to visitors through the local angling associations and owners (contact the local tourist office for details).

Several thousand sea trout are still caught each year in the Nith, a testimony to hard work, for the river was badly polluted in the early part of the twentieth century. Sea trout have been in decline almost everywhere in Scotland but the Nith seems to be bucking the trend, retaining a relatively buoyant population. Some large salmon are also

River Nith, near Thornhill, Dumfries: One of the most varied South West rivers, the Nith has excellent runs of sea trout and salmon. It also has good native brownies and grayling too. Through its deep-cut gorge sections to its wide open pools there is great diversity and sport available from what is a relatively small river.

THE RIVER NITH

Location Details
Flowing through some of the loveliest south west Scottish countryside, the Nith runs through Dumfries before meeting the sea within the Solway Firth.

Type of Fishery
A salmon and sea trout river of justifiably high renown.

Description
Mixed river: rocky gorges, swift-flowing pools and deep dubs and slower meandering glides. Highly attractive and productive.

Species
Salmon (good runs) and sea trout (excellent sea trout stream) wild brownies and grayling.

Season Details
25th February to 30th November for salmon – later than most Scottish rivers.
Brown trout – statutory season (March15th to 6th Oct)

Permit Contact(s)
Upper-Nithsdale Angling Club: Pollock and McLean, 61 High Street, Sanquhar. Tel 01659 502241.
Mid-Nithsdale Angling Association: 110 Drumlanrig Street, Thornhill. Tel 01844 330555.
The Factor, Buccleugh Estates, Drumlanrig Castle Mains, Thornhill. Tel 01848 600283.
Smiths Gore, 28 Castle Street, Dumfries. Tel 01387 263066.

Favourite Flies & Baits
Salmon: Shrimp patterns (Ally's Shrimp and GP), Willie Gunn, Blue Charm on tubes and standard irons.
Sea trout: Stoat's Tail, Teal Blue and Silver, Peter Ross
Brownies: Dry Flies, especially olives and Iron Blue Duns
Grayling: Red Tag, GRHE and Greenwell's nymphs
Spinning with Devons and Flying C's is successful.

How to Fish
Conventional approach to salmon fishing and to dusk/night-time sea trouting.
Dry fly (upstream) for brownies, and downstream nymphs for grayling.

The Upper River Border Esk, near Langholm: The lovely pools of the Border Esk hold some specimen sea trout.

THE RIVER BORDER ESK

Location Details

Flowing through Langholm and Canonbie with its outflow in the Solway Firth.

Type of Fishery

A fine river of medium size with many large sea trout and also salmon and grilse. Brown trout are present throughout, but it is the sea trouting that attracts most anglers.

Description

A lovely river of swift streams and wide pools – just the territory for sea trouting – and often overhung with shade-providing trees.

Species

Sea trout, salmon and wild brown trout, with grayling is some reaches.

Season Details

1st February to End November, statutory brown trout season.

Permit Contact(s)

Buccleugh Estate, Ewesbank, Langholm, Dumfriesshire. Tel 01387 380202.

Esk & Liddle Fishery Assocn., The Old School, Hagg-on-Esk, Canonbie. Tel 01387371416.

Mr Lavericks, Burnfoot House, Langholm Dumfireshire. Tel 01387 370611.

Favourite Flies & Baits

Shrimp patterns for salmon: Ally's Shrimp or Curry's Red Shrimp. Standard irons like Willie Gunn and Hairy Mary, Tube flies like Comet do well.

Sea trout will take Dark Mackerel, Peter Ross, Teal Blue & Silver, Silver Stoat's Tail. Silver Invicta, and Silver March Brown.

Brown trout like dries and nymphs: GRHE, Greenwell's and Iron Blues.

How to Fish

Like all sea trout rivers it pays to have reconnoitred well in advance of your night-time fishing. The river does have some deep holes (best avoided when wading!) and the trees do have spaces for a well-placed back-cast (otherwise roll cast).

Standard tactics for salmon (down and across allow the fly to track slowly over the lies).

Sea trout are fairly easy to spook so wait until last light and wade very quietly. Fish the runs and deeper pots early, then the tails of the pools later.

Upstream dries and downstream nymphs for the fine brownies.

Border Esk:
In low water conditions at the height of summer, the best time to fish for Border Esk fish is when the darkness hides what you are up to – don't enter the water and disturb the fish.

caught each year, perhaps not quite as big as the one hooked by Jock Wallace, a 'weel-kent' local poacher, who claimed to have hooked the fish (illegally) at eight o'clock in the morning and not landed it until 6 o'clock in the evening. Whether it is strictly true is not wholly relevant, but he is said to have then cheekily presented it to the local laird who recorded its weight at 67 lbs – even larger than the accredited Scottish record set much later in 1921 by Miss Ballantine on the Tay.

The Rivers Bladnoch and Cree are fine small rivers flowing through the elegant countryside of Galloway. Primarily a grilse river, the Bladnoch has good grilse runs when summer rain fills the pools and salmon are present from mid-spring time. It runs out of Loch Maberry through quite varied water to join the River Cree on the Solway sands near Wigtown. In the upper reaches, sluggish stretches abound with perch and pike – that presumably feed on juvenile salmonids – but elsewhere the river flows swift and true providing good and accessible sport.

The River Cree enjoys a fair number of salmon in the earlier part of the year although the season starts quite late on March 1st. The early fish are supplemented by good runs of grilse in June and July and a heavier run of larger salmon at the 'back-end'. The Cree is accessible to visiting anglers who should book through the Newton Stewart Angling Association water or some of the estate beats.

River Nith, Drumlanrig Estate, near Dumfries:
If you had to catch a salmon to save your life in the South West – the Nith would be a very good option. Fine pools and tempting glides make it a classic salmon river, and excellent for grayling and trout too.

THE RIVER ANNAN

Location Details
From the hinterland in the border hills the Annan runs by Lochmaben and Moffat to the sea in the Solway Firth.

Type of Fishery
A multi-ownered fishery with excellent salmon, sea trout and brown trout fishing.

Description
Swift headstreams and slower mid and lower reaches, the Annan is essentially a spate river which requires substantial rainfall to bring in migratory fish (this is exacerbated by water abstraction and by huge afforestation).

Species
Salmon: many hundreds are caught each year, and sea trout (good runs) with superb brown trout and grayling in some sections. There are even chub and other coarse fish to fish for.

Season Details
25th February to the 15th of November, statutory brown trout season.

Permit Contact(s)
The Factor, Annadale Estate, Lockerbie, Dumfriesshire. Tel 01576 470317.
Anthony Steel, Kirkwood, Lockerbie. Tel 01576 510200.
Annan & District AC, 63-65 High Street, Annan, Dumfrieshire. Tel 01461 202616.
The Clerk ,'Royal Four Towns Waters', Prestonhouse Rd, Hightae, Lockerbie. Tel 01387 810220.

Favourite Flies & Baits
For salmon: Shrimp patterns (Ally's and GP), tube flies of Willie Gunn tying, standard dressings of Hairy Mary, Comet, Thunder & Lightning.
Sea trout: Peter Ross, Silver Stoat's Tail, Teal Blue and Silver.
Brown trout and grayling: Hare's Lug and Iron Blue nymphs. Dry flies: Badger Quill, Greenwell's Glory and Wickhams Fancy and wet flies like Red Tag (grayling), Grouse & Claret and March Brown.

How to Fish
Most of the time you will fish with a floating line with a medium length salmon rod. Although a slow sink/intermediate/sink-tip is also useful if the water is higher. Fish down and across, absolutely conventionally.
Trout like upstream dries and downstream nymphs (as do grayling).
Sea trout are best left until you can't see the stones in the river when you stand in the water at dusk then, and only then, do you start.

River Annan, upstream of Lockerbie:
Large brown trout rise contentedly to hatching ephemerid flies, sea trout leap for no apparent reason and silver salmon lunge about as though they are bored waiting for your fly.

Useful Contacts

Whether you need to speak to someone about something unusual, report an incident, or wish to obtain detailed information, the following list of organisations should help you to take that important first step.

THE NATIONAL BODIES

SCOTTISH ANGLERS NATIONAL ASSOCIATION (SANA)
The governing and representative body for game angling in Scotland. Services include competitions, coaching (accreditation through its SGAIC qualification), environmental matters, youths, ladies & consultative affairs.
Caledonia House
South Gyle
Edinburgh
EH12 9DQ
Tel: 0131 339 8808

THE SALMON AND TROUT ASSOCIATION (S&TA)
Represents Scottish salmon and trout anglers, defending their rights and interests. Closely involved with Scottish environmental affairs.
Coaching accreditation through STANIC qualification.
The Caledonia Club
32 Abercrombie Place
Edinburgh
EH3 6QE
Tel: 0131 558 3644

THE SCOTTISH FEDERATION OF SEA ANGLERS
Represents sea angling throughout Scotland. Publishes helpful guides and supplies useful information.
Caledonia House
South Gyle
Edinburgh
EH12 9DQ
Tel: 0131 317 7192

SCOTTISH FEDERATION FOR COARSE ANGLING
Represents the interests of Scottish coarse anglers.
Contact: Steve Clerkin
Tel: 01592 642242

THE PIKE ANGLERS CLUB (SCOTLAND)
Represents the interests of Scottish pike anglers.
Contact: Alistair McPhee
Tel: 01259 210877

ANGLERS CLEARWATER ASSOCIATION (ACA Scotland)
Mainly involved with the quest for pure water & legal pursuit of polluters.
Campaigns for the cleaning up of watercourses. Represents clubs and individuals with problems arising from pollution.
1 Caenlochan Road
West Ferry
Dundee
DD5 1JX
Tel: 01382 730308

SCOTTISH EXECUTIVE RURAL AFFAIRS DEPARTMENT (FISHERIES DIVISION)
The Scottish Government's department dealing with all fishery matters.
Pentland House
47 Rob's Loan
Edinburgh
EH14 1TY
Tel: 0131 244 6227

FRESHWATER FISHERIES LABORATORY
The headquarters of the Scottish freshwater fisheries research department and laboratories.
Faskally
by Pitlochry
Perthshire
PH16 5LB
Tel: 01796 472060

SCOTTISH ENVIRONMENT PROTECTION AGENCY (SEPA)
The organisation responsible for the formal consent of discharges, and the monitoring and control of potential pollution. Contact the SEPA if you find what you think is a instance of pollution.
1 South Street
Perth
PH2 8NJ
Tel: 01738 627989

SCOTTISH NATURAL HERITAGE (SNH)
The agency involved with all matters of natural history in Scotland. Legal matters, protection of rare species, SSSI and SAC control.
12 Hope Terrace
Edinburgh
EH9 2AS
Tel: 0131 447 4784

SCOTTISH TOURIST BOARD
Co-ordinates the work of regional tourism services.
23 Ravelstone Place
Edinburgh
EH4 3EU
Tel: 0131 332 2433

THE FISHERIES TRUSTS

These organisations are committed to the improvement of the fishing in their local catchment areas. Their staff are extremely knowledgeable about fishing in general – both scientifically and locally – and are willing to help visiting anglers and those with genuine queries.

AWE FISHERIES TRUST
Contact: Dr Colin Bell
Ardchonnel Old School House
Eredine
Dalmally
Argyll
PA33 1BW
Tel: 01866 844293

Opposite:
River South Esk.

WEST GALLOWAY FISHERY TRUST
Contact: Callum Sinclair
12 Victoria Street
Newton Stewart
DG8 6BT
Tel: 01671 403011

RIVER CLYDE FISHERIES TRUST
Contact: Jim MacAloon
12 Chalmers Crescent
Murray 7
East Kilbride
G75 0PE
Tel: 01355 221724

LOCHABER & DISTRICT FISHERIES TRUST
Contact: Dr Jon Watt
Arienskill Cottage
Lochailort
Inverness-shire
PH38 4LZ
Tel: 01687 470350

WEST SUTHERLAND FISHERIES TRUST
Contact: Dr Shona Marshall
Gardeners Cottage
Scourie
Sutherland
IV27 4SX
Tel: 01971 502259

WESTER ROSS FISHERIES TRUST
Contact: Dr James Butler
Rose Cottage
Eilean Darach Estate
Garve
Wester Ross
Tel: 01854633349

WESTERN ISLES FISHERY TRUST
Contact: Mark Bilsby
Creed Lodge
Marybank
Stornoway
Lewis
HS2 9JN
Tel: 01851 701526

THE TOURIST OFFICES

There are 14 divisional tourist offices in Scotland and most towns have their own tourist information centre. This is probably the best reference point for finding out about fishing in any area. Most fisheries have pamphlets or information sheets available through their local tourist office, and those that do not will be on the office's register so that you can contact them directly.

ABERDEEN & GRAMPIAN
27 Albyn Place
Aberdeen
AB10 1YL
Tel: 01224 288800
website:www.agtb.org

ANGUS & CITY OF DUNDEE
7-21 Castle Street
Dundee
DD1 3AA
Tel: 01382 434664
website:
www.angusanddundee.co.uk

ARGYLL, THE ISLES, LOCH LOMOND, STIRLING & THE TROSSACHS
Old Town Jail
St John Street
Stirling
FK8 1EA
Tel: 01786 445222
website:
www.scottish.heartlands.co.uk

AYRSHIRE AND ARRAN
Block 2
45 Skye Road
Prestwick
KA9 2TE
Tel: 01292 470700
website:
www.ayrshire-arran.com

DUMFRIES & GALLOWAY
64 Whitesands
Dumfries
DG1 2RS
Tel: 01387 245550
website: www.galloway.co.uk

EDINBURGH & LOTHIANS
4 Rothesay Terrace
Edinburgh
EH3 7RY
Tel: 0131 473 3800
website: www.edinburgh.org

GREATER GLASGOW AND CLYDE VALLEY
11 George Square
Glasgow
G2 1DY
Tel: 0141 204 4400
website: www.seeglasgow.com

THE HIGHLANDS OF SCOTLAND
Peffery House
Strathpeffer
IV14 9HA
Tel: 01997 451160
website: www.host.co.uk

KINGDOM OF FIFE
70 Market Street
St Andrews
Fife
KY16 9NU
Tel: 01334 474609
website: www.standrews.co.uk

ORKNEY ISLANDS
6 Broad Street
Kirkwall
Orkney
KW15 1NX
Tel: 01856 872856
website: www.orkney.com

PERTHSHIRE
Lower City Mills
West Mill Street
Perth
PH1 5QP
Tel: 01738 627958
website: www.perthshire.co.uk

BORDERS
Murray's Green
Jedburgh
TD8 6BE
Tel: 01835 863435
website:
www.scot-borders.co.uk

SHETLAND
Market Cross
Lerwick
ZE1 0LU
Tel: 01595 693434
website:
www.shetland.tourism.co.uk

WESTERN ISLES
26 Cromwell Street
Stornoway
Isle of Lewis
HS1 2DD
Tel: 01851 703088
website: www.witb.co.uk

Bibliography & Acknowledgements

BIBLIOGRAPHY

It has been said that more has been written about fishing than anything else. I don't know. What is indisputable, however, is that there are some excellent books that describe Scottish angling and which are suitable for novices and experts alike. The following list is not exhaustive but it offers width and depth of knowledge of Scottish angling accumulated by genuine anglers in Scotland – surely nothing exceeds good, honest, hard-won experience.

Biggart, David A., *SNACA 1880 – 1980 The First Hundred Years.* The Scottish National Angling Clubs Association, 1979.

Currie, Willam B., *The River Within.* Merlin Unwin Books Ltd, 1993.

Headley, Stan, *Trout and Salmon Flies of Scotland.* Merlin Unwin Books Ltd, 1997.

Little, Crawford, *Success with Salmon.* David and Charles Ltd., 1988.

Mills, Derek & Graesser, Neil, *The Salmon Rivers of Scotland.* Cassells Ltd., 1992.

Sandison, Bruce, *Rivers and Lochs of Scotland – The Angler's Complete Guide.* Merlin Unwin Books Ltd., 2000.

ACKNOWLEDGEMENTS

I am hugely indebted to the superb staff of Colin Baxter Photography, for their vital guidance and contributions during the creation of this book.

The quality of the Glyn Satterley's images are a tribute to the creativity and skill of a master photographer, for that is undoubtedly what Glyn is. Those who dabble with a camera while they enjoy our countryside will appreciate how difficult it is to catch rivers and lochs in that fleeting moment which conveys their innermost character. Glyn's dedication and skill shine so brightly. I am very fortunate to number him amongst my friends.

I am particularly grateful to Paul Young for his generous foreword.

My thanks go to the huge range of fisheries staff, tackle shops and manufacturers, estate managers, ghillies, fishery scientists, angling clubs, associations and national angling bodies, hotels, guest houses, publishers, boat owners, tourist facilities and fellow anglers who combine to provide such excellent fishing in Scotland – and to their support and assistance to me while I was writing the text. Thank you all. Anglers owe you so much, and regrettably appreciate you so little.

Lastly, I offer my deepest appreciation to my wife Maureen, and to my daughters Elaine and Claire. They had to put up with my absence and distraction while I wrestled with the text. Without their patience and encouragement this book simply would not have come to pass.

Colin Baxter Photography wishes to thank Nigel Houldsworth (*www.fishingmaps.co.uk*) for his maps of the salmon pools of the rivers Tay, Tweed and Spey; Heather Brunton of the Scottish Life Archive; Ian Mitchell of the Robert D. Clapperton Photographic Trust and Andrew Graham Stewart for their kind assistance.

Night Fishing, River Tweed, and an exceptional 12½ pound sea trout.

Index

Entries in bold indicate pictures